The Most Famous Battles of the Ancient World: Salamis, Cannae, and the Teutoburg Forest

By Charles River Editors

A modern illustration depicting an Ancient Greek phalanx formation

About Charles River Editors

Charles River Editors provides superior editing and original writing services across the digital publishing industry, with the expertise to create digital content for publishers across a vast range of subject matter. In addition to providing original digital content for third party publishers, we also republish civilization's greatest literary works, bringing them to new generations of readers via ebooks.

Sign up here to receive updates about free books as we publish them, and visit Our Kindle Author Page to browse today's free promotions and our most recently published Kindle titles.

Introduction

The Battle of Marathon (490 BCE)

Adam Carr's picture of the site of the battle today

"The Athenians...charged the barbarians at a run. Now the distance between the two armies was little short of eight furlongs [about a mile]. The Persians, therefore, when they saw the Greeks coming on at speed, made ready to receive them, although it seemed to them that the Athenians were bereft of their senses, and bent upon their own destruction; for they saw a mere handful of men coming on at a run without either horsemen or archers. Such was the opinion of the barbarians; but the Athenians in close array fell upon them, and fought in a manner worthy of being recorded. They were the first of the Greeks, so far as I know, who introduced the custom of charging the enemy at a run, and they were likewise the first who dared to look upon the Persian garb, and to face men clad in that fashion. Until this time the very name of the Persians had been a terror to the Greeks to hear." - Herodotus

The Ancient Greeks have long been considered the forefathers of modern Western civilization, but the Golden Age of Athens and the spread of Greek influence across much of the known world only occurred due to one of the most crucial battles of antiquity: the Battle of Marathon. In 491 B.C., following a successful invasion of Thrace over the Hellespont, the Persian emperor Darius sent envoys to the main Greek city-states, including Sparta and Athens, demanding tokens of earth and water as symbols of submission, but Darius didn't exactly get the reply he sought. According to Herodotus in his famous *Histories*, "Xerxes however had not sent to Athens or to Sparta heralds to demand the gift of earth, and for this reason, namely because at the former time when Dareios had sent for this very purpose, the one people threw the men who made the demand into the pit and the others into a well, and bade them take from thence earth and water and bear them to the king."

Thus, in 490 B.C., after the revolt in Ionia had been crushed, Darius sent his general Mardonius, at the head of a massive fleet and invading force, to destroy the meddlesome Greeks, starting with Athens. The Persian army, numbering anywhere between 30,000 and 300,000 men, landed on the plain at Marathon, a few dozen miles from Athens, where an Athenian army of 10,000 hoplite heavy infantry supported by 1,000 Plataeans prepared to contest their passage. The Athenians appealed to the Spartans for help, but the Spartans dithered; according to the Laws of Lycurgus, they were forbidden to march until the waxing moon was full. Accordingly, their army arrived too late. Thus, it fell upon the Athenians to shoulder the burden. With their army led by the great generals Miltiades and Themistocles, the Athenians charged the outnumbering Persians. Outmatched by the might of the heavy, bronze-armored Greek phalanx, the inferior Persian infantry was enveloped and destroyed, causing them to flee for their ships in panic. The Athenians had won a colossal victory against an overwhelming and seemingly invincible enemy.

Somewhat ironically, the Battle of Marathon has been best commemorated by the race that bears its name, a tradition that started based on a legend that a Greek man named Pheidippides ran the 26.2 miles back to Athens in order to announce the Greek victory and subsequently collapsed and died as soon as he had done so. However, the importance of the battle itself cannot be overstated. The Battle of Marathon proved to be one of the biggest sources of enmity between the Greeks and Persians, and Darius's son Xerxes would seek to undo the results with his own invasion just years later. As it was, the rivalry between the Greeks and Persians would last for over 150 years and culminated with Alexander the Great's destruction of the Achaemenid Persian capital city of Persepolis. Marathon also positioned the city-state of Athens as a major power not only in Greece but throughout the Mediterranean and Near East, as their military, diplomatic, and economic influence grew after the battle.

The Greatest Battles of the Greco-Persian Wars chronicles the decisive Greek victory that ended the First Persian War and ensured the safety of mainland Greece. Along with pictures and a bibliography, you will learn about the Battle of Marathon like never before.

The Battle of Thermopylae

Bronze monument of Spartan King Leonidas at Thermopylae

"Although extraordinary valor was displayed by the entire corps of Spartans and Thespians, yet bravest of all was declared the Spartan Dienekes. It is said that on the eve of battle, he was told by a native of Trachis that the Persian archers were so numerous that their arrows would block out the sun. Dienekes, however, undaunted by this prospect, remarked with a laugh, 'Good. Then we will fight in the shade...'" – Herodotus

There are few battles in history in which the vanquished are better remembered and celebrated than the victors, and even fewer where a defeat is considered a victory. But that has become the enduring legacy of the Battle of Thermopylae, a battle as unique as it is famous. The story of the battle and the willing sacrifice of the Greek defenders to buy the rest of the retreating Greeks time is well known across the world and still resonates with audiences to this day. Last stands are the stuff of martial legends, and Thermopylae is the greatest of them all.

Though there was another contingent of Greeks fighting alongside them, Thermopylae is remembered for the stand of the 300 Spartans, who, with no compulsion binding them, chose to fight and die in the remote mountain pass against insurmountable odds. Their story has been told in literature, art, film, and even in graphic novels.

But the battle was more than the ultimate self-sacrifice, the embodiment of the famous statement that "greater love has no one than this, that one lay down his life for his friends". It was also a veritable clash of civilizations, and one that, though in and of itself it was a defeat, helped set the stage for the eventual Greek victory that might very well have changed the course of history. It was a showdown between various Greek city-states, including Sparta and democratic Athens, against the autocratic, absolutist Persian Empire. Had the Persians triumphed, the Golden Age of Athens would have been snuffed out, and Ancient Greece would never have formed the backbone of Roman and Western culture. Simply put, the West as we know it today might never have existed.

Of course, the Greeks themselves couldn't have known that and doubtless never viewed it that way. Famous as this battle is – it is likely that anyone with even a passing interest in military history has a basic understanding of what happened at Thermopylae – there still exist a vast number of misconceptions on the subject, first and foremost the idea that the Persian horde was faced exclusively by the elite 300 Spartans. In actuality, until the last day of the battle, between 5,000 and 7,000 Greeks took their place in the battle-line, including Arcadians, Corinthians, Myceneans, Mantineans, Tegeans, Thespians, Phocians, Locrians and Thebans. Likewise, the idea that the Greeks themselves fought for democracy or any such political ideal is a fallacy; they were frequently at war with each other and in this case banded together simply to fight for the individual independence of their own city-states and the continuing freedom of Greece itself.

The Greatest Battles of the Greco-Persian Wars separates the facts from the legends to explain who fought the battle, how the battle was fought, and the results and aftermath of the battle. Along with art depicting important people, places, and events, you will learn about the Battle of Thermopylae like never before.

The Battle of Salamis

A depiction of the victorious Greeks returning home after Salamis

"Forward, sons of the Greeks,

Liberate the fatherland,

Liberate your children, your women,

The altars of the gods of your fathers,

And the graves of your ancestors:

Now is the fight for everything." – The Greek battle hymn sung before the Battle of Salamis according to Aeschylus

When the Spartans' famous and sacrificial stand at the Battle of Thermopylae ended, the Athenian fleet was forced to fall back, and Xerxes' massive Persian army marched unopposed into Greece before advancing on Athens. The Greek armies were scattered and unable to face the might of Persia, so Athens was forced to do the unthinkable: evacuate the entire population of the city to Salamis, from where the Athenians watched in horror as Xerxes' troops plundered the defenseless city, set it aflame, and razed the Acropolis.

However, the Athenians remained belligerent, in part because according to the oracle at Delphi, "only the wooden wall shall save you." Indeed, this would prove true when Themistocles managed to lure the Persian fleet into the straits of Salamis. There, on a warm day in September 480 BCE, hundreds of Greek and Persian ships faced each other in a narrow strait between the Attic peninsula of Greece and the island of Salamis. The battle that ensued would prove to be epic on a number of different levels, as it set a precedent for how later naval battles were fought in the ancient Mediterranean, turned the tide in the Greeks' favor against the Persians in the Persian Wars, and ultimately played a role in Athens' rise to a preeminent role in the Hellenic world.

Bereft of much of his fleet after Salamis, Xerxes feared being stranded on the wrong side of the Hellespont, as there was a chance Themistocles might take the allied navy north to destroy his bridge across the straits. Accordingly, he retreated with the greater part of his army, back through Thermopylae and then from there to Persia, and many of his men perished from lack of adequate supplies and disease. Thus, it can safely be said that while Thermopylae continues to be more celebrated and better remembered, Salamis was the decisive battle of the Second Persian War.

A careful examination of the Battle of Salamis and its aftermath reveals that perhaps the most important aspect that the battle had on Greece was the fulfillment of the oracle's prophecy that a "wooden wall" would protect the Greeks against the Persians. The wooden wall of Greek ships proved to not only protect the Greeks from the invaders but also helped to propel the Greeks, particularly the Athenians, to a position of hegemony in the Mediterranean that was not surpassed until the rise of Rome several hundred years later.

The Battle of Cannae

Jorg Schulz's picture of a modern monument near the battlefield

"Few battles of ancient times are more marked by ability...than the battle of Cannae. The position was such as to place every advantage on Hannibal's side. The manner in which the far from perfect Hispanic and Gallic foot was advanced in a wedge in échelon...was first held there and then withdrawn step by step, until it had reached the converse position...is a simple masterpiece of battle tactics. The advance at the proper moment of the African infantry, and its wheel right and left upon the flanks of the disordered and crowded Roman legionaries, is far beyond praise. The whole battle, from the Carthaginian standpoint, is a consummate piece of art, having no superior, few equal, examples in the history of war." – Theodore Dodge, military historian

Although the Romans gained the upper hand over Carthage in the wake of the First Punic War, the legendary Carthaginian general Hannibal brought the Romans to their knees for over a decade during the Second Punic War. While military historians are still amazed that he was able to maintain his army in Italy near Rome for nearly 15 years, scholars are still puzzled over some of his decisions, including why he never attempted to march on Rome in the first place.

Regardless, Hannibal was such a threat that the Romans responded in an unprecedented nature when the Carthaginians resumed the campaigning season in the spring of 216 BCE by capturing the city of Cannae, a crucial supply hub, and placing themselves along the line that convoys from the ports and warehouses of the south needed to travel to reach Rome. This was something the Romans could not and did not take lying down; Rome raised the largest army in their city's history, a force of between 80,000 and 100,000 men, and marched south with Consuls Varro and Paullus at the head of the army. This military behemoth disregarded the delaying tactics that Maximus had favored, fully determined to destroy Hannibal once and for all as quickly as possible. Polybius described the incredible size of this Roman army: "The Senate determined to bring eight legions into the field, which had never been done at Rome before, each legion consisting of five thousand men besides allies. ...Most of their wars are decided by one consul and two legions, with their quota of allies; and they rarely employ all four at one time and on one service. But on this occasion, so great was the alarm and terror of what would happen, they resolved to bring not only four but eight legions into the field."

Despite the massive horde headed his way, Hannibal was ready for them. He encamped his army near the Aufidus, a river not far from Cannae, and waited. His intelligence told him that Consul Varro, the more influential of the two Roman generals, was a firebrand, talented in attack but with a tendency to overreach himself, and Hannibal resolved to use this flaw to his advantage. Hannibal arrayed his army in the open, sure that Varro would be unable to resist the temptation to offer battle, and then deliberately placed his weakest infantry in the center of his battle-line. Varro led the Roman legions straight at the center of Hannibal's formation, proceeding in characteristic bull-headed fashion and spearheading the assault himself. Hannibal's troops in the center yielded before the legions, as Hannibal had anticipated, sucking the bulk of the Roman force deep into the centre of Hannibal's formation. Meanwhile, the wings of Hannibal's infantry automatically swung against the flanks of the Roman force while Hannibal's cavalry, led by his celebrated general Maharbal, crushed the Roman cavalry and light infantry deployed to protect the formation's flanks and rear and, in so doing, succeeded in encircling it completely. The Roman force now found itself unable to run or maneuver, completely surrounded by Hannibal's forces. It was one of the earliest examples of the pincer movement in the history of warfare.

The result was a massacre, one of the most vicious battles in the history of the world. Around 75% of the Roman army was cut down in the ensuing melee, which would be in the vicinity of between 50,000-80,000 soldiers depending on which initial estimates are considered to be accurate. Among the casualties was the luckless Consul Paullus, two-thirds of the city's Military Tribunes, a host of officials and noblemen from the most prominent Roman families, and almost a full third of the Senate. Hannibal's army killed so many prominent Romans that his men collected more than 200 gold signets from dead Romans, and he had the rings sent to Carthage to demonstrate his complete victory.

Livy described the scene, "So many thousands of Romans were dying ... Some, whom their wounds, pinched by the morning cold, had roused, as they were rising up, covered with blood, from the midst of the heaps of slain, were overpowered by the enemy. Some were found with their heads plunged into the earth, which they had excavated; having thus, as it appeared, made pits for themselves, and having suffocated themselves." If the casualty numbers are accurate, Hannibal's army slaughtered an average of 600 Roman soldiers every minute until nightfall ended the battle, and less than 15,000 Roman troops escaped, which required cutting their way through the center of Hannibal's army and fleeing to the nearby town of Canusium.

Cannae is still considered one of the greatest tactical victories in the history of warfare, and the fact the battle was a complete victory resulting in the wholesale annihilation of the enemy army made it the textbook example for military commanders to try to duplicate. Of course, others usually were unsuccessful. Cannae was the kind of complete victory that every commander from Caesar to Frederick the Great to Napoleon to Robert E. Lee sought, and that few generals save Caesar and Napoleon bagged whole armies is a testament to the near impossibility of achieving a victory like Cannae.

Not surprisingly, after the serious threat Hannibal posed during the Second Punic War, the Romans didn't wait much longer to take the fight to the Carthaginians in the Third Punic War, which ended with Roman legions smashing Carthage to rubble. As legend has it, the Romans literally salted the ground upon which Carthage stood to ensure its destruction once and for all. Despite having a major influence on the Mediterranean for nearly five centuries, little evidence of Carthage's past might survives. The city itself was reduced to nothing by the Romans, who sought to erase all physical evidence of its existence, and though its ruins have been excavated, they have not provided anywhere near the wealth of archaeological items or evidence as ancient locations like Rome, Athens, Syracuse, or even Troy.

The Battle of the Teutoburg Forest

This is a cenotaph of Marcus Caelius, a Roman centurion killed in the battle. The inscription reads, "To Marcus Caelius, son of Titus, of the Lemonian district, from Bologna, first centurion of the 18th legion. 53½ years old. He fell in the Varian War. His bones may be interred here. Publius Caelius, son of Titus, of the Lemonian district, his brother, erected (this monument)."

"The details of this terrible calamity, the heaviest that had befallen the Romans on foreign soil since the disaster of Crassus in Parthia, I shall endeavor to set forth, as others have done, in my larger work. Here I can merely lament the disaster as a whole. An army unrivaled in bravery, the first of the Roman troops in discipline, vigor and military experience, was thus brought through supine leadership, the perfidy of the foe, and a cruel Fortune into an utterly desperate situation. The troops did not even have the opportunity of fighting, as they wished . . . and hemmed in by woods, lakes and the bands of ambushed enemies, were entirely cut off by those foes, whom they had used to slaughter like cattle. Their leader, Varus, showed some spirit in dying, though none in fighting - for, imitating the example of his father and grandfather, he ran himself through with his sword. Of the two praefects of the camp Lucius Eggius gave an honorable example, but Ceionius one of baseness, for after the bulk of the army had perished, Ceionius advised a surrender, preferring to die by the executioner than in battle. Numonius Vala, Varus's lieutenant, a man hitherto of good reputation, this time proved guilty of foul treachery, for leaving the infantry unguarded he fled with the allied cavalry, trying to reach the Rhine. But Fortune avenged his crime; he perished in this act of deserting his countrymen. The savage enemy mangled the half-burned body of Varus. His head was cut off and sent to Marobodus [a barbarian king] and by him sent to the Emperor; and so at length received honorable burial in the sepulcher of his family." – Velleius Paterculus, ancient Roman historian

Every great nation or empire has had at least one horrific military loss or disaster in their history, and the Roman Empire, perhaps the greatest empire that ever existed in the Western world, was no exception to this rule. While Rome certainly suffered defeats and outright massacres over the course of its long and storied history, none of them were as disturbing for the Empire as the battle of the Teutoburg Forest in 9 CE. This battle, which took place in Germany, is also known as the Varian disaster, named after the governor of the Roman province, Germania Publius Quinctilius Varus. Varus was not only the Roman governor of the Roman controlled sections of Germania, he was also the highest military authority, being able to make decisions as to the who, what, where, when, why and how of military maneuvers and operations. It was Varus, then, who was in direct command of the Roman legions destroyed in the battle.

The battle remains pertinent not only to military historians and archeologists but also to modern military officers around the world as well. As recently as 2009, the United States of America's Army Command and General Staff College published a work that focused upon the Roman legions in the Teutoburg Forest. This work was an examination of the battle in order to help understand the failures made by Varus, and how to avoid them. While it may seem unusual for a modern military to examine the mistakes of the past, it isn't; the Army used the battle as an example of how a theoretically inferior force, the Germanic warriors, were able to defeat a superior force in the Roman legions.

Indeed, the Battle of the Teutoburg Forest featured some of the finest fighting forces in the world – the Roman legionaries – and a group of people whom the Romans didn't consider human at all – the Germanic tribes. Nonetheless, the battle between these two forces, in the narrow confines of the Teutoburg Forest, would be a turning point in the histories of both nations. Never again would Rome seek to establish a colony and create a functioning province out of the Germanic area; in fact, the Romans never ventured east of the Rhine River after the disastrous expedition. For the Germanic tribes, while they would later suffer from punishment excursions by various Roman legions following the battle of the Teutoburg Forest, they proved that they could hold their own against the might of the Roman Empire and that their land was indeed their own.

The Most Famous Battles of the Ancient World: Marathon, Thermopylae, Salamis, Cannae, and the Teutoburg Forest

About Charles River Editors

Introduction

The Battle of Marathon

   Primary Sources

   Chapter 1: The Ionian Revolt

   Chapter 2: The Achaemenid Persian Perspective of Athens and Ionia

   Chapter 3: The Persians Prepare to Invade Greece

   Chapter 4: The Order of Battle

   Chapter 5: The Greek and Persian Ways of War

   Chapter 6: The Athenians Take the Field

   Chapter 7: The Greek Center Collapses

   Chapter 8: The Persian Retreat

   Chapter 9: A Shield Signal?

   Chapter 10: How the Greeks Won the Battle of Marathon

   Chapter 11: The Marathon Runner

   Chapter 12: The Results and Aftermath of the Battle of Marathon

   Bibliography

The Battle of Thermopylae

   Chapter 1: A New King Comes to Power in the Achaemenid Empire

   Chapter 2: The Geography of Thermopylae and the Build-up to the Battle

   Chapter 3: The First and Second Days of the Battle

   Chapter 4: Tonight We Dine in Hades

   Chapter 5: The Aftermath and Legacy of Thermopylae

   Bibliography

The Battle of Salamis

   Chapter 1: The Athenians Build Their Navy

   Chapter 2: The Evacuation of Attica

   Chapter 3: The Persians Advance Through Attica

   Chapter 4: Naval Warfare in the Ancient World

   Chapter 5: The Order of Battle

   Chapter 6: The Battle of Salamis

   Chapter 7: Why the Greeks Won at Salamis

   Chapter 8: Monuments and Trophies from the Battle of Salamis

- The Battle of Cannae
  - Prelude to the Second Punic War
  - Hannibal's Invasion of Italy
  - Opposing Forces
  - Preparing the Trap at Cannae
  - The Battle Plans
  - The Battle of Cannae
  - The Aftermath
- The Battle of the Teutoburg Forest
  - Varus
  - Arminius
  - Before the Ambush
  - The Teutoburg Forest and the Opposing Forces
  - Laying the Trap
  - The Battle
  - The Aftermath
  - Online Resources
  - Bibliography

The Battle of Marathon

Primary Sources

As with any historical study, historians' examination of the Battle of Marathon is based on primary sources, and the most complete source concerning the Battle of Marathon is the ancient Greek historian Herodotus' *The Histories*. Herodotus' account has continued to be the base for most modern accounts of the battle, but it's important to recognize inherent flaws in the author's work. While Herodotus is remembered as the "Father of History" for being the first of his kind to write the kind of historical narratives people are familiar with today, he wrote his seminal work decades after the battle and never witnessed the event personally. As a result, his account is based on a number of different oral testimonies, which can be full of inherent problems (Vansina 1985, 3-32).

An ancient bust depicting Herodotus

Herodotus' account is also relatively short and lacks some important details. For example, the time of year or week of the battle is never given, and he doesn't specify how many days the whole episode lasted, from the preparations on the field to the time when the Persians sailed back to Asia. To corroborate Herodotus, modern scholars also have the 1st century CE Greek geographer Pausanias and his work *Description of Greece*. Pausanias is perhaps best used as an auxiliary to Herodotus, as he wrote much later and his descriptions of Marathon were more concerned with burial sites of the fallen warriors then the battle itself.

The final sources for the reconstruction of the Battle of Marathon then are modern archaeologists and historians. Modern scholars have helped to fill in considerable gaps in knowledge concerning the Battle of Marathon by conducting digs that have verified different aspects of the Herodotus account and by using philology to better understand the detailed nuances of what the ancient Greek historian wrote.

By combining all of these sources, not only can a reasonable reconstruction of the Battle of Marathon be made, but perhaps some new ideas may come to light.

Chapter 1: The Ionian Revolt

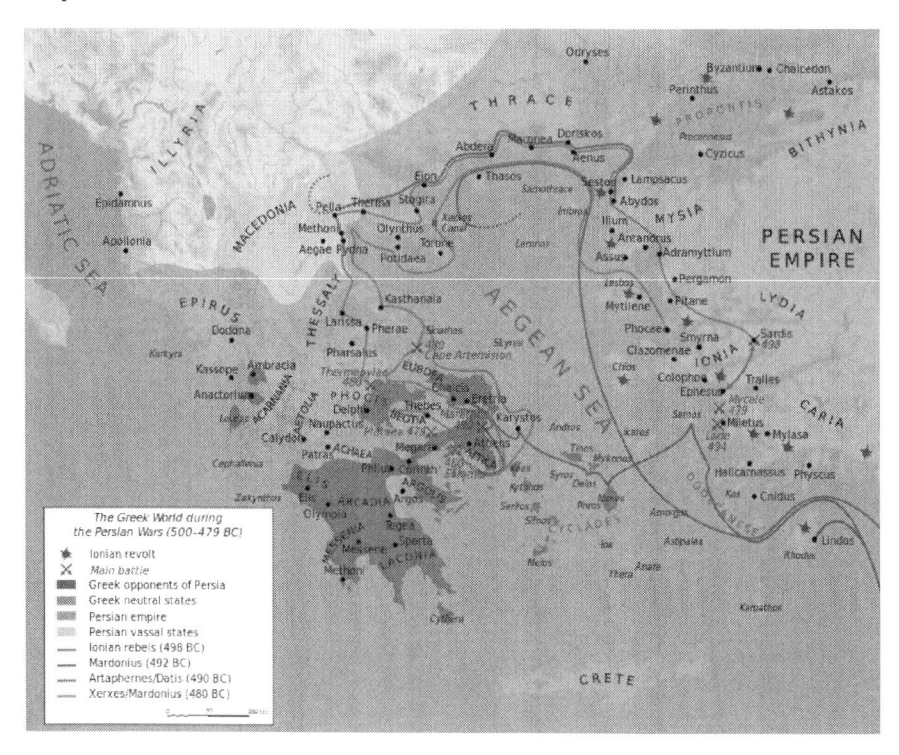

A map of the region at the time of the wars

A 5th century depiction of a Greek hoplite (right) fighting a Persian soldier

The Battle of Marathon was part of the wider Greco-Persian Wars (499-479 BCE), which began on the Ionian coastline (modern day western Turkey) but would later spread to directly affect mainland Greek city-states such as Athens and Sparta. In 500 BCE, Sparta and Athens were not terribly interested in the affairs of the Achaemenid Persian Empire, and for the most part, the status of the Ionian Greeks, who were under Persian control, also mattered very little to them. Sparta stood at the head of an alliance/league of Peloponnesian city-states who were more concerned with their region, while Athens had recently abolished tyranny and was learning the intricacies of democratic government (Forrest 2001, 37).

While Athens was uninvolved, perhaps following the cue of their Athenian cousins, some of the Ionian, Aeolian, and Doric city-states in Anatolia revolted against their own tyrants, which was tantamount to rebellion against their Persian overlords (Forrest 2001, 37). Herodotus provided the best account of the Ionian Revolt, which was largely instigated by a former tyrant named Aristagoras, who believed that a successful revolt would place him in a powerful position. Herodotus wrote, "Certain substantial citizens of Naxos, forced by the commons to leave the island, took refuge in Miletus, which had been put under Aristagoras, son of Molpagoras, as deputy governor. He was nephew and son-in-law of Histiaeus, the son of Lysagoras, who was being detained by Darius at Susa . . . The first thing they did when they got there was to ask Aristagoras to lend them some troops, in the hope of recovering their position at home. This suggested to Aristagoras that if he helped the exiles to return he himself would be ruler of Naxos; so using their friendship with Histiaeus to cloak his purpose, he made them an offer." (Herodotus, *The Histories*, V, 30).

Aristagoras had a keen sense of political acumen and a feel for the times, as a large part of his strategy was to gain the favor of the Ionians Greeks by promising the reward of democracy. First, he had to abdicate his own tyranny, which he did in public fashion. According to Herodotus, "To induce the Milesians to support him, he began by professing to abdicate his tyranny in favor of a popular government, and then went on to do the same thing in the other Ionian states, where he got rid of the tyrants." (Herodotus, *The Histories*, V, 37).

At the same time, Aristagoras knew that enticing the Ionian states to rebel would not be enough to defeat the mighty Achaemenid Empire. For that, he would need the support of one, or both, of the Ionian's mainland Greek cousins. However, Aristagoras' efforts to obtain the aid of Sparta and Athens against the Persians would lead to his demise and set the Athenians on a crash course with the Persians that would reach its apex at Marathon.

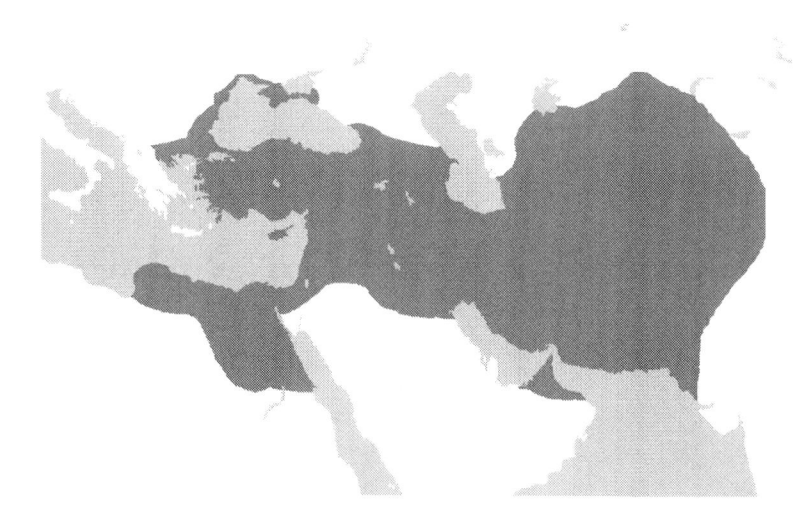

A map depicting the enormous extent of the Achaemenid Empire

Perhaps owing to the fierce reputation of the Spartan warriors, or simply due to the fact that Sparta was farthest from Ionia, Aristagoras visited Sparta first to plead for assistance against the Persians. At the time, Sparta's government was a type of republican-monarchy, in which adult males had voting rights at their councils but two kings presided over the city and largely decided on affairs of state such as diplomacy and war (Plutarch, *Lycurgus*, 7). When Aristagoras finally made it to Sparta, he met with the only reigning king of the time, Cleomenes, and at first tried to appeal to his patriotism, then his pride, and finally his greed. Herodotus' account of Aristagoras' plea to Cleomenes reads, "I hope Cleomenes, that you will not be too much surprised at my anxiety to visit you. The circumstances are these. That Ionians should have become slaves in place of free men is a bitter shame and grief not only to us, but to the rest of Greece, and especially to you, who are the leaders of the Greek world. We beg you, therefore, in the name of the gods of Greece, to save from slavery your Ionian kinsmen. It will be an easy task, for these foreigners have little taste for war, and you are the finest soldiers in the world. The Persian weapons are bows and short spears; they fight in trousers and turbans – that will show you how easy they are to beat! Moreover, the inhabitants of that continent are richer than all the rest of the world put together – they have everything, gold, silver, bronze, elaborately embroidered clothes and beasts of burden and slaves. All this you may have if you wish." (Herodotus, *The Histories*, V, 49).

Cleomenes' interest was apparently piqued until Aristagoras showed him a map of the vast Achaemenid Empire, to which the Spartan replied, "Your proposal to take Lacedaemonians a three months' journey from the sea is a highly improper one." (Herodotus, *The Histories*, V, 50).

Unfazed by the Spartans' denial of his proposal, Aristagoras began to sail back to Ionia, but he stopped in Athens to present the citizens of that city-state with a similar offer. Aristagoras approached the Athenians at an opportune time, as they had recently expelled their tyrant Hippias, who was supported by the Persians, so they were already inclined to campaign against them (Herodotus, *The Histories*, V, 97). Aristagoras used many of the same arguments he tried with the Spartans, including the weakness of the Persian military and the riches of the Achaemenid Empire, but he also appealed to common ancestry that the Athenians and Ionians shared. Herodotus noted, "In addition to this he pointed out that Miletus had been founded by Athenian settlers, so it was only natural that the Athenians, powerful as they were, should help her in her need. Once persuaded to accede to Aristagoras' appeal, the Athenians passed a decree for the dispatch of twenty ships to Ionia, under the command of Melanthius, a distinguished Athenian." (Herodotus, *The Histories*, V, 97).

Athenian support for the Ionian cause was lukewarm at best, and the entire Ionian coalition soon crumbled under the weight of the mighty Achaemenid Empire. When the Persians were finally able to reestablish their rule over the rebellious Ionian city-states, Aristagoras fled and later died in exile, and the rebellious cities, especially Miletus, suffered under brutal punitive measures. (Herodotus, *The Histories*, V, 126). Herodotus graphically wrote about the punishment the Persians meted out to the Ionians: "Once the towns were in their hands, the best-looking boys were chosen for castration and made into eunuchs; the most beautiful girls were dragged from their homes and sent to Darius' court, and the towns themselves, temples and all, were burnt to the ground." (Herodotus, *The Histories*, VI, 32).

The ruthless suppression of the Ionian Revolt by the Achaemenid Persians proved to be the first act in the greater Greco-Persian Wars, and if the Athenians thought that their limited involvement in the affair would mitigate the ire of the Persian king Darius I (ca. 550-486 BCE), they were sorely mistaken. Through their involvement in the Ionian Revolt, despite the fact it was minimal for the most part, the Athenians set themselves at odds with the Persian emperor, putting them on a crash course that would culminate at the Battle of Marathon about nine years later.

An ancient depiction of Darius I

Chapter 2: The Achaemenid Persian Perspective of Athens and Ionia

When the Battle of Marathon took place in 490 BCE, Athens was a powerful city-state, but it was just one among many that were as prone to fight each other as they were non-Greeks. The Persians on the other hand commanded the greatest empire the known world had ever witnessed – the Achaemenid Empire – which spanned from Bactria (present day Afghanistan) in the east to Egypt in the west (Briant 2002, 366). Besides possessing the already ancient and venerated kingdom of Egypt, the Achaemenid Persians also controlled the city of Babylon and the regions of Mesopotamia and the Levant, which were home to such illustrious previous cultures as Israel, the Phoenicians, and the Assyrians just to name a few. When viewed from this perspective, the Greek Ionian city-states were a small fraction of the total empire, and the more distant Athenians may have appeared to the Persians as little more than minor interlopers who were playing a dangerous game that was out of their league. That said, despite the fact that the Persians in general may have disregarded any military threat that the Athenians posed, Ionia was still viewed as an important part of the Achaemenid Empire.

The Achaemenid Empire was divided in satrapies, or provinces, which were generally based more on ethnicity than geographical area, although the two often coincided (Cameron 1973). The number of satrapies also fluctuated, although there were usually at least 20 at any time (Briant 2002, 390). A number of extant Persian satrapal lists are known from the reign of Darius I, which includes ones from the royal palace at Persepolis, Darius' royal tomb, and a colossal statue of the ruler discovered in the ruins of Susa in 1972 (Roaf 1974, 149). Herodotus also gives a list of 20 satrapies and the type and amount of tribute they brought to Persepolis in Book III of *The Histories*. Ionia was listed in some of these lists as a satrapy, and Herodotus' account in particular noted that the Ionia was responsible for a yearly tribute payment of 400 talents of silver (Herodotus, *The Histories*, III, 90). The satrapy of Ionia was clearly an important possession to the Achaemenid Persians, which in their eyes justified the level of brutality they used in order to bring the province back into line.

The Athenians no doubt raised the ire of Darius I when they supported the Ionian Revolt, but their direct interference in the affairs of the Achaemenid Empire was not their first transgression against the Persians. Before the Athenians inserted themselves into the Ionian Revolt, they were involved in a war with Sparta, and when that did not go well for them, they looked to Persia for an alliance. The Athenians sent envoys to the city of Sardis in Ionia to meet with the Persian governor, Artaphernes, who requested that the Greeks give a symbolic gift of earth and water to him. Herodotus explained, "To strengthen their position they sent representatives to Sardis, in the hope of concluding an alliance with Persia. When they got there and delivered their message, Artaphernes the son of Hystaspes, the governor, asked in reply who these Athenians were that sought an alliance with Persia, and in what part of the world they lived. Then, having been told, he put the Persian case in a nutshell by remarking that, if the Athenians would signify their submission by the usual gift of earth and water, then Darius would make a pact with them;

otherwise they had better go home. Eager that the pact should be concluded, the envoys acted on their own initiative and accepted Artapherenes' terms – for which they were severely censured on their return to Athens." (Herodotus, *The Histories*, V, 73).

As Herodotus wrote, the Athenian envoys were admonished for their act of obeisance towards the Persians, but the political damage had been done; the Athenians broke Persian protocol and tradition when they offered earth and water but did not give their obedience. Furthermore, around the time of the Athenian earth and water fiasco, Hippias, the tyrant who was expelled from Athens in 510 BCE, showed up in Sardis and urged Artapherenes and the Persians to restore him as tyrant of Athens (Olmstead 1948, 151-52). In fact, when the Persians finally set forward with their invasion plan of Greece, Hippias was with the Persian fleet, which indicates that the invasion was at least partially intended to restore Athens to tyranny (Doenges 1998, 2).

By breaking the standard Persian political protocol, the Athenians had placed themselves on the imperial radar of the Persians, but when they supported the Ionian Revolt, Darius I took the matter personally. The Persians were not the only one who committed atrocities during the Ionian Revolt, as a combined force of Ionian Greeks and Athenians captured and sacked the city of Sardis and reduced its temple to rubble. When Darius I learned of the Athenians role in the sack of Sardis, he exploded. According to Herodotus, "The story goes that when Darius learnt of the disaster, he did not give a thought to the Ionians, knowing perfectly well that the punishment for their revolt would come; but he asked who the Athenians were, and then, on being told, called for his bow. He took it, set an arrow on the string, shot it up into the air and cried: 'Grant, O God, that I may punish the Athenians.'" (Herodotus, *The Histories,* V, 105).

To Darius I, the matter was settled: the Athenians must be taught a lesson and brought under the yoke of the Achaemenid Empire.

Chapter 3: The Persians Prepare to Invade Greece

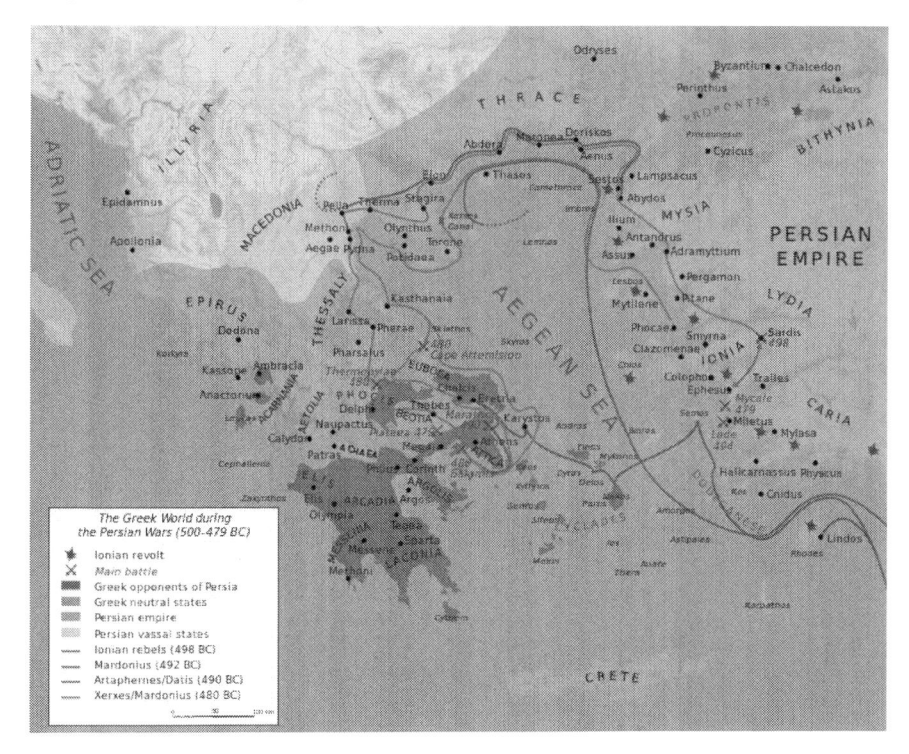

A map of the region from 500-479 BCE

In the ancient world, it took a lot of time and resources to plan a large-scale military campaign, and the Persian invasion of Greece was no exception. The heart of the Achaemenid Empire was thousands of miles from Greece, so any major invasion would involve many logistical concerns, especially transportation of troops and resources, but Darius I was up for the challenge. The Persian army was led by the general Mardonius, who mustered his forces on land and sea in Ionia in 491 BCE, and his expedition into Greece would be the largest military expedition that world had ever seen. In fact, it was most likely intended to subjugate not only Athens but all of Greece.

From Ionia, Mardonius led the Persian army north along the Aegean coastline until they marched through Thrace and Macedonia. At this point, they encountered a storm that destroyed most of their ships (Herodotus, *The Histories*, VI, 44). The disastrous loss of the Persian fleet only proved to be a temporary setback though, as the rich Achaemenid Empire was able to muster a new army, which was led by a general named Datis. Datis was ordered by Darius I to "reduce Athens and Eretria to slavery and to bring the slaves before the king." (Herodotus, *The Histories*, VI, 94).

Datis had many advantages over the Greeks, as he commanded overwhelming naval superiority and had the military intelligence of Hippias, the former tyrant of Athens, at his disposal (Doenges 1998, 2). Instead of following Mardonius' route the previous year around the Aegean, Datis led the Persian army by ships directly across the Aegean, reducing the island of Naxos to slavery but sparing Delos (Herodotus, *The Histories*, VI, 95-98).

When Datis and the Persians arrived in Greece, they first set their sights on laying waste to Eretria. According to Herodotus, the Eretrians prepared themselves for a long siege but were betrayed by some of their own people: "The Eretrians had no intention of leaving their defenses to meet the coming attack in the open; their one concern (the proposal not to abandon the town having been carried) was to defend their walls – if they could . . . then on the seventh, two well-known Eretrians, Euphorbus the son of Alcimachus and Philagrus the son of Cyneas, betrayed the town to the enemy. The Persians entered, and stripped the temples bare and burnt them in revenge for the burnt temples of Sardis, and, in accordance with Darius' orders, carried off all the inhabitants as slaves." (Herodotus, *The* Histories, VI, 101)

With Eretria reduced to rubble, Datis then turned his attention south to the Attica peninsula and the city of Athens, but unlike the Eretrians, the Athenians would be better prepared and would leave their city to meet the Persians on the plain near Marathon.

Chapter 4: The Order of Battle

A picture of reconstructed Persian ships on the beach near the Battle of Marathon

Before the Battle of Marathon, the Athenians had plenty of time to plan and mobilize for war, and after the Persians defeated the Ionians and then obliterated Eretria, the Athenians were able to put a plan into action that is still admired and studied by military historians. Although Athens was a decent sized city-state for the Hellenic world, it was puny compared to the Achaemenid Empire, making it impossible to make up for the numerical disparity in a number of ways.

Nonetheless, Athens was still formidable. All Athenian citizens between the ages of 18-42 were eligible for military service (Sage 1996, 38), and the army was sub-divided by tribes, which were then commanded by lieutenants known as *taxiarchs* (Sage 1996, 38). Although the requirements for and basic structure of the Athenian military are known, much less is known about the men's training. During the period of the Battle of Marathon, there is no evidence for any formal training of hoplites in Athens, and the only Greek city-state where any significant training is recorded comes from Sparta (Sage 1996, 35). In other words, the Athenian military at the time of the Battle of Marathon was a sort of "home guard," where each male citizen was responsible for his part militarily and thus always prepared for war.

As noted before, Herodotus is the most complete primary source concerning the Battle of Marathon, but others do exist or at least once did, that can help complement Herodotus' account. The oldest sources that depicted the Battle of Marathon were actually a series of pictures that were painted in the Poecile Stoa by the artists Micon and Paenus around 460 BCE, about 30 years after the battle (Hammond 1968, 26). Unfortunately, the pictures are no longer extant, but the Greek geographer Pausanias gave a partial description in his geographic survey of Greece: "At the end of the painting are those who fought at Marathon; the Boeotians of Plataea and the Attic contingent are coming to blows with the foreigners. In this place neither side has the better, but the centre of the fighting shows the foreigners in flight and pushing one another into the morass, while at the end of the painting are the Phoenician ships, and the Greeks killing the foreigners who are scrambling into them." (Pausanias, *Description of Greece*, I, 5.3). Pausanias' description of the Poecile Stoa is useful because it corroborates Herodotus' accounts, namely that the Plataeans were the only other Greeks besides the Athenians who fought the Persians. It also indicates the chaos of the Persians' retreat.

The battle of Marathon itself is believed to have taken place in September 490 BCE (Hammond 1968), and it is also thought to be the first amphibious battle in world history (Doenges 1998, 4). The Persians landed their invasion force near Marathon because it was believed to be good ground for them to maneuver their cavalry, which the Persian commander Datis believed would give him the edge over the Greek hoplites (Hammond 1968, 33). Although the plain around Marathon was good ground for cavalry and was no doubt a large part of the Persian decision to land there, its proximity to Eretria also played a role. Herodotus wrote, "The part of Attic territory nearest Eretria – and also the best ground for cavalry to maneuver in – was at Marathon. To Marathon, therefore, Hippias the son of Pisistratus directed the invading army, and the Athenians, as soon as the news arrived, hurried to meet it. The Athenian troops were commanded by ten generals, of whom the tenth was Miltiades." (Herodotus, *The Histories*, VI, 102-103).

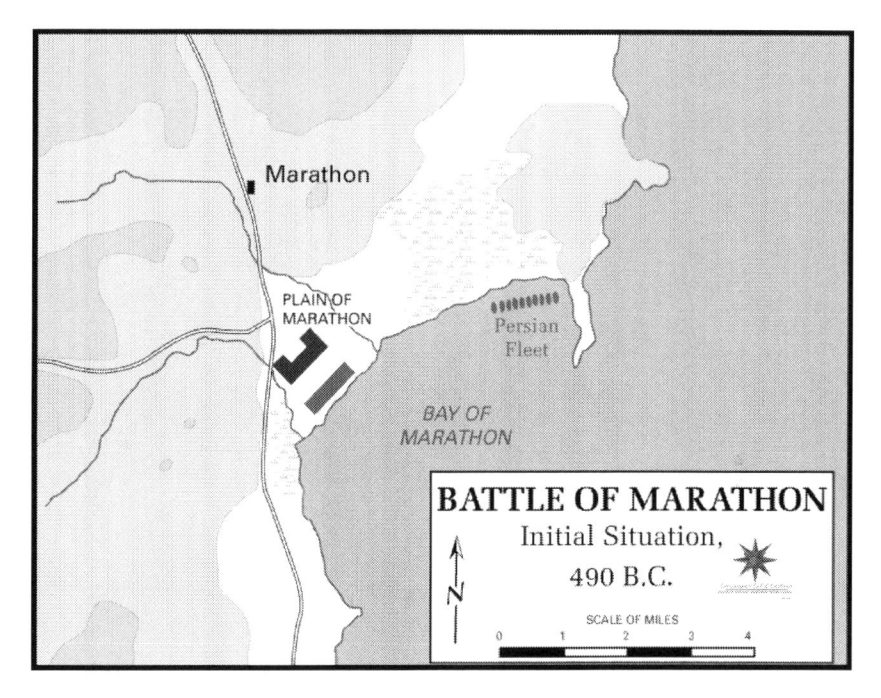

Disposition of the forces at Marathon

The appearance of the former Athenian tyrant, Hippias, is also important because he apparently provided useful intelligence to Datis and the Persians that revealed Marathon to be the best place for cavalry operations. It was also close to the recently conquered Eretria, and the close proximity to Eretria was logistically important to the Persians and their potential success not only at Marathon but also if they were to subject all of Attica and possibly Greece itself. Since the Persian army was so far removed from the nearest Achaemenid colonies (which were across the Aegean in Ionia), they were forced to use Eretria as a temporary base and source of their supply lines (Hammond 1968, 32). The short distance between Eretria and Marathon across the bay also provided a safe and quick route for the Persians to move goods and men.

As a result, the Persians assembled their army near Marathon, but the exact size of the army is still open to conjecture. Unfortunately, Herodotus never gave a number for the combatants in the Persian army – only ships – so modern historians are forced to make educated guesses based on the size of the field, the number that Herodotus listed as killed, and the number of Persian ships. A recent study estimates that the number of Persian fighting men may have been around 12,000-15,000 men, which would not be much more than the army the Greeks fielded at Marathon (Doenges 1998, 6), but earlier studies, such as Hammond's, places the total number of the

Persian army as high as 90,000. That said, Hammond noted that many of them would have been sailors and not infantry (Hammond 1968, 33).

Chapter 5: The Greek and Persian Ways of War

Numbers aside, the two forces fought in a completely different way, which each side had perfected over decades, perhaps centuries, in their respective theaters of war. The Persian army was formed of contingents mustered from the furthest reaches of its vast empire, and though one might expect what was, in effect, a "multinational" force to adopt vastly different styles of fighting, ancient historians writing of the battle indicate there was a degree of standardization in their equipment. That said, it is possible the ancient historians who wrote of the battle, all of whom were Greek, decided to lump all Persian forces together by assuming one unit would have much the same equipment as the next, as was the case for the Greek soldiers. The Persian army that faced the Spartans and their Greek allies at Thermopylae was made up of infantry, cavalry and chariot units, each of them apparently equipped in a similar fashion. The infantry was what would be categorized by military historians as "light", thus not bearing heavy armor or weapons. Each individual Persian infantryman would be equipped with a light, short thrusting spear (which could also be thrown if necessary), a shortsword or saber, a light double-curved bow and a wicker shield. Shield sizes appear to have varied from unit to unit, but archaeological evidence from Persian sculpture seems to suggest that, generally speaking, the shields would cover the soldiers wielding them from knee to neck, while not being wide enough to create significant overlap with the ranks on either side.

Wicker might seem like a foolish material to construct a shield out of, but it was in fact remarkably effective in its own right. The wicker was, of course, extremely light, making it very easy to wield, but it was also effective in stopping slashes from light weapons and could also trap thrust weapons that penetrated it, making them extremely hard to withdraw. The cavalry and charioteers also shared similar equipment, being armed with longer curved sabers for slashing, double-curved bows and javelins. It appears as though some units, particularly those from the Persian heartland, were also armed with double-headed axes, fearsome weapons which would have in all likelihood made them the Persian shock troops.

Armor for the Persian soldiers appears to have also been fairly standardized as well. This is because for much of the Persian infantry it was virtually non-existent. Though it's hard to imagine today, especially considering the Persians were going up against heavily armored hoplites, Persian soldiers appear to have worn no greaves, vambraces or any other form of arm or leg armor, and most units seem to have forgone helmets in favor of knotted rags about their heads, or light caps of metal or leather. To protect their torsos, the soldiers either wore nothing at all, or light back-and-breasts of leather, chain mail, or (very rarely) bronze scales. The elite Persian infantry, recruited from the Persian heartlands, and the famous "Immortals", the Emperor's 10,000 strong personal guard, might have been more heavily armored, but generally speaking they were far from protected.

The reasons for this extremely light equipment are simple: aside from the monumental cost of equipping such a massive army like the one the Persians fielded with heavy armor and weapons, they were simply not suited to the climate in which the Persian army conducted much of its operations. The scorching desert plains of Asia Minor and Egypt, the near-impassable mountains of Afghanistan and the Hindu Kush, and the sweltering heat of the Punjab were not battlefields suited for heavy iron, steel or bronze armor, which weighed soldiers down and, in such extremes of temperature, might well carry them off altogether from heatstroke or fatigue. Thus, the standard Persian tactic was to shower similarly lightly-armed opponents with waves of arrows and javelins from a distance before closing with the weakened ranks of the enemy and cutting them to pieces with their short swords and sabers. The cavalry and charioteers would also most likely fight in a similar fashion, rather than in the knee-to-knee heavy cavalry charge of the middle ages or the Napoleonic battlefields more familiar to the West.

The Greeks, by contrast, fought in a vastly different manner. To begin with, while many of the Persian soldiers were conscripts (with the exception of some elite corps, like the Immortals, service in which was one of the greatest honors available in the Persian Empire), all of the Greek infantrymen were volunteers, and generally far better-trained ones. Each city-state required its volunteers to undertake city-wide annual or bi-annual military exercises, and the Spartans, the backbone of the Greek force, literally spent their entire life training and preparing for war, with manual labor entrusted to their serfs, the helots. It is not entirely clear why Sparta placed such a great emphasis on having a militaristic society, but it resulted in making military fitness a preoccupation for the Spartans from birth. Spartan babies with even the slightest hint of physical deformities were left to die, while the fortunate ones began their military training at the age of 7 years old. Every Spartan male had to join the army at 18.

Thus, the backbone of the Greek way of war was the citizen-soldier, and aside from some notable exceptions, like Boeotia, they fielded armies made up almost exclusively of infantry. While that might sound like a disadvantage against more diverse opposing forces that included archers or chariots, the Greeks weren't using just any infantry. Their main strength was the hoplite – a soldier about as different from his Persian counterpart as could possibly be.

Most historians believe that the hoplite became the dominant infantry soldier in nearly all the Greek city-states around the 8th century B.C. Hoplites were responsible for acquiring their own equipment, so not every hoplite might have been equally armed, but considering the style of warfare, they needed as much uniformity as possible.

Like the Persian infantry, the hoplites also carried spears, but while the Persian weapons were short and light, the Greek spears were thick shafts anywhere between seven and nine feet long. These spears were topped by a 9-inch spearhead, with a "lizard-sticker" buttspike at the bottom which could be used as a secondary spearhead if the main weapon was snapped off, or to plant the spear upright when at rest. Each hoplite also carried a shortsword, designed specifically for thrusting in the close confines of a melee (the Spartan weapon, the *xiphos,* was so short as to be virtually a dagger, its blade barely over a foot long). Unlike the Persian infantry, the hoplites did not carry bows. Though the Greeks did employ light infantry, in the form of slingers, javelineers and archers, their role was extremely secondary to that of the heavy infantry.

This was largely due to the armor which each hoplite wore into battle, which consisted of bronze greaves covering the wearer from ankle to knee, a skirt of leather or quilted linen to protect the groin area, and a heavy breastplate made either of bronze or quilted linen under overlapping bronze scales. To protect their heads, the hoplites wore the famous helmet that is perhaps their most iconic feature, a full-face bronze helmet with high flaring cheek-pieces and a thick nasal that obscured and protected their faces completely, topped by a horsehair crest that added another foot to their height. Helmets were worn front-to-back for line infantry and sideways for officers, to make them more recognizable to their own troops in the heat of battle.

Armored from head to foot in iron and bronze, the hoplite was the tank of his age, but the most important feature of his equipment was undoubtedly his shield. Weighing in at over 30 pounds, the *hoplon* or *aspis* was a great wooden bowl over three feet in diameter, made of heavy oak fronted with bronze and covering each hoplite from knee to neck, as well as providing a significant overlap with the shields of his companions in the battle-line. Obviously, these armaments did not lend themselves to the style of fighting the Persians favored. There could be no standing off and engaging the enemy at a distance with the Greek hoplites carrying short swords and thrusting spears, and because of the weight of their equipment (which was up to 70-90 pounds all told),

Greek art depicting hoplites fighting

19th Century illustration of a Hoplite

For the Greeks, a hoplite was only as strong as the hoplite next to him; without hoplites on the sides, both flanks were exposed, and heavy infantry units are not mobile. Thus, the Greeks implemented the phalanx formation, one of history's most important military innovations. The phalanx was a line of infantry as wide across as the battlefield dictated, anything from five to 30 men deep, with each rank of men officered by a veteran. The formation also included an additional, expert file-closer at the back of each file, to keep the formation cohesive.

The phalanx advanced slowly to maintain its tight formation and unit cohesion, speeding up in unison just before reaching combat. The vast hoplite shields overlapped one another significantly, forming an uninterrupted wall of oak and bronze over which the first rank, while holding out their shields, would use their short swords to stab at the enemy in front of him, while the ranks immediately behind the first rank would slash at enemies with their spears over the top of the first line. Because each soldier's right flank was shielded by his companion's shield (all shields were strapped to the left arm, to preserve the integrity of the formation; left-handed fighters did not exist), the phalanx, especially in the case of less well-trained units, had a tendency to edge to the right, which the Greeks countered by placing their elite troops to the right as a bulwark. The rows in back of the first line would also use their shields to help hold up the hoplites in the front and help them maintain their balance. The formation and method of attack was designed to physically overpower the enemy and scare them, lowering their morale. The phalanx as a fighting unit fell out of favor by the height of the Roman Empire, but the principles behind it remained in use for subsequent infantry formations lasting past the American Civil War. As the Greeks relied on the hoplite to defend other hoplites and concentrate their attack, infantry units in the gunpowder age relied on concentrated gunfire to stun and scare the enemy. And as military commanders learned time and again throughout the ages, if soldiers were not packed shoulder to shoulder in a tight formation, they were far more likely to flee.

Ultimately, though this is a subject of some contention, much of the consensus argues that the main strength of the hoplite phalanx was its utter inexorability when it operated as a cohesive, immaculately drilled unit – an unstoppable juggernaut which relied less on the initial clash of shield-walls (hoplites never advanced at a run, to preserve their formation) than on the relentless pushing force of their advance to shatter the enemy formation.

Chapter 6: The Athenians Take the Field

"With you it rests, Callimachus, either to bring Athens to slavery, or, by securing her freedom, to be remembered by all future generations. For never since the time that the Athenians became a people were they in so great a danger as now. If they bow their necks beneath the yoke of the Persians, the woes which they will have to suffer...are already determined. If, on the other hand, they fight and overcome, Athens may rise to be the very first city in Greece." – Miltiades to the polemarch [an honored dignitary of Athens] before the battle, according to Herodotus

Since Athens was a democracy, major decisions of state were decided by a majority vote of either an assembly of the citizens, or as often in the case of war, a vote of the 10 generals mentioned above. The first major decision that the Athenians would face was to either prepare the city's defenses for a siege or wait for help from other Greeks, such as the Spartans, to arrive. The other choice was to meet the much larger Persian force on the battlefield near Marathon. There was merit to both arguments, and in true Greek fashion both sides were heard, but ultimately it was the general Miltiades who swayed the opinion of the other generals to meet the Persians on the battlefield: "Amongst the Athenian commanders opinion was divided: some were against risking a battle, on the ground that the Athenian force was too small to stand a chance of success; others – and amongst them Miltiades – urged it . . . To Callimachus, therefore, Miltiades turned. 'It is now in your hands, Callimachus,' he said, 'either to enslave Athens, or to make her free and to leave behind you for all future generations a memory more glorious than even Harmodius and Aristogeiton left. Never in our history have we Athenians been in such peril as now. If we submit to the Persians, Hippias will be restored to power – and there is little doubt what misery must then ensue: but if we fight and win, then this city of ours may well grow to pre-eminence amongst all the cities of Greece' . . . Miltiades' words prevailed, and by the vote of Callimachus the War Archon the decision to fight was made." (Herodotus, *The Histories*, VI, 109-110).

The Athenians thus decided to meet the Persians on the battlefield, and it is generally believed that they took the northern route from Athens to Marathon, which is about 25 miles long (Doegnes 1998, 7). The only other road to Marathon was slightly longer at about 28 miles and would have left the Greeks more exposed to a cavalry attack (Doegnes 1998, 7). After the Greeks arrived, the two sides faced each other in an uneasy calm that lasted for a few days before the battle, which helped the Greeks fortify their forces and better prepare for battle.

Once the Greeks arrived on the plain, they camped at a site that was considered to be sacred to the hero Hercules, and they were then joined by the Plataean Greek contingent. According to Herodotus, "The Athenian troops were drawn up on a piece of ground sacred to Heracles, when they were joined by the Plataeans, who came to support them with every available man." (Herodotus, *The Histories*, VI, 108).

The total number of Greeks who were camped at the plain near Marathon is estimated to be around 10,000 total, with about 1,000 of the hoplites being Plataeans (Hammond 1968, 34). Although most of the Athenian hoplites traveled to Marathon to confront the Persians, a small skeleton crew stayed behind in Athens in order to defend the city in case the Persian forces split and part attacked the city (Hammond 1968, 34).

Datis and the Persians were eager to engage the Greeks in battle as they had the advantage with numbers and cavalry, but the Greeks were not yet done with their preparations that would help give them the ultimate advantage. In the days before the actual battle, the Greeks probably gradually advanced their position, felling trees along the way and then using those trees to obstruct the Persian cavalry (Hammond 1968, 39). Thus, by the time the Greeks had advanced to the actual battlefield, they tried to be protected in their rear and flanks by the rugged hillsides, which effectively made the Persian cavalry useless (Hammond 1968, 39). This strategy was a major factor in how the Greeks won the battle, because the vaunted and feared Persian cavalry played almost no role in the Battle of Marathon, and the Greek hoplites were much better armored and trained than the average Persian soldiers, who wore little armor.

Chapter 7: The Greek Center Collapses

In essence, Miltiades and the Greeks knew that in order to defeat the larger Persian army they had to plan accordingly and win the battle before the first blow was struck, while Datis became too reliant on his cavalry and was unwilling to improvise. Still, while the decisions made by Miltiades and Datis before the actual battle may have ultimately decided the victor, the two sides still had to fight, and it turned out to be an epic battle that has rightfully earned its legendary reputation.

In pre-modern warfare, the standard order of battle usually involved the belligerent armies lining up in shield wall, or *phalanx*, across from each other and then fighting with the ultimate goal of breaking through the enemy's line. Herodotus' description of the Battle of Marathon appears to follow this method: "When it did come, the Athenian army moved into position for the coming struggle. The right wing was commanded by Callimachus – for it was the regular practice at that time in Athens that the War Archon should lead the right wing; then followed the tribes, in their regular order; and, finally, on the left wing, were the Plataeans." (Herodotus, *The Histories*, VI, 111).

The fact that the Athenian field marshal (War Archon), Callimachus, was on one of the wings instead of the center is another important aspect of the battle that will be discussed further below, but as the two armies met, the Greeks were forced to compensate for their numerical inferiority, so Callimachus, Miltiades and the other Greek generals were faced with a choice: concentrate their forces in the center (where the initial Persian thrust would probably be focused) or place the majority of their forces on the wings in order to prevent being flanked. According to Herodotus, the Greeks chose the second option: "One result of the disposition of Athenian troops before the battle was the weakening of their center by the effort to extend the line sufficiently to cover the whole Persian front; the two wings were strong, but the line in the centre was only a few ranks deep. The dispositions made, and the preliminary sacrifice promising success, the word was given to move, and the Athenians advanced at a run towards the enemy, not less than a mile away . . . They were the first Greeks, so far as we know, to charge at a run, and the first who dared to look without flinching at Persian dress and the men who wore it; for until that day came, no Greek could hear even the word Persian without terror." (Herodotus, *The Histories*, VI, 112).

Perhaps the most interesting and strategically important aspect of this passage is the fact that the Greeks ran to meet the Persians. At first, one may think that running to meet the enemy on the battlefield would be disadvantageous, especially a mile away, because it could tire the runners out, but there are some advantages to the strategy as well. Combatants in pre-modern battles had to be in good physical shape given the nature of the hand-to-hand fighting, so a brisk run to meet the enemy would raise soldiers' heart rates and help get them in the proper frame of mind as the battle began. In effect, the mile or so that the Greek hoplites ran across the plain of Marathon to meet the Persian army was a warm-up for the main event, which was the actual battle.

Modern scholars have also pointed out that when the Greeks sprinted to meet the Persians, they eliminated one of the advantages that the Persians had: cavalry. Once the two armies became engaged and the Greek flanks were protected by the hilly terrain, the Persian cavalry threat was eliminated (Hammond 1968, 40). The other Persian advantage – numerical superiority – was countered by the Greek formation of the battle line, which would prove to be the ultimate undoing of Datis and his army.

However, once the battle began, it was not long before the thin Greek center collapsed. A burial mound that was discovered and excavated in modern times marks where the Greek center stood, and also where the Greeks suffered most of their casualties (Hammond 1968, 18). Herodotus' account tells how the Persians pushed through the center: "The struggle at Marathon was long and drawn out. In the centre, held by the Persians themselves and the Sacae, the advantage was with the foreigners, who were so far successful as to break the Greek line and pursue the fugitives inland from the sea; but the Athenians on one wing and the Plataeans on the other were both victorious . . . Drawing their two wings together into a single unit, they turned their attention to the Persians who had broken through in the center." (Herodotus, *The Histories*, VI, 113).

The wings were instrumental to Greek victory, as they essentially ceded the center to the Persians but then collapsed on their enemy from the wings. Herodotus, who had no military experience and was not well versed in military affairs, does not mention if the Greeks planned the maneuver in such a way, but logic would seem to indicate that they did. Up until this point in the battle, everything that Miltiades and Callimachus did was precise and well-thought out, from the road they took to Marathon, to where they chose to camp, and even the decision to sprint to engage the Persians. As such, it would be hard to believe that the Greek generals did not plan to collapse the wings as well. Hammond noted, "Now it is obvious that the action of the Athenians and the Plataeans on the wings, which were separated from one another by a considerable distance, had been preconcerted; for Miltiades, having thinned his centre and packed his wings, must have anticipated the actual developments in the fighting and issued orders in advance to the effect that the men on the wings, if and when victorious, were to turn towards the centre, to form line and to go to the aid of the Greek troops of the centre." (Hammond 1968, 29).

Hannibal's victory against the Romans at Cannae has often been considered the seminal use of a pincers attack of this type, and it is still considered a masterpiece of generalship that was imitated about 2,000 years later by Napoleon at Austerlitz, but if Hammond is correct, Miltiades and Callimachus orchestrated a pincers attack at Marathon centuries before Hannibal did. Either way, it's clear that Miltiades and the other Greek generals aided their cause and evened the odds by planning for contingencies. On the other hand, despite numerous advantages, Datis and the Persians were unable to capitalize on their superior numbers at the center of the line, and their cavalry was useless (Doenges 1998, 12).

Chapter 8: The Persian Retreat

"The two armies fought together on the plain of Marathon for a length of time; and in the mid-battle the barbarians were victorious, and broke and pursued the Greeks into the inner country; but on the two wings the Athenians and the Plataeans defeated the enemy . Having so done, they suffered the routed barbarians to fly at their ease, and joining the two wings in one, fell upon those who had broken their own center, and fought and conquered them. These likewise fled, and now the Athenians hung upon the runaways and cut them down, chasing them all the way to the shore, on reaching which they laid hold of the ships and called aloud for fire." - Herodotus

Once the Greek flanks collapsed on the Persian center, Datis knew that phase of the battle was lost, so he ordered the Persians to retreat to the ships. Herodotus wrote very little about the Persian retreat other than that the Greeks captured seven Persians ships and that two Greek generals, Callimachus and Stesilaus, were killed pursuing the Persians (Herodotus, *The Histories*, VI, 114-115), but Pausanias helps fill in the gaps. He wrote that the disastrous Persian retreat may have been partially due to them not knowing the terrain and running into a marsh: "There is at Marathon a lake which for the most part is marshy. Into this ignorance of the roads made the foreigners fall in their flight, and it is said that this accident was the cause of their great losses." (Pausanias, *Geography of Greece*, I, 32,7).

Datis and the Persians were losing, but they were not yet defeated, so he and his surviving army that made it to the ships set sail around the Attic peninsula for Athens (Morkot 1996, 75). The quickest way for the Persians to reach Athens from Marathon was by land, and preferably on horseback, but once the Greeks defeated them at Marathon, they had to sail the entire way to Athens (Hodge 2001, 247). At this point, the Greek victory on the battlefield of Marathon was assured, but all may have been lost if Datis and the Persians could reach Athens before them. Plutarch succinctly captured the Greek urgency as they raced back to Athens on foot: "When the Athenians had routed the Barbarians and driven them aboard their ships, and saw that they were sailing away, not toward the islands, but into the gulf toward Attica under compulsion of wind and wave, then they were afraid lest the enemy find Athens empty of defenders, and so they hastened homeward with nine tribes, and reached the city that very day. But Aristides was left behind at Marathon with his own tribe, to guard the captives and the booty." (Plutarch, *Aristides*, 4-5).

Chapter 9: A Shield Signal?

As the Greeks raced on foot to protect their precious city, Datis had one last hand to play: traitors within Athens. This may be perhaps the most mysterious aspect of the fighting, as Herodotus' account seems to raise more questions than answers. According to Herodotus, members of the powerful Alcmaeonidae family conspired with Datis and the Persians in some manner. Herodotus wrote, "The Persians laid a course round Sunium for Athens, which they hoped to reach in advance of the Athenian army. In Athens the Alcmaeonidae were accused of suggesting this move; they had, it was said, an understanding with the Persians, and raised a shield as a signal to them when they were already on board. While the Persian fleet was on its way round Sunium, the Athenians hurried back with all possible speed to save their city, and succeeded in reaching it before the arrival of the Persians." (Herodotus, *The Histories*, VI, 116).

Plutarch's later account of the race to Athens by both the Persians and Greeks corroborates Herodotus' account, but the aspect of traitorous elements within Athens is not repeated by later historians, so modern scholars are left to other methods to judge the validity and importance of the account. Herodotus clearly noted that a shield was raised as a signal to the Persian fleet, but he did not specify exactly *how* that shield was used as a signal or what type of message it could have conveyed. It is important to recognize that a hoplite shield could not have given a flash because of its convex shape (Hodge 2001, 237), so this would rule out the shield signal as a heliographic device, and it's unclear whether heliography was even used as a method of communication at the time. But what if what Herodotus described as a shield was really a flat, bronze sheet that was capable of reflection? In theory, this could be done at a range of up to almost three miles, but there are obvious problems with this theory. If the signaler flashed the bronze in a steady transmission for five to ten minutes, then those on the Persian ships would only see split-second flashes, which would mean that they would have to anchor for a period of time in order to decipher the message (Hodge 2001, 245-46). Modern heliographic techniques have primarily used Morse Code as a language, so any ancient heliographic methods would have employed a code yet unknown to modern scholars.

If the Marathon shield signal was not used as a heliographic device, then it was probably raised or waved by the bearer to the fleet that was near the shore (Hodge 2001, 239). This means that the signal was probably pre-arranged, and that the Persians would have known where and when to look for it on the coastline (Hodge 2001, 239). The signal also had to have been simple enough to just relate a two-way choice (Hodge 2001, 239). Perhaps if the bearer waved the shield above his head, it meant one thing, but if he held the shield low, it meant something else.

Whatever the actual movement of the shield was, there can be no doubt that the one wielding it was an Athenian traitor who was probably at the Battle of Marathon (Hodge 2001, 246), and the origin of the traitorous shield bearer can be determined by assessing the context of the situation. Both armies were in a race south for Athens, with the Greeks by land and the Persians by sea, so anyone signaling the Persian fleet had to have been at Marathon and know that both armies were headed south. The Greeks who stayed behind in Athens did not yet know the outcome of the battle, or that the two armies were headed their way.

As such, if there was a shield signal, it was a message to Datis and the Persians that relayed the movements and intents of the Greek army (Hodge 2001, 246). It will probably never be known what message the signal sent, but Hodge thinks that it meant "Abort Loutsa! Plan B, go round Sounion" (Hodge 2001, 253). Hodge points out that a landing at Loutsa would have been opposed by the Greek army, so the Persians hoped to land at Sounion unopposed, though they were ultimately stymied when the Greeks arrived there before them (Herodotus, *The Histories*, VI, 116). Herodotus wrote that the Persians then anchored outside of the Athenian harbor before sailing back to Asia (Herodotus, *The Histories*, VI, 116).

To add to the mystery of the shield signal, Herodotus somewhat doubted his own account. He wrote that "the tale of the Alcmaeonidae treacherously signaling to the Persians with a shield is, to me, quite extraordinary, and I cannot accept it." (Herodotus, *The Histories*, VI, 121). Herodotus' argument is that the Alcmaeonidae family helped expel the tyrants so it is difficult to believe that they would conspire with the Persians in order to re-install Hippias as tyrant. Of course, this does not necessarily mean that an Athenian traitor did not signal the Persians – it may have been a non-Alcmaeonidae or even an Alcmaeonidae with his own agenda – but at this point, the mystery of the shield signal will probably remain a permanent enigma.

As the fog from the battlefield cleared, Spartan reinforcements finally showed up, but they were no longer needed. Herodotus explained, "After the full moon, two thousand Spartans set off for Athens. They were so anxious not to be late that they were in Attica on the third day after leaving Sparta. They had, of course, missed the battle; but such was their passion to see the Persians, that they went to Marathon to have a look at the bodies. That done, they praised the Athenians on their good work, and returned home." (Herodotus, *The Histories*, VI, 120). What is most interesting about this passage is not that the Spartans showed up late for the battle - Herodotus was detailed in his explanation of their initial refusal to fight – but how quickly the Spartans were able to make it to Marathon.

Chapter 10: How the Greeks Won the Battle of Marathon

As the Persian fleet sailed back to Ionia, the Greeks were finally able to claim victory over their foreign adversaries, but the victory was not an easy one, and there were several factors that played a role. Some of these factors were tangible and concrete, while others were more abstract, but they were all important.

The most notable factor was the battlefield strategy. Even a cursory reading of Herodotus makes it abundantly clear that Miltiades and the other Greek generals were clearly superior in their craft to Datis. Every move the Greeks made was thought out and done with consideration to what the Persian counter may be. The Greeks chose a specific route from Athens to Marathon in order to block the Persians from marching past them, then camped and advanced on terrain that made the Persian cavalry maneuvers difficult, and finally charged on foot to further mitigate what was left of any cavalry advantage. To compensate for the inferior numbers, the Greeks spread their line thin but concentrated their strongest units on the wings, where they could encircle and slaughter the Persians. On the other hand, it appears that Datis went into the battle simply thinking that his superior numbers and cavalry would be enough to carry the day. When the Greeks took his cavalry out of the equation, he apparently had no contingency plan. Even worse, he apparently didn't notice that the Greeks were concentrating their forces on the wings.

Clearly, the Greeks were one step ahead of Datis and the Persians at every stage in the battle, which may be attributed to the dictatorial style of leadership that the Persian general employed and possibly even the types of governments that the Persians and Greeks, particularly the Athenians, lived under. As Herodotus explained, the Greeks were led by a council of generals who had to come to a consensus before important strategic decisions were made. This system was an obvious benefit at the Battle of Marathon, and it was also a reflection of Athenian society, which was something that the Greeks who fought at Marathon did not want to lose. All Athenians born to Athenian citizens were conferred with citizenship rights at birth, which meant that they were able to enjoy benefits that others throughout the world, including other parts of Greece, did not have (Lloyd 1973, 42). In 490 BCE, Athens was free of her tyrants and Athenians had started to enjoy and appreciate the democratic constitution that they had instituted in their city-state. Herodotus believed that the freedom the Athenians enjoyed even made them better fighters: "For while they were oppressed under tyrants, they had no better success in war than any of their neighbors, yet, once the yoke was flung off, they proved the finest fighters in the world. This clearly shows that, so long as they were held down by authority, they deliberately shirked their duty in the field, as slaves shirk working for their masters; but when freedom was won, then every man amongst them was interested in his own cause." (Herodotus, *The Histories*, V, 78).

It is difficult to measure if the Athenians became better fighters after they instituted democracy, as Herodotus argued, but they were cognizant of the difference in political status between them and the Persians, and even their Ionian Greek cousins. Athenians were citizens who had certain rights protected by a constitution, while the Persians and even Ionians were all merely subjects of a king. It is easy to see how the Athenians would have fought much more to preserve their rights and status then the countless soldiers of the Persian army who were forced to fight.

The Athenians had much to lose in terms of their freedoms and rights, which gave them an advantage over the Persians, but defending their land was also an intangible factor that spurred the Greeks to be better fighters on the plain of Marathon. Since the Greeks were fighting in their homeland, they had the advantage of knowing how to use the terrain to their advantage, which was evidenced by the route they took to Marathon and where they camped before the battle, as well as the route they took back to Athens after the battle. Lack of knowledge of the land and terrain also played a role in the Persian retreat going awry (according to Pausanias account), as the soldiers ran into a marsh where they were then cut down.

Fighting on and for their homeland also provided the intangible benefit of fear that aroused the Greeks to fight more fiercely. After the Greeks learned the fate of Eretria, they knew that Athens would be subjected to similar destruction, which no doubt meant that every Greek fought that much harder. By 490 BCE, the Greeks also knew the fate of their Ionian cousins, who according to Herodotus were reduced to slavery. The fear of losing one's family and city can be a much more powerful incentive than any desire to capture riches that the Persian army may have had.

Pride in their status as citizens and free men definitely played a role in propelling the Greeks to victory at Marathon, but as powerful as pride can be, shame can also be strong, and it also apparently played an important role in the Greek victory at Marathon. Although Greek support for the Ionian Revolt was lukewarm at best, their withdrawal part way through the revolt was viewed by many in the Greek world as cowardly and became a source of immense shame for the Athenian people. Herodotus wrote that the Athenian shame manifested itself in a popular play that depicted the Ionian Revolt: "The Athenians, on the contrary, showed their profound distress at the capture of Miletus in a number of ways, and in particular, when Phrynichus produced his play, *The Capture of Miletus*, the audience in the theatre burst into tears. The author was fined a thousand drachmas for reminding them of their own evils, and they forbade anybody ever to put the play on stage again." (Herodotus, *The Histories*, VI, 21). The Athenian desertion of the Ionians was no doubt still fresh on the minds of the Greek warriors who took the field at Marathon as they sought to rectify a wrong that their city had done to fellow Greeks.

There were a number of intangibles that clearly contributed to Greek victory at Marathon, but perhaps the greatest Greek advantage was concrete and tangible. The standard Greek soldiers, known as hoplites, were heavily armed and well-trained fighters. Hoplites began to appear in the Hellenic world in the middle of the 8th century BCE and are named after the large shields, *hoplon*, that they used (Sage 1996, 25). Besides the shield, hoplites wore a metal (usually bronze) helmet, a bronze plate corselet, and metal greaves to protect the shins and calves (Sage 1996, 26). The primary offensive weapon of hoplites was a heavy thrusting spear that would be used when they fought in their standard *phalanx* formation, which was a type of shield wall (Sage 1996, 26). When and if the phalanx was broken, then the hoplites used short stabbing swords for close quarter combat (Sage 1996, 26). The 1st century BCE Greek historian Diodorus described how the hoplites changed weapons during a battle between the Spartans and Plataeans in the 4th century BCE: "For the most capable foot-soldiers of that time, Boeotians and Lacedaemonians, whose lines were drawn up facing one another, began the contest, exposing their lives at every risk. After the first exchange of spears in which most were shattered by the very density of the missiles, they engaged with swords." (Diodorus Siculus, *The Library of*

History, XV.86, 2).

An ancient depiction of a hoplite

A 6th century BCE depiction of phalanx formations

A display of hoplite armor

The superior arms and armor of the Greek hoplites was one of the major selling points that Aristagoras argued to both the Spartans and Athenians in hopes of enticing them to join the Ionian Revolt, which he contrasted with the lack of weaponry carried by the Persian army. The Persian army was comprised of soldiers drawn from throughout the Achaemenid Empire, but at its core was a cadre of Persian fighters known as the Immortals. The Immortals were the Persian king's personal bodyguards and always numbered around 10,000, no matter the losses incurred in a battle, which is how they earned the moniker (Briant 2002, 261-63). Primary source evidence is scant concerning the armor of the Immortals, but modern scholars believe they wore a quilted corselet and carried a wicker shield (Sage 1996, 90). Remains of glazed brick reliefs from the Persian city of Susa depict the Immortals wearing long gowns with no visible armor and carrying spears with bows and quivers slung over their shoulders (Harper, Aruz, and Tallon 1992, 226-27). The Immortals may have been elite warriors, but at Marathon they were no match for the better armored Greek hoplites.

Sculpted depictions of ancient Persian warriors

A frieze from Darius I's palace believed to depict Immortals

Chapter 11: The Marathon Runner

One of the most legendary aspects of the Battle of Marathon, at least in terms of how it resonates in modern society, is the story of the runner named Phillippides or Pheidippides. According to the later Greek historian Plutarch and the 2nd century CE Greek writer Lucian, Pheidippides ran a little over 26 miles from the battlefield of Marathon to Athens in order to tell the citizens of that city that the Greeks had won the battle. Lucian wrote, "Phillippides, the one who acted as courier, is sad to have used it first in our sense when he brought the news of victory from Marathon and addressed the magistrates in session when they were anxious how the battle had ended; "Joy to you, we've won." he said, and there and then he died, breathing his last breath with that, "Joy to you." (Lucian, *A Slip of the Tongue in Greeting*, 3).

Lucian was a fiction writer and not a historian, so this account is probably more legend than historical reality, but it does reveal a couple of key aspects about the Battle of Marathon that lingered in the minds of Greeks several centuries later. First, the account shows that even those who were not historians and military officials viewed the battle as incredibly important; even if the account is purely fictional, Lucian, or whomever the fictional account began with, saw the actual battle as important enough to use as part of a literary device.

Most notably, the account has a certain resonance that has endured not only in the hearts and minds of Greeks for centuries but throughout the world. The idea of a man running to his death to give a message of victory seems to strike a chord that is difficult to describe with words, but it is eloquently done by Lucian. Of course, it is from this legend that the modern standard marathon length has been set at 26.2 miles, which is roughly the distance between Athens and the Marathon battlefield.

However, a closer examination of Herodotus' account reveals that Pheidippides probably ran a much farther distance and was nowhere near the battlefield. According to him, Pheidippides was sent by the Athenian high command to Sparta in order to elicit that city-state's support against the Persians at Marathon. He wrote, "Before they left the city, the Athenian generals sent off a message to Sparta. The messenger was an Athenian named Pheidippides, a professional long-distance runner. According to the account he gave the Athenians on his return, Pheidippides met the god Pan on Mt Parthenium, above Tegea." (Herodotus, *The Histories*, VI, 105).

As this translation of Herodotus notes, Pheidippides was one of many professional runners, who were known as *hemerodromi* in Greece and were important to interstate communication between the ancient Greek city-states (Christensen, Nielsen, and Schwartz 2009, 149). The *hemerodromi* played a vital role in ancient Greek military intelligence, as they were entrusted with classified messages that they delivered orally only to specific people (Christensen, Nielsen, and Schwartz 2009, 160). In other words, Herodotus' account of Pheidippides running to Sparta is nothing outside of the norm of standard ancient Greek military culture and therefore believable at face value. That said, Herodotus credited him with covering 500 kilometers (about 311 miles) in three days and two nights, which is much harder to take at face value (Christensen, Nielsen, and Schwartz 2009, 151).

The historicity of Pheidippides running from Athens to Sparta and back has been questioned by scholars and lay people alike for centuries, and it was apparently even the object of speculation in Herodotus' time. He noted, "The Athenians believed Pheidippides' story, and when their affairs were once more in a prosperous state, they built a shrine to Pan under the Acropolis, and from the time his message was received they have held an annual ceremony, with a torch-race and sacrifices, to court his protection. On the occasion of which I speak – when Pheidippides, that is, was sent on his mission by the Athenian commanders and said that he saw Pan – he reached Sparta the day after he left Athens and delivered his message to the Spartan government." (Herodotus, *The Histories*, VI, 105-6).

That the Athenians and Herodotus believed this story does not necessarily make it so, but modern research has revealed that the run was not only possible but even probable. In modern times, athletes have competed in numerous competitions that replicate those of the ancient Greeks, including long distance running, and in 1984, a Greek man named Giannis Kourus ran one leg of Pheidippides' journey, 250 kilometers, in under 21 hours (Christensen, Nielsen, and Schwartz 2009, 155n).

If this time was doubled, then it would be within the time that Herodotus gave, but there are other factors such as weather and diet that need to be considered. Herodotus noted that although Pheidippides successfully told the Spartans of the impending battle at Marathon, the Spartans declined on religious grounds. The account asserts, "The Spartans, though moved by the appeal, and willing to send help to Athens, were unable to send it promptly because they did not wish to break their law. It was the ninth day of the month, and they said they could not take the field until the moon was full." (Herodotus, *The Histories,* VI, 106).

Although Herodotus gave no dates concerning this event (or any having to do with the Battle of Marathon for that matter), modern scholars believe that the law in question was in relation to a festival for Apollo Karneios, which would place the date of Pheidippides' run, and the Battle of Marathon, in September 490 BCE (Christensen, Nielsen, and Schwartz 2009, 161). September in Greece is hot, which would mean that Pheidippides would have had to have consumed plenty of liquids and a high carbohydrate diet similar to other modern long distance runners in east Africa and Latin America (Christensen, Nielsen, and Schwartz 2009, 162-63). With all of these factors considered, Pheidippides would had to have averaged 10 kilometers every 48 minutes, with short breaks to eat, in order to have completed the run in the span that Herodotus mentioned (Christensen, Nielsen, and Schwartz 2009, 161).

With those factors in mind, the run would have been difficult but possible for a well-trained, professional runner. Also, as with any athletic or physical competition, a large part of the performance barriers are psychological, which Pheidippides may have overcome by meditation on the various gods, such as Pan, in order to break through the physical limitations (Lloyd 1973, 15). Fear may also have played a role in his successful run; the carnage that the Persians wrought on Eretria was no doubt still fresh on his mind as he undertook his mission to do his part to save his city. Even as the Spartans were observing their religious duties, Datis was moving the Persian army onto the plain of Marathon.

Chapter 12: The Results and Aftermath of the Battle of Marathon

After the Battle of Marathon, Darius I was not done with his punitive plans for Athens. According to Herodotus, the Persian loss at Marathon only incensed the Achaemenid king even more: "When the news of the battle of Marathon reached Darius, son of Hystaspes and king of Persia, his anger against Athens, already great enough on account of the assault on Sardis, was even greater, and he was more than ever determined to make war on Greece. Without loss of time he dispatched couriers to the various states under his dominion with orders to raise an army much larger than before; and also warships, transports, horses, and grain. So the royal command went round; and all Asia was in an uproar for three years, with the best men being enrolled in the army for the invasion of Greece, and with the preparations. In the year after that, a rebellion in Egypt, which had been conquered by Cambyses, served only to hard Darius' resolve to go to war, not only against Greece but against Egypt too." (Herodotus, *The Histories*, VII, 1).

Darius would never get his chance to exact revenge against the Athenians, as he died soon after in 487 BCE (Forrest 2001, 41), but the Greco-Persian Wars would continue with his son and successor, Xerxes, who would lead an even greater army into Greece. Some Greeks also anticipated another Persian invasion. The Spartan king Leonidas was the main advocate of this theory, sustaining it even when Darius died and was succeeded by his son Xerxes in 486 BCE. Under Leonidas and their other king, Agesilaus, the Spartans waged a series of campaigns in the years following the Battle of Marathon to bring reluctant allies and Persian sympathizers into the fold and ensure a united Greek front would greet all Persian attempts to invade.

That invasion, just as Leonidas had prophesied, came in 480 BCE, when Xerxes, at the head of an army which Herodotus claimed numbered over a million men, bridged the Hellespont (the Dardanelles straits) via a colossal pontoon bridge and marched his army into Thrace, threatening Greece proper. But ultimately, the Persian invasion under Xerxes would also end in failure thanks to legendary battles like Thermopylae and Salamis (Forrest 2001, 41), and given that perspective in hindsight, the Battle of Marathon was the pivotal event, and the Athenians were the major agent, in the Greco-Persian Wars. It was the Athenians who instigated the Ionian Greeks into rebellion and subsequently provoked the wrath of the Persians, and it was the Athenians that soundly defeated the Persians at Marathon, which set the stage for the later battles of Thermopylae, Salamis, and Plataea.

Achaemenid Persian historical records say nothing of the Battle of Marathon and little concerning the Greco-Persian wars, which is not surprising since the Persian historical tradition was essentially inherited from other ancient Near Eastern traditions that depicted the sovereign as always victorious (Cameron 1983, 80-81). Even had the Persians followed more modern or Hellenic historiographical traditions, they still would have ignored their loss at Marathon due to its one-sidedness. According to Herodotus, the final casualty count of the battle was 5,400 Persians killed while the Greeks only lost 192 men (Herodotus, *The Histories*, VI, 117).

Whatever the actual numbers, the dead Greek hoplites were buried at the site of the Battle of Marathon, which led to the site becoming both a sacred place and an archaeological treasure trove in later centuries. Modern archaeological excavations at Marathon have revealed that a mound at the site, called the "Soros," was in fact the burial place of the fallen Athenian hoplites (Hammond 1968, 14). In terms of recreating the Battle of Marathon, the mound is believed by modern scholars to be the place where the Greek center was broken and where they suffered the most casualties (Hammond 1968, 18). Excavations have shown that the hoplites were cremated *en masse* on a large pyre following ancient Greek funerary traditions. Those present for the funeral then had a large feast, placed earth over the pyre, and then laid wreaths, which effectively made the site into a memorial.

Hundreds of years later the Greek geographer Pausanias visited the site and gave a detailed report of what he witnessed. He wrote, "There is a parish called Marathon, equally distant from Athens and Carystus in Euboea. It was at this point in Attica that the foreigners landed, were defeated in battle, and lost some of their vessels as they were putting off from land. On the plain is the grave of the Athenians, and upon it are slabs giving the names of the killed according to their tribes; and there is another grave for the Boetian Plataeans and for the slaves, for slaves fought then for the first time by the side of their masters. There is also a separate monument to one man, Miltiades, the son of Cimon, although his end came later, after he had failed to take Paros and for this reason had been brought to trial by the Athenians. At Marathon every night you can hear horses neighing and men fighting. No one who has expressly set himself to behold this vision has ever got any good from it, but the spirits are not wroth with such as in ignorance change to be spectators. The Marathonians worship both those who died in the fighting, calling them heroes, and secondly Marathon, from whom the parish derives its name, and then Heracles, saying that they were the first among the Greeks to acknowledge him as a god. . . Although the Athenians assert that they buried the Persians, because in every case the divine law applies that a corpse should be laid under the earth, yet I could find no grave." (Pausanias, *Description of Greece*, I. 32. 3).

Picture of the mound at Marathon

Pausanias' account is not only interesting but also fills in gaps of Herodotus' account and corroborates it in other ways. Pausanias noted that the names of all the Athenian fallen were written on slabs at the site, which could corroborate Herodotus' number of fallen Greeks. Although Herodotus wrote his history decades after the Battle of Marathon, some of the veterans were still alive, so he may have consulted them as sources, but it is improbable that senior citizens could have given him such accurate numbers on the fallen. For that, he probably consulted the inscriptions that Pausanias described.

Another important point raised by Pausanias was that the Plataeans and slaves were given a separate grave. Herodotus made no mention of slaves fighting on the Greek side, but he did describe how the Plataeans came to side with the Athenians at Marathon. He wrote that the Plataeans were essentially compelled to fight on the side of the Athenians due to the latter's past assistance of the former and that the "people of Plataea put themselves into Athenian hands, and which led to their coming to support of Athens at Marathon." (Herodotus, *The Histories*, VI, 108). Perhaps Pausanias, who lived much later, confused the Plataeans' inferior status with some sort of servitude towards Athens, but unless more evidence is discovered, this will remain a question.

Pausanias' mention of the hero of Marathon, Miltiades, is also important, as the account notes that the general was given a memorial at Marathon but was also disgraced and faced legal problems later in his life. Herodotus gave a much more detailed account of Miltiades tragic life: "After the slaughter at Marathon, the already high reputation of Miltiades in Athens was greatly increased. Consequently, when he asked for a fleet of seventy ships together with troops and money, without even telling the Athenians the object of the expedition he had in mind, but merely saying he would enrich them if they followed him, because it was a place where they could easily get as much money as they wanted, they were so carried away by excitement that they made no objections whatever. They let him have the ships and the men, whereupon he set sail for Paros . . . All he had achieved after twenty-six days' siege was to destroy the crops in the countryside; he failed to annex the island, and he did not bring home a single penny." (Herodotus, *The Histories*, VI, 132-35).

Things only went from bad to worse for the hero of Marathon. During the siege of Paros, Miltiades suffered an injury to his leg, which became infected when he entered the sacred shrine of Demeter. On top of that, his Athenian investors pursued criminal charges against him. Herodotus wrote, "Miltiades on his return to Athens became the talk of the town; many were loud in their censure of him, and especially Xanthippus, the son of Ariphron, who brought him before the people to be tried for his life on the charge of defrauding the public. Miltiades, though present in court, was unable to speak in his own defense because his leg was gangrened; he lay on a couch and his friends spoke for him, basing their defense upon his past services to his country. They had much to say about the battle of Marathon . . . The popular verdict was to spare his life, but to fine him fifty talents for his offence. Shortly afterwards the gangrene in his thigh grew worse; mortification set in and he died. The fifty talents were paid by his son Cimon." (Herodotus, *The Histories*, VI, 136). Thus, Miltiades, the great hero of Marathon, died an early, painful, and inglorious death as a convicted criminal and pauper.

While Miltiades' life after the Battle of Marathon veered from fame to infamy, he was not the only veteran of the epic battle who was remembered in later centuries. In Pausanias's account of the Marathon battlefield, he noted that another temple was erected at the site to commemorate the Greek victory, and that a famous Greek playwright was among the veterans. He wrote, "Still farther off is a temple to Glory, this too being a thank-offering for the victory over the Persians who landed at Marathon. This is the victory of which I am of opinion the Athenians were proudest; while Aeschylus, who had won such renown for his poetry and for his share in the naval battles before Artemisium and at Salamis, recorded at the prospect of death nothing else, and merely wrote his name, his father's name, and the name of his city, and added that he had witnesses to his valor in the grove at Marathon and in the Persians who landed there." (Pausanias, *Description of Greece*, I.14.5).

Although Aeschylus was recognized as a veteran of the Battle of Marathon by ancient historians, none of his surviving works tell such stories, so it was left to other writers to glorify the Greeks. Of course, Herodotus' account is the most complete to survive, and as was the custom with ancient Greek historians, Herodotus recited his history to live audiences, which included a reading at Athens in 446/445 BCE that no doubt was in front of some of the veterans of the Battle of Marathon (Hammond 1968, 28). The Battle of Marathon also inspired the writer Lucian enough to include it in his famous *Dialogues of the Gods*, in which the god Pan discussed his attributes: "But I won't disgrace you father. I'm a musician and play the pipe loud and true. Dionysus is lost without me, and has made me his companion and fellow-reveler; I'm his dance-leader, and if you could see how many flocks I have around Tegea and on Parthenium, you'd be delighted. I'm lord and master of all Arcadia. Besides that, the other day, I fought so magnificently on the side of the Athenians at Marathon that a prize of valor was chosen for me – the cave under the Acropolis. Anyhow, go to Athens and you'll soon find out what a great name Pan has there." (Lucian, *Dialogues of the Gods*, 272).

Perhaps the greatest effect that the Battle of Marathon had on the Greek world was the level of confidence that it bestowed upon Athens. Indeed, the beginning of the 5th century BCE would usher in the Golden Age of Athens, which involved some of the city's most famous men, like Socrates and Plato. Before Marathon, Athens struggled with tyrants and numerous other Greek enemies, but after the epic battle, the Athenians went on to lead the Hellenic League, along with Sparta, successfully against the Xerxes and the Persians.

Of course, the successes would also lead Athens and Sparta on a collision course towards the Peloponnesian War in the late 5th century, a war so devastating that it would help bring about the collapse of Greek independence altogether.

Bibliography

Briant, Pierre, 2002. *From Cyrus to Alexander: A History of the Persian Empire*. Translated by Peter T. Daniels. Winona Lake, Indiana: Eisenbraums.

Cameron, George C. "The Persian Satrapies and Related Matters." *Journal of Near Eastern Studies* 32 (1973): 47-56.

Christensen, Dirk Lund, Thomas Heine Nielsen, and Adam Schwartz. 2009. "Herodotos and *Hemerodromoi:* Pheidippides' Run from Athens to Sparta in 490 BCE from Historical and Physiological Perspectives." *Hermes* 137: 148-169.

Cameron, George C. 1983. "Ancient Persia." In *The Idea of History in the Ancient Near East*, ed. Robert C. Denton, 77-98. New Haven, Connecticut: American Oriental Society.

———. "The Persian Satrapies and Related Matters." *Journal of Near Eastern Studies* 32 (1973): 47-56.

Diodorus Siculus. 2004. *The Library of History*. Translated by C.H. Oldfather. Cambridge, Massachusetts: Harvard University Press.

Forrest, George. 2001. "Greece: The History of the Archaic Period." In *The Oxford History of Greece and the Hellenistic World*, edited by John Boardman, Jasper Griffin, and Oswyn Murray, 14-46. Oxford: Oxford University Press.

Hammond, N.G.L. 1968. "The Campaign and Battle of Marathon." *Journal of Hellenic Studies* 88: 13-57.

Harper, Prudence O., Joan Aruz, and Françoise Tallon, eds. 1992. *The Royal City of Susa: Ancient Near Eastern Treasures in the Louvre*. New York: Metropolitan Museum of Art.

Herodotus. 2003. *The Histories*. Translated by Aubrey de Sélincourt. London: Penguin Books.

Hodge, A. Trevor. 2001. "Reflections on the Shield at Marathon." *The Annual of the British School at Athens* 96: 237-259.

Lloyd, Alan. 1973. *Marathon: The Story of Civilizations on Collision Course*. New York: Random House.

Lucian. 1959. *Works*. Translated by K. Kilburn. Cambridge, Massachusetts: Harvard University Press.

Morkot, Robert. 1996. *The Penguin Historical Atlas of Ancient Greece*. London: Penguin Books.

Olmstead, A.T. 1948. *History of the Persian Empire.* Chicago: University of Chicago Press.

Pausanias. 1964. *Description of Greece*. Translated by W.H.S. Jones. Cambridge, Massachusetts: Harvard University Press.

Plutarch. 2005. *On Sparta*. Translated by Richard Talbert. London: Penguin Books.

———. *Lives*. 1968. Edited and translated by Bernadotte Perrin. Cambridge, Massachusetts: Harvard University Press.

Sage, Michael M. 1996. *Warfare in Ancient Greece: A Sourcebook*. London: Routledge.

Schmidt, Erich F. 1953. *Persepolis I: Structures, Reliefs, Inscriptions.* Chicago: University of Chicago Press.

Vansina, Jan. 1985. *Oral Tradition as History*. Madison: University of Wisconsin Press.

The Battle of Thermopylae

Chapter 1: A New King Comes to Power in the Achaemenid Empire

After the Battle of Marathon, Darius I was not done with his punitive plans for Athens. According to Herodotus, the Persian loss at Marathon only incensed the Achaemenid king even more: "When the news of the battle of Marathon reached Darius, son of Hystaspes and king of Persia, his anger against Athens, already great enough on account of the assault on Sardis, was even greater, and he was more than ever determined to make war on Greece. Without loss of time he dispatched couriers to the various states under his dominion with orders to raise an army much larger than before; and also warships, transports, horses, and grain. So the royal command went round; and all Asia was in an uproar for three years, with the best men being enrolled in the army for the invasion of Greece, and with the preparations. In the year after that, a rebellion in Egypt, which had been conquered by Cambyses, served only to hard Darius' resolve to go to war, not only against Greece but against Egypt too." (Herodotus, *The Histories*, VII, 1).

Furious, Darius began laying the initial plans and stockpiles for a colossal, all-out invasion of Greece on a scale hitherto unseen, and one which took years to prepare. Darius was still intent on making sure everything was in place when he died in 487 BCE, and after the emperor's unexpected death, the Achaemenid Persian Empire saw a number of its satrapies (colonized foreign peoples/provinces) rebel against the central authority (Briant 2002, 525). On top of the problems with rebellion, the Persians faced the more pressing problem of who would be the next Great King of the empire.

Although it is known that Xerxes I became Darius I's successor, the method of succession remains problematic for modern scholarship (Briant 2002, 518-25) and is an important factor when considering reasons why the Persian king initiated the second round of the Greco-Persian Wars. Herodotus (The Histories, VII, 2-4), gives a long account of Xerxes accession to the throne, which he attributed to a combination of the crown prince's mother, Atossa, and the fact that Xerxes was born while Darius I was king, unlike his older brothers who were born before he was king. Old Persian cuneiform inscriptions from the ancient Persian city of Persepolis attribute Xerxes' rise to power to the god Ahuramazda. A text known as "Xerxes Persepolis a" (XPa) states, "Saith Xerxes the King: Other sons of Darius there were, (but) – thus unto Ahuramazda was the desire – Darius my father made me the greatest after himself. When my father Darius went away from the throne, by the will of Ahuramazda I became king on my father's throne. When I became king, I built much excellent (construction). What had been built by my father, that I protected, and other building I added." (Kent 1953, 150).

The text is clearly aimed at proving the new king's legitimacy to rule the Achaemenid Empire, which suggests that there may have been questions within the royal family about Xerxes' right to rule. The text also relates that Xerxes dedicated at least a portion of his time and resources to building projects, which was a way that many kings from various ancient Near Eastern cultures legitimized their rule.

Given that he had rebellions to suppress and possibly questions about his legitimate right to rule, it's fair to wonder why Xerxes embarked on a Herculean effort to invade Greece shortly after his father had been defeated. In answering that question, Herodotus relates in detail that when Xerxes came to power in 486 BCE, his geopolitical interests were to the south of Greece, in Egypt. As Xerxes prepared his punitive expedition against the Egyptians, the Persian general Mardonius, who was famous for losing the Persian fleet in Greece during the reign of Darius I, convinced the Great King to also invade Greece. Herodotus wrote:

> "Xerxes at first not at all interested in invading Greece but began by building up an army for a campaign in Egypt. But Mardonius – the son of Gobryas and Darius' sister and thus cousin to the king – who was present in court and had more influence with Xerxes than anyone else in the country, used constantly to talk to him on the subject. 'Master,' he would say, 'the Athenians have done us great injury, and it is only right they should be punished for their crimes. By all means finish the talks you already have in hand; but when you have tamed the arrogance of Egypt, then lead an army against Athens. Do that, and your name will be held in honour all over the world, and people will think twice in future before they invade your country.' And to the argument for revenge he would add that Europe was a very beautiful place; it produced every kind of garden tree; the land there was everything that land should be – it was, in short, too good for any mortal except the Persian king." (Herodotus, The Histories, VII, 5).

Mardonius' influence was apparently effective, because Xerxes heeded the call to arms with the further incentives of upholding family honor and retribution for the Athenians' destruction of the city of Sardis during the Ionian revolt. Xerxes proclaimed, "I will bridge the Hellespont and march an army through Europe into Greece, and punish the Athenians for the outrage they committed upon my father and upon us. As you saw, Darius himself was making his preparations for war against these men; but death prevented him from carrying out his purpose. I therefore on his behalf, and for the benefit of all my subjects, will not rest until I have taken Athens and burnt it to the ground, in revenge for the injury which the Athenians without provocation once did to me and my father. These men, you remember, came to Sardis with Aristagoras the Milesian, a slave of ours, and burnt the temples and sacred groves." (Herodotus, The Histories, VII, 8).

These two passages reveal both Xerxes' initial reluctance to attack Greece and his passionate personality, both of which were important for how the fighting turned out, but either way, once the emperor was in favor of an invasion of Europe, the great Persian army would have to be mobilized and moved from Asia to Europe.

The Persian army's mobilization and mustering was no doubt the largest type in history until that time and was probably the largest until the First Crusade about 1,500 years later. The logistical feat of just assembling the army took years, and according to Herodotus, the amount of materials consumed by the army was immense. The historian wrote, "For the four years following the conquest of Egypt the mustering of troops and the provision of stores and equipment continued, and toward the close of the fifth Xerxes, at the head of his enormous army, began his march. . . All these armies together, with others like them, would not have equaled the army of Xerxes. Was there a nation in Asia that he did not take with him to Greece? Save for the great rivers, was there a stream his army drank from that was not drunk dry? Some nations provided ships, others formed infantry units; from some cavalry was requisitioned, from others horse-transports and crews; from others, again, triremes for floating bridges, or provisions and naval craft of various kinds." (Herodotus, The Histories, VII, 20-21).

The mustering of the army took place in Sardis from 484-481 BCE, after which they then set out in the spring of 480 for their long trek to Greece following the Aegean coastline. Before the army left Sardis, Xerxes sent representatives throughout Greece to demand the symbolic "earth and water" from the various kingdoms and city-states (Herodotus, The Histories, VII, 32). Earth and water, if given, was a symbol of a ruler's obeisance and fealty towards the Persian king; the Persian king in turn agreed to leave the subordinate ruler in power and to do no harm to any of his temples or people (Briant 2002, 145). At the same time, however, Xerxes sent no demand for earth and water to the two most important Greek city-states – Athens and Sparta – because the Persian messengers were killed when his father, Darius I, sent demands for earth and water during the first war (Herodotus, The Histories, VII, 133). It would also have been contrary to the partly punitive aspect of Xerxes' expedition against Athens to demand earth and water, since Xerxes did not want the obedience of the Athenians but to destroy and enslave them.

According to Herodotus, the entire army – soldiers, sailors, marines, and various support personnel – numbered 1,700,000 (Herodotus, The Histories, VII, 60) and it took them an entire week to bridge and cross the Hellespont, which is a channel in the Aegean that separates Asia from Europe (Herodotus, The Histories, VII, 56). While it's almost certain that number was inflated, the most important number concerning the size of the Persian army in relation to the Battle of Salamis was the 1207 triremes (war ships) that Herodotus said comprised the Persian fleet. Since Persia was a landlocked country, nearly the entire navy was gathered from other peoples, including 300 of the ships being manned by Phoenicians and 200 sailed by Egyptians (Herodotus, The Histories, VII, 89-96).

Of course, Xerxes and the Persians were not the only ones who prepared for the coming war. As the great Persian army began its long march into Europe, the Greeks, particularly the Athenians, also made preparations that would ultimately ensure their victory at the Battle of Salamis. Recognizing that war was in all likelihood an inevitability, the Athenians had begun the construction of a giant fleet, but because Athens could not hope to bear the expense of both treasure and manpower of funding both a standing army and a fleet, they had sought support elsewhere. The chief Greek states, ignoring the ambassadors that Xerxes sent to demand earth and water in 481 BCE, met at Corinth to decide on what was to be done. Their resolve was an indication of the measure of the crisis they faced, for the Greek city-states were notoriously fractious and only came together in times of the greatest emergency.

Chapter 2: The Geography of Thermopylae and the Build-up to the Battle

View of the pass at Thermopylae. At the time of the battle, the coastline was roughly where the road is today, and the trees on the left side of the picture would most likely have been absent.

"Xerxes however had not sent to Athens or to Sparta heralds to demand the gift of earth, and for this reason, namely because at the former time when Dareios had sent for this very purpose, the one people threw the men who made the demand into the pit and the others into a well, and bade them take from thence earth and water and bear them to the king." – Herodotus, *Histories*, Book Seven, section 133.

At the Hellespont, Xerxes planned to cross the straits via a gigantic bridge of boats, an incredibly ambitious endeavor and one that ends with one of antiquity's most colorful legends. Herodotus reported that the Persians' first attempt to bridge the Hellespont failed after a storm destroyed the flax and papyrus cables of the bridges. Enraged, Xerxes ordered his men to whip the Hellespont with 300 lashes and throw fetters into the water.

Illustration of Xerxes ordering his men to whip the Hellespont, 1909

After the meeting at Corinth, a force of 10,000 allied troops, under the command of the Spartans, was sent to blockade the pass of Tempe, in Thessaly, only to discover that Xerxes had stolen a march on them. Despite the first failure, the Persians had actually accomplished the unthinkable and physically bridged the Hellespont in 480 B.C., crossing into northern Greece to the south of the hoplites waiting at Tempe. There was now only one way to stop Xerxes; to cross into Greece proper, the Persians would be forced to travel through the narrow defile of the mountain pass at Thermopylae, a site which had already seen its fair share of battle due to its strategic nature. If the Greeks could hold Xerxes off at Thermopylae, and concurrently if the allied fleet could stop the Persian navy at Artemisium to prevent a bypass, then the invasion of Greece could be defeated.

The Spartans, as expected, were put in command of all allied land forces. Their prowess in battle, born of the fact that all Spartan citizens trained from boyhood in the ruthless warrior academy of the *agoge* to be perfect in the pursuit of feats of athletics and arms (and something they were able to do free of constraints as they delegated all manual labor to the helots) was legendary, and their fame rightly acquired. The Spartan hoplites were very rarely defeated, and the sight of their red-cloaked hoplites, with the Lambdas (Greek letter "L", shaped line an inverted "V", for Laekedaemon, the Spartan heartland) stark on their shields, was often enough to prompt enemies to flee the field altogether.

The Greeks set about making their preparations while Xerxes' army advanced south through Thessaly and Macedonia, a horde to end all hordes. There has been intense speculation and debate among historians as to just how large the Persian army was, with ancient accounts reporting that it drank rivers dry and stripped entire regions of their crops. Though Herodotus and the other Greek sources talk of a force numbering anything between a million and two and a half million fighting men, with equivalent numbers of support personnel, these figures are in all likelihood exaggerated, the product of either Greek propaganda or Persian misinformation. Modern scholars believe Xerxes' army was a more manageable but still extremely formidable 300,000-500,000 men, and the lowest modern estimates put the number at 100,000. Even the celebrated Spartans would have their work cut out for them.

Indeed, the campaign might well be over before it had properly begun, for the timing of Xerxes' advance could not have been more unfortunate for the Greeks. As the Persians approached Thermopylae, the Spartans were engaged in celebrating the festival of Carneia, the traditional period of peacetime in Laekedaemon during which time no armies could march, on pain of offending the Gods in the gravest way possible. One of the two Spartan kings, Leonidas (the Spartans always had two monarchs, so that if one should fall in battle Sparta would still have a ruler), beseeched the Ephors, the Spartan high priests, for a special permission to dispatch a unit to Thermopylae. Given the extraordinary circumstances, the Ephors granted him the right to take the King's Bodyguard, a unit of three hundred men, to war.

Leonidas was sure he was marching to his death, since the renowned oracle at Delphi had predicted that Sparta must mourn a king in order to achieve victory. According to ancient accounts, the oracle foretold:

"For you, inhabitants of wide-wayed Sparta,
Either your great and glorious city must be wasted by Persian men,
Or if not that, then the bound of Lacedaemon must mourn a dead king, from Heracles' line.
The might of bulls or lions will not restrain him with opposing strength; for he has the might of Zeus.
I declare that he will not be restrained until he utterly tears apart one of these."

Seeking to fulfill the prophecy, Leonidas personally picked 300, all of which had living sons so their bloodlines would not be extinguished. According to Plutarch, when Leonidas was asked upon his departure by his wife Gorgo, Queen of Sparta, what she should do in his absence, he replied, "Marry a good man and bear good children."

Statue of Leonidas

The Spartans were willingly creating a suicide unit, but to the men who joined Leonidas it was undoubtedly a high honor to be selected. The ancient Roman historian Plutarch captured the essence of the Spartans' thinking and culture in recounting a story about one of the men who was not chosen, "When Paedaretus was not chosen to be one of the Three Hundred, an honor which ranked highest in the State, he departed cheerful and smiling, with the remark that he was glad if the State possessed three hundred citizens who were better than himself."

Thus, in the summer of 480 BC, Leonidas and his men marched towards Thermopylae. Alongside the vaunted 300 Spartans were a further 600 of the *perioikoi,* the Spartan "peers", which enjoyed similar rights to full-blooded Spartan citizens, and an equal number of helot servants and light infantrymen, for a total of 1,500. The Spartans were quickly joined along the march by another 3,000 hoplites from Corinth, Arcadia, Mantinea, Tegea and Mycenae, and more troops joined them as they progressed out of the Peloponnese and into Northern Greece. The Thespians sent 700 hoplites, the Thebans 400, and when the allied army reached Thermopylae the Phokians and Locrians, who inhabited the lands directly to the south of the pass, sent all 2,000 men they had, according to Herodotus. Thus, to bolster Leonidas' ranks, the Greeks either had around 6,000 men according to Herodotus or 7,500 according to ancient historian Diodorus Sicilus. Whatever the actual number, the Greeks were facing what even modern historians have estimated as being upwards of half a million men. Based on modern estimates, at best the Greeks were facing odds of 20-1, but it's more likely there were 50-80 Persians for every Greek.

Obviously the Greeks heading toward Thermopylae knew they were going to be outnumbered by an astounding amount ahead of time, so they were obviously determined to stand and fight there no matter how many men Xerxes had. As Plutarch so aptly put it, "The Spartans used to ask about the enemy, it was not important how many there are, but where the enemy was." But the Greeks weren't heading to Thermopylae simply to die a glorious death; they chose it because it was the best defensive ground.

To bolster their defense, the Greeks planned to occupy the narrowest point of the pass at Thermopylae, what was known as the "Middle Gate". At that spot, there still stood the ruins of an ancient wall built by the Phokians, which would help the defense of the pass. Some of the Peloponnesian allies, once they had surveyed the site, offered the opinion that they should abandon Phokis and Locris to their fate and fall back to the isthmus of Corinth, where it would be easier to summon reinforcement, but Leonidas was adamant that they must make their stand at Thermopylae, or not at all, not least because he had 2,000 Phokian and Locrian soldiers at his orders now. But Leonidas' considerations were tactical as well as political. Simply put, Thermopylae, "The Hot Gates" in Greek (named from the hot springs that made it a sought-after spa location for travellers from all across Greece), was the best possible place for a numerically inferior enemy to contest Xerxes' passage. Though the geography of the pass has changed considerably over the millennia, in ancient times it consisted of a track running at the bottom of a defile about 100 yards across, snaking its way along the coast. To one side of the path, the land fell away sheer to the rocky coast below, while to the other the pass was hemmed in by impassable cliffs. There was a single mountain path which could allow a small force to bypass Thermopylae, a fact which the Greeks knew but the Persians did not. Accordingly, Leonidas dispatched a thousand of his men to guard the path, while he arrayed the rest of his troops defensively across the narrow aperture known as the Middle Gate (there were three such tightenings of the pass all told) with the hastily reinforced Phokian wall as a fallback defensive position. In the narrow pass, Xerxes' massive advantage in numbers would be nullified. Now all Leonidas and his men could do was wait.

Chapter 3: The First and Second Days of the Battle

"When someone else wished to know why Sparta was without walls, [Agesilaus] pointed to the citizens in full armor and said, 'These are the Spartans' walls.'" – Plutarch, *Life of Agesilaus*

Some time after Leonidas, his Spartans and their allies had set up their defensive position at Thermopylae, and with the allied fleet standing to off Artemisium, Xerxes' army finally arrived. In August of 480 B.C., the Spartan scouts (possibly the *Skiritai,* the celebrated Spartan light infantry, who always fought on the extreme left of the Spartan battle-line, directly opposite the enemy elite troops) spotted a great horde of armed men moving on the far side of the Malian Gulf. Tens, then hundreds of thousands of armed men, followed by an equal or even greater number of slaves and camp followers, and more bullocks, horses, camels and assorted cattle than the assembled Greeks had ever seen in their lives.

Xerxes' horde was big enough to blacken the ground from horizon to horizon, and all that stood between it and Greece were six, perhaps seven thousand hoplites. Yet, remarkably, or perhaps as a testament for the respect he had for Greek heavy infantry, Xerxes did not attack at once. Instead, he chose to talk. He dispatched an envoy to the Leonidas and the Greeks, asking them to stand down and grant him passage, and promising that the Spartans themselves would receive untold honors if they would but submit. The Greeks, Xerxes' envoy argued, would still be free; inclusion in the Persian Empire would mean riches and privilege for all. Leonidas, however, did not see things quite that way. Capitulation, he and the Greek allied generals argued, was tantamount to slavery. At Leonidas' stubborn refusal to see sense, Xerxes' envoy grew irate and insisted the Spartans and their allies lay down their weapons. According to Plutarch, Leonidas replied with the famous phrase "molòn labé", "Come and take them."

The words molṑn labé inscribed on the marble of the Leonidas Monument at Thermopylae. Today this is the motto of the Greek 1st Army Corps.

Five days passed while the Greeks waited and Xerxes determined what was to be done. His navy could not hope to force the passage at the straits of Artemisium without suffering extremely heavy casualties, and might well be turned back altogether. Likewise, outflanking the small Greek force at Thermopylae appeared impossible. The Persians would have no choice, then, except to make a fight of it. On the morning of the fifth day after the Persian army's arrival, Xerxes gave his orders. 5,000 archers moved forward into position towards the Greek encampment at the Phokian wall. The battle of Thermopylae had begun.

With the Spartans in the vanguard, Leonidas ordered the Greeks to take up the phalanx formation across the pass and arrayed them before the wall as the Persian archers advanced to within a hundred yards of the Greeks. From there, the Persians unleashed a colossal volley of arrows against them. Like all good archers, it is likely that at that range the Persians could shoot three volleys while their first arrow was still in the air, and the Greeks soon found themselves under a veritable hail of darts. However, to the Persians' great consternation, the Greeks literally shrugged them off. The light Persian bows were a far cry from the longbows or compound bows of the English and Mongols, which could punch through armor at three hundred yards, and the Greeks' thick bronze shields, helmets and armor completely protected them from the storm of arrows, which the ancient historians claimed caused only a few light flesh-wounds. Shaken, Xerxes ordered his archers to fall back and sent in his hammer-blow: ten thousand of his best infantry, natives of the Persian heartland of Media and Cissia, which included among their officers a number of Xerxes' own relatives, scions of the royal family. It was time for the Spartans to prove why they were the best heavy infantry in the world.

Like a wave, the Medes and Cissians swept forward towards the Greek positions, where the Spartans, *Periokoi*, and other Peloponnesians had taken up their place in the van with Leonidas, who was in his 60th year and thus considerably older than he has historically been portrayed. Nevertheless, like a wave hitting a cliff, as the Persians smashed against the Greek phalanx they broke. The Persians had just encountered the famous "Wall of Bronze", and these initial attackers were powerless against it. Their courage and valor could not be disputed, but their training and equipment were completely inadequate to the task. The Persians had shorter spears, making it hard for them to even reach the Greek phalanx before getting speared themselves. And even if they did make contact, the lighter shields and shorter spears and swords of the Persians prevented them from effectively engaging the Greek hoplites. Their light spears shivered against the great bronze-fronted shields and thick armor of the hoplites, their sabers and short swords cut ineffectually at the crested helmets and bronze-wrapped shins, and their own light armor and wicker shields could do nothing to prevent the heavy Greek spears from punching through them like paper, splitting the men wielding them.

Despite their advantage in numbers and the great number of men they poured into the pass, try as they might the Persians could make no headway against the Greek forces. Indeed, they soon found themselves on the receiving end of what the hoplites had spent countless soul-numbing hours practicing: *Othismos.* This was the "mass shove" of the hoplite phalanx, which began pushing the Persians in their front backwards and chewing up their line like a meat-grinder. Thousands of the Medes and Cissians were cut down, while still more were crushed to death by the press of men or were literally hurled off the cliffs to drown or smash into the rocks below. According to Herodotus, this was achieved at the cost of only a few Spartan dead. The carnage was so catastrophic for the Persians that Xerxes, who was watching the battle from the heights above, leapt up from his chair three times in mortal anguish for his men, who were being cut to pieces in the defile below. The Greek historian Ctesias wrote that the Persians' first wave was "cut to ribbons", yet only only two or three Spartans were dead.

Fighting in the phalanx, even for trained warriors, was incredibly taxing physically. The need to be constantly reactive, often at a split second's notice, in order to block a thrust or slash or strike back in turn, coupled with wearing over 60 pounds of armor and constantly shoving against a solid-packed mass of men was so exhausting that it could only be endured for a handful of minutes at a time, even by the Spartans. Because of this, the Greek troops rotated their units (generally divided by city of origin) in and out of the battle-line to ensure a constant supply of fresh hoplites to the meat-grinder of the phalanx. According to Herodotus, this was also an indication that the Greeks had sufficient numbers to block the entire pass. The Greek soldiers were so exhausted from fighting that, as soon as they were relieved, they dropped to the ground as though dead, while the helots rushed to assist them. The ground, which had been hard-packed and parched in summer, was churned with blood.

In the early afternoon, a lull fell on the battlefield as the Persian forces pulled back, which allowed the Greeks a chance to catch their breath and tend to the small wounds which, despite their armor, were a natural consequence of fighting in the Phalanx. Given that fighting in the phalanx formation consisted largely of a confused shoving brawl where weapons burst into fragments of wood and iron and people lunged with knives, swords, spears and axes, it's quite likely that a significant number of wounds would be the result of "friendly fire" by overly enthusiastic fellow hoplites. And though they reportedly suffered few casualties in the first wave of fighting, the Greeks were impressed by the bravery of the Persians, who despite being decidedly outmatched had continued to hurl themselves at the phalanx, even tearing with their own bare hands at the weapons and shields of the enemy in an attempt to disarm them so that their comrades might get a spear-thrust in.

The Medes and Cissians had acquitted themselves nobly if futilely, and they had been bloodily repulsed, but Xerxes was far from done. The Spartans and their allies had barely dented his great horde, and now he dispatched the hammer-blow that he assumed would fell them in earnest. Against troops already bone-weary from the morning's battle, he sent in his famed 10,000 man crack unit, the Immortals. Unlike the Medes and Cissians, the Immortals advanced into battle in tomb-like, utter silence (as the Spartans did themselves), in a deliberate attempt to avoid battle-frenzy and instill fear into the waiting enemy. The Greek hoplites rose to their feet, shouldered their shields, and took up their positions in the phalanx. The Persians were coming again.

Depiction of the Immortals in the Palace of Darius I

The Persians' elite corps remains the subject of much intrigue, including over the origins of their name. It was Herodotus who referred to the force as the "Immortals", claiming that the name referred to the fact that the force was always 10,000 strong, and that there was thus always a new member to replace a wounded or dead one. Though there is evidence from Persia that the unit did exist, no name was attached to them, and modern historians believe that Herodotus and/or his source mistook the name Anûšiya ("companions") with Anauša ('Immortals')."

Herodotus wrote in his *Histories* of all the extra perks the Immortals received, including concubines and food designated only for them, but they were about to receive the same treatment from the Greeks that their counterparts had received earlier. Xerxes may very well have hoped or even assumed that his vaunted Immortals would make short shrift of the tired Greeks, especially because it was not even the Spartans but one of the allied contingents who first rose to take their place in the battle-line against them. However, once again the superior training and armament of the hoplites proved decisive. Though slightly more heavily armored than their Mede and Cissian counterparts, the Immortals were no match for the phalanx, who suckered the Immortals deeper into the pass by feigning a retreat and tempting the Persians to chase after them. Once again, Xerxes was forced to watch in horror as his vaunted infantry was cut to ribbons in the pass.

At last, as darkness fell, the decimated Immortals fell back, yielding the field of battle to the Greeks, who were so tired that many of them needed their comrades to physically force food and water into their mouths because they were incapable of taking sustenance themselves.

Though the night passed without incident, the dawn of the second day of the battle brought no respite for the Greeks. Though his elite shock troops had failed, Xerxes still had tens of thousands or even hundreds of thousands of completely fresh troops to throw at the Hot Gates. Counting on the fact that the Spartans and their allies would be exhausted and/or injured by wounds, and incapable of putting up a spirited resistance, Xerxes launched an all-out assault against the Phokian wall.

Yet again, Xerxes could not have been more wrong. Driven to extremes of valor and endurance by a desire to match up to the notorious Spartans, the allied Greeks performed like prodigies on the second day, and once again the phalanx proved to be a bulwark that could take any amount of enemy damage, shrugging off the Persian attacks without faltering. Now, however, fatigue began to tell in earnest, and as the Greeks became more sluggish, the number of casualties began to rise. Dozens were killed, and many more wounded, including a significant number of Spartans. Despite their casualties and exhaustion, however, the Greeks managed to push back the advancing Persians once more and, towards midday, Xerxes' men fell back to their encampment, now by all accounts terrified by the apparent utter invincibility of their foes.

It was at this crucial moment, when Xerxes was pondering if even attrition could destroy the Spartans and their allies, that he received what amounted to a gift from the gods. A native of Thracis named Ephialtes deserted to his side and revealed to his generals that there existed a remote mountain path, through which the Persians could march to the rear of Thermopylae. This would allow the Persians to envelop the defending Greek forces and destroy them. Ephialtes' name would later become so reviled as a traitor that his name virtually disappears from Greek histories altogether, indicating the shame associated with it. Even in modern Greece, the name Ephialtes is synonymous with traitor, and his name has become the word for "nightmare" in modern Greek.

According to Herodotus, two other men were accused of betraying the hidden trail to the Persians: Onetas, a native of Carystus and son of Phanagoras; and Corydallus, a native of Anticyra. However, Herodotus was certain that it was actually Ephialtes because, as he wrote, "the deputies of the Greeks, the Pylagorae, who must have had the best means for ascertaining the truth, did not offer the reward on the heads of Onetas and Corydallus, but for that of Ephialtes of Trachis."

Whatever the case, Xerxes no longer needed to force his way past the hoplites guarding the Hot Gates. Now he could simply outflank them and appear in both their front and rear.

Chapter 4: Tonight We Dine in Hades

"Come back with your shield or on it." – The phrase Spartan mothers uttered to their sons departing for war. Plutarch, *Moralia*

Leonidas at Thermopylae, by Jacques Louis David, 1814. The famous painting is a juxtaposition of various historical and legendary elements from the Battle of Thermopylae.

At dawn of the third day of the battle, General Mardonius, at the head of 10,000 Immortals (whose numbers were immediately filled by selecting eligible recruits from other units) and a further 10,000 Persian troops, moved up the path that Ephialtes had revealed, surprising the 1,000 Phokian hoplites who were guarding it. Faced with overwhelming odds and without a similarly effective defensive position to protect, the Phokians fell back to a hilltop nearby, where they planned to make a final stand, but the Persians contented themselves with keeping them at a distance with volleys of arrows while the main force proceeded at the double down the path.

A Phokian runner raced ahead of them, bearing the grave news to Leonidas; in a few hours at most, his troops would be encircled. Staring calamity in the face, Leonidas convened a council of war with his surviving generals. Despite their previous successes, all the Greeks knew that staying to fight meant death. Accordingly, many of the generals leading the Greek contingents chose retreat as the only viable option, but not Leonidas. With the weight of prophecy, Spartan military tradition, and simple common tactical sense on his shoulders, he bade the other Greek contingents disperse, but he and his Spartans were determined to stand and die. According to

Plutarch, Leonidas exhorted his men, "Eat well, for tonight we dine in Hades."

The reason for Leonidas' decision is simple, and it has less to do with bombast and the will of the gods than it does with a desire not to see his entire command annihilated. By fighting a rearguard action, he could ensure that the slow-moving hoplites would be able to escape before Xerxes' cavalry, unleashed on the vast plains behind Thermopylae, could run them down and cut them to pieces. Thus, those who would stay behind to fight were doing so in an effort to save those who fled.

Whether it was because so many other Greeks were just as brave as the Spartans or because they realized the tactical situation, what was left of the 700 Thespians refused to leave even when ordered to do so, as did 400 Thebans. The helots who had accompanied the Spartans into battle also refused to retreat. Thus, while the majority of the Greek forces departed the battlefield, a mixed unit of around 1,700 men stayed back to defend the pass against Xerxes and the Persians.

As daylight washed across the battlefield, Xerxes made his customary morning sacrifices and, having established that the Immortals were now advancing towards the rear of what remained of the Greek forces, ordered a fresh wave of ten thousand infantry to advance against the Phokian wall.

This time, however, the Greeks did not remain on the defensive. Rather, in a last, desperate, glorious attempt to take as many of the enemy with them as they could, they advanced into the wider part of the path, meeting the Persians where every Greek spear and sword could be brought to bear. The struggle was brutal and vicious, and despite the odds it lasted for hours as the Greeks inflicted carnage upon the Persian forces but began to be slowly whittled down. According to Herodotus, when all their spears were shattered, and even their buttspikes had been smashed to kindling, the Greeks fought on with swords, daggers and captured Persian weapons, continuing a desperate melee where all form of fighting order broke down completely.

At the height of this fighting, Leonidas himself was killed, feathered with shafts by Persian archers, and a massive running fight broke out between the Greeks, desperate to keep his body in their possession, and the Persians who sought to despoil it. It was at this point, when the fighting was at its most bitter, that two of Xerxes' own brothers were killed, but both sides could not sustain a massacre of such ferocity for long. Greeks and Persians alike fell back to draw breath and, with the Immortals now approaching from their rear, the remnants of the Greek force dragged their dead and wounded back to a hill not far behind the Phokian wall to make one final stand.

It was at this point that Herodotus claims the Thebans had a change of heart. Historians have largely assumed the Thebans were brought as hostages to Thermopylae, as Herodotus himself suggested, which makes it unclear why the departing Greeks didn't take the hostages back with them. Some historians speculate the Thebans that remained were loyal to the Greek cause, but here Herodotus seems to dispel that notion in writing that they "moved away from their companions, and with hands upraised, advanced toward the barbarians..." Shouting that they surrendered, they advanced towards the Persians, casting their weapons aside. Many were cut down either out of vengeance or because the Persians suspected a trick, but eventually the rest were seized and borne away in chains.

The final act of the drama was about to unfold. The Persians swept in against the beleaguered Greeks who stood, back to back, atop the knoll they had chosen to die on. Their armor was in pieces, their shields stove in or long gone, and their weapons were little more than sticks and blunted, twisted pieces of metal. Herodotus described the final scene, "Here they defended themselves to the last, those who still had swords using them, and the others resisting with their hands and teeth." Finally, furious at the losses he had suffered, Xerxes ordered his men to fall back and, with his archers standing in at a distance, had the remaining Greeks slaughtered with a hail of arrows.

The Battle of Thermopylae was over.

Chapter 5: The Aftermath and Legacy of Thermopylae

"Stranger, announce to the Spartans that here
We lie, having fulfilled their orders." – Epigram for the Spartans of Thermopylae written by Simonides of Ceos

With the desperate fighting finally over, the Greeks had lost between two and three thousand men, but they had succeeded in holding the pass for three days and inflicted several times their number of casualties. It was a defeat, obviously, but one that had the flavor of victory. In fact, Thermopylae so enraged Xerxes that he ignored Persian customs honoring valiant enemy warriors and had Leonidas' corpse beheaded and crucified. Though the Greeks who had stayed behind to contest the passage of Xerxes' troops had perished to the last man, their sacrifice would echo throughout Greece, an inspiration for the men preparing for the battles yet to come, when the fate of all the Hellenic world would be decided.

Thermopylae had been the gates of Greece, and after the battle Xerxes advanced with both his army and navy into the heart of his enemies' territory. Greece's allied fleet retreated from its blockading position at Artemisium towards Salamis, where they helped ferry the Athenians away from their city and onto the island not far from the shore. Meanwhile, the Persian army advanced into the interior, putting Boeotia (including Thespiae) to the torch before marching on Athens itself. Finding the city deserted by almost all of its citizens, Xerxes vented his spite upon the Greeks and took revenge for his father's defeat at Marathon by putting the entire city to the torch, forcing the Athenian citizens to watch as their city was turned to rubble.

In the aftermath of the campaign, a stone lion was erected on the site of the last stand of Leonidas' men at Thermopylae, and most of the bodies were interred there, Spartan, Helot and Allied (although Leonidas' bones were eventually returned to Sparta). Over them was laid a plaque bearing the epitaph written by the celebrated poet Simonides, one that has since spawned countless variations like, "Go tell the Spartans, stranger passing by, that here, according to their laws, we lie".

The legend of Thermopylae has endured, but therein remains the overarching question. How much of the accounts of the battle has any basis in historical fact? There is almost no doubt that the quotes attributed to Leonidas and the Spartans by ancient historians like Herodotus and Plutarch are apocryphal and meant to demonstrate the Spartans' short, laconic phrases and wit, historically accurate characteristics that they were known for. Moreover, the estimated size of the Persian force varies wildly, the accounts of the first two days of fighting are clearly too good to be true for the Greeks, and anecdotes like Xerxes standing up in awe during the fighting were either added for color or somehow passed down through oral tradition. From a historical perspective, it's possible only to make educated guesses about a battle that took place over 2,500 years ago and has no surviving first-hand accounts.

In the case of Thermopylae, however, seeking out historical accuracy actually misses the forest for the trees. After all, regardless of what did or did not happen at Thermopylae, Xerxes still managed to subdue much of the Greek mainland before Salamis and Plataea, which took place about a year after Thermopylae. And even by all ancient Greek accounts, Thermopylae ends with the Persians victorious. From a strategic perspective, the last stand at Thermopylae at best bought the Greeks a few days and at worst was a debacle that resulted in the Greek navy fleeing and the Greek defenders dead or retreating. In fact, that is all that can be said with certainty about the Battle of Thermopylae and the results. But none of this is the reason Thermopylae has endured as one of antiquity's most famous or fascinating battles, and it could even be said that Thermopylae has remained legendary in spite of all of that.

Instead, Thermopylae was and remains significant because it took place during a war in which the fate of Greece and the West hung in the balance, and the nature of the last stand embodies the values held dear by the Greek culture (and by extension Western culture). Moreover, the story captures the very ethos of Sparta, the militaristic city-state that wowed even its ancient contemporaries. Given that perspective, whether the Persians had 100,000 or 2 million soldiers does not matter; all that matters is that the Greeks faced impossible odds and still decided to make history's most famous last stand, stoically fighting to the last man. Whether the Greeks actually lost 3 men in the first day's fighting or 3,000 does not matter; all that matters is none of the defenders lived at the end. And whether Thermopylae was a Pyrrhic victory for the Persians or a strategic debacle for the Greeks, the end result of the Persian invasion still ends with a Greek victory.

Thus, getting the historically accurate account of Thermopylae is no more useful than having Herodotus' colorful and distorted account because the value and significance of Thermopylae has always been psychological, for the very same reasons that the Alamo remains one of the most famous battles in American history. Across the Western world, making a last stand or fighting on in the face of near certain death and defeat has long been considered the epitome of courage and even something worth celebrating, whether it was Thermopylae, the Alamo, the Charge of the Light Brigade, or Pickett's Charge. During the Battle of Berlin near the end of World War II in Europe, the Nazi Luftwaffe had a "Leonidas Squadron" that flew "self-sacrifice missions" against the advancing Soviets.

As the last 2,500 years have shown over and over again, the legend of the Battle of Thermopylae *is* the history of the Battle of Thermopylae.

Bibliography

Readers interested in learning more about Thermopylae, and the Spartans in general, should consult an annotated version of Herodotus' *Histories*, Plutarch's *Moralia*, and Plutarch's Lives of Lysander and Agesilaus.

For a more modern take, Ernle Bradford's *Thermopylae: The Battle for the West*, Rupert Matthews's *The Battle of Thermopylae: A Campaign in Context*, or Paul Cartledge's *The Spartans: An Epic History*.

For a fictionalized but highly researched and entertaining account of the battle, see Steven Pressfield's excellent *Gates of Fire: An Epic Novel of the Battle of Thermopylae*.

The Battle of Salamis

Chapter 1: The Athenians Build Their Navy

Ancient Athens is remembered militarily for its prowess on the sea, but if not for some fortuitous circumstances, the Athenians would never have become a maritime power and the Persians may have won the Battle of Salamis. In 483 BCE, while the Persian army was mustering in Sardis, a large deposit of silver was discovered about 25 miles south east of Athens in a place that would later be named Laurium (Hale 2009, 7). This serendipitous discovery by the Athenians proved to be a boon to their economy, but the city leaders came to an impasse over how to spend the money; most of the city leaders wanted to put the 600,000 drachmas of silver towards a dole fund, but Themistocles, the great hero of the Battle of Salamis, had other ideas (Hale 2009, 11). Themistocles argued that the silver surplus should be used to build a navy, which the Athenians in turn would use to fight the Greek city-state of Aegina. Herodotus explained, "Themistocles, however, persuaded them to give up this idea and, instead of distributing the money, to spend it on the construction of two hundred warships for use in the war with Aegina. The outbreak of this war at that moment saved Greece by forcing Athens to become a maritime power." (Herodotus, The Histories, VII, 144).

Depiction of Themistocles

Herodotus' account is corroborated by the later historian and biographer Plutarch, who also gives more details concerning Themistocles' intelligence and personality. Plutarch wrote, "And so, in the first place, whereas the Athenians were wont to divide up among themselves the revenue coming from the silver mines at Laureium, he, and he alone, dared to come before the people with a motion that this division be given up, and that with these moneys triremes be constructed for the war against Aegina. This was the fiercest war then troubling Hellas, and the islanders controlled the sea, owing to the number of their ships. Wherefore all the more easily did Themistocles carry his point, not by trying to terrify the citizens with dreadful pictures of Darius or the Persians – these were too far away and inspired no very serious fear of their coming, but by making opportune use of the bitter jealousy which they cherished toward Aegina in order to secure armament he desired. The result was that with these moneys they built a hundred triremes, with which they actually fought at Salamis against Xerxes." (Plutarch, Themistocles, IV, 1-2).

Themistocles' oratory skills, intelligence, and guile convinced the other Athenian leaders to go with his plan, which ultimately saved their city from the Persians, but he was also successful in convincing them of the type of navy they should build. Themistocles specified that the navy would be comprised of fast, light triremes, which were designed for ramming, not carrying large numbers of marines (Hale 2009, 20). In Themistocles' judgment, it was the Persian navy that was its Achilles heel, so a well-trained and equipped Athenian navy would be the only way to defeat Xerxes and his army. Despite defeating the Persian army on the plane of Marathon, the force that Xerxes was bringing with him south on land was so much larger that the Greeks had thought to find another way to defeat the Persians this time around. The Persian navy was also vast, but unlike its army, which had a solid core of Persian fighters, it was primarily made up of subject peoples who were forced to fight (Hale 2009, 34).

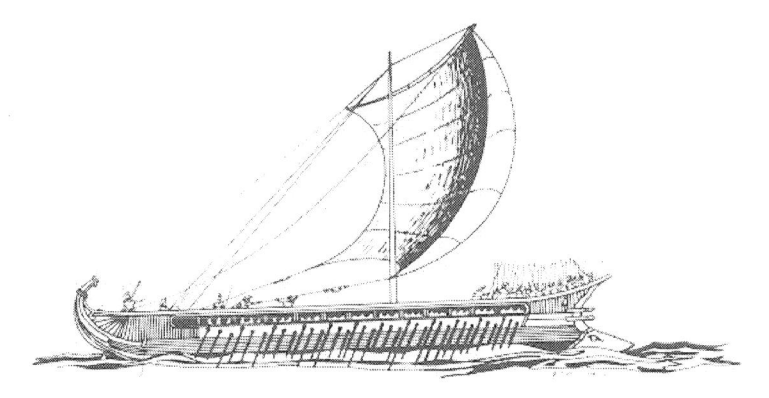

An illustration of a Greek trireme

Themistocles was able to build the Athenian navy through his silver tongue with the silver discovered in Attica, and he then used even more duplicitous methods to become the general of the Athenian fleet. According to Plutarch, there were not many men who desired to lead the Athenians against the Persians, due in large measure to fears of Persian reprisals should Xerxes defeat the Greeks. However, fear did not stop all candidates, and Themistocles and an apparently corrupt man named Epicydes were finalists for the position until the former used his guile to displace the latter. Plutarch explained, "At last, when the Mede was descending upon Hellas and the Athenians were deliberating who should be their general, all the rest, they say, voluntarily renounced their claims to the generalship, so panic-stricken were they at the danger; but Epicydes, the son of Euphemides, a popular leader who was powerful in speech but effeminate in spirit and open to bribes, set out to get the office, and was likely to prevail in the election; so

Themistocles, fearing lest matters should got to utter ruin in case the leadership fell to such a man, bribed and bought off the ambition of Epicydes." (Plutarch, Themistocles, VI, 1).

With Themistocles firmly in the position as general, the Athenians had a capable leader who could defeat the Persian fleet. The Athenians also temporarily rescinded all ostracisms in 480 BCE, which allowed notable and wealthy citizens to return to defend their possessions. Athens later benefited from this policy at the Battle of Salamis since the formerly banished Aristides, the second most important Athenian at the battle, fought valiantly alongside his countrymen (Plutarch, Aristides, VIII, 1).

The Greeks then had two final acts of preparation to make before Xerxes and the Persian army arrived in Attica: they had to evacuate most of the Attic peninsula and consult their oracles. The ancient Greeks were a very religious people who saw the influence and actions of their gods in most events, great and small. Poseidon protected Greek mariners, Athena did the same to her eponymously named city, and Zeus sat on Mount Olympus presiding over all mortals and immortals alike. When the Greeks had important questions that pertained to worldly events and situations, they consulted oracles for answers, and the most important oracle in the Greek world was Apollo's oracle in the city of Delphi (Parker 2001, 320). Thus, the Athenians approached the oracle and asked directly what course of action they should take against the approaching Persian army, and Herodotus recorded that the oracle replied:

> "Why sit you, doomed ones? Fly to the world's end, leaving
>
> Home and the heights your city circles like a wheel.
>
> The head shall not remain in its place, nor the body,
>
> Nor the feet beneath, nor the hands, nor the parts between;
>
> But all is ruined, for fire and the headlong god of war
>
> Spending in a Syrian chariot shall bring you low.
>
> May a tower shall he destroy, not your alone,
>
> And give to pitiless fire many shrines of gods,
>
> Which even now stand sweating, with fear quivering,
>
> While over the roof-tops black blood runs streaming
>
> In prophecy of woe that needs must come. But rise.
>
> Haste from the sanctuary and bow your hearts to grief." (Herodotus, The

Histories, VII. 140).

The oracle's answer both upset and confused the Athenians, who then decided to approach the oracle a second time with olive branches in their hands as signs of their supplication (Herodotus, The Histories, VII, 141). The second prophecy was still enigmatic, but it proved be the final statement on the matter. Herodotus wrote that this time, the oracle said:

> "Not wholly can Pallas win the heart of Olympian Zeus,
>
> Though she prays him with many prayers and all her subtlety;
>
> Yet will I speak to you this other word, as firm as adamant:
>
> Though all else shall be taken within the bound of Cercrops
>
> And the fastness of the holy mountain of Cithaeron,
>
> Yet Zeus the all-seeing grants to Athene's prayer
>
> That the wooden wall only shall not fall, but help you and
>
> your Children.
>
> But await not the host of horse and foot coming from Asia,
>
> Or be still, but turn your back and withdraw from the foe.
>
> Truly a day will come when you will meet him face to face.
>
> Divine Salamis, you will bring death to women's sons
>
> When the corn is scattered, or the harvest gathered in." (Herodotus, The Histories, VII, 141).

The second prophecy was a bit clearer, but a new question arose: what was the wooden wall? Determining what the oracle meant by the wooden wall immediately became a new source of debate amongst the Athenians, and while one party believed that it referred to the wooden palisade around the Acropolis in Athens, another faction believed it was in reference to the new Athenian fleet (Herodotus, The Histories, VII, 142).

The Athenians, with their democratic nature, appeared to be at an impasse once more, and it would be bridged not by a priest or oracle but by Athens' supreme commander and orator, Themistocles. The Athenian commander had invested too much into the Athenian fleet to let it slip away through a misinterpreted prophecy, so he did what any far-sighted military commander would have done by interpreting the prophecy himself. Herodotus noted, " There was however, a man in Athens who had recently come into prominence – Themistocles called Neocles' son; he now came forward and declared that there was an important point in which the professional interpreters were mistaken. If, he maintained, the disaster referred to was to strike the Athenians, it would not have been expressed in such mild language. 'Hateful Salamis' would surely have been a more likely phrase than 'divine Salamis', if the inhabitants of the country were doomed to destruction there. On the contrary, the true interpretation was that the oracle referred not the Athenians but to their enemies. The 'wooden wall' did, indeed, mean ships; so he advised his countrymen to prepare at once to meet the invader at sea." (Herodotus, The Histories, VII, 143).

Themistocles' charm, charisma, and oratorical skills prevailed once more as the Athenians decided to evacuate Athens and Attica and to make their stand on the sea in the narrow channel between the Attic peninsula and the island of Salamis, but before the Greeks would make their retreat further south to the island of Salamis and even further to the Peloponnesian peninsula, they had to form a formal alliance. Thus, as Xerxes and the Persian army was rampaging its way south through the kingdoms of Thrace and Macedon, a number of Greek city-states held a conference and formed the Hellenic League, with Sparta playing the role of military leader (Herodotus, The Histories, VII, 145). Once the Athenians had chosen a leader, built a navy, and recruited allies, it was time for them to put their plan into motion.

Chapter 2: The Evacuation of Attica

With the Persians marching south, the Greeks decided that they would meet Xerxes and his forces in order to give their people more time to evacuate Attica. After the meeting at Corinth, a force of 10,000 allied Greek troops, under the command of the Spartans, was sent to blockade the pass of Tempe in Thessaly, only to discover that Xerxes had stolen a march on them. Despite the first failure, the Persians had actually accomplished the unthinkable and physically bridged the Hellespont in 480 BCE, thereby crossing into northern Greece to the south of the hoplites waiting at Tempe. There was now only one way to stop Xerxes; to cross into Greece proper, the Persians would be forced to travel through the narrow defile of the mountain pass at Thermopylae, a site which had already seen its fair share of battle due to its strategic nature. If the Greeks could hold Xerxes off at Thermopylae, and concurrently if the allied fleet could stop the Persian navy at Artemisium to prevent a bypass, then the invasion of Greece could be defeated.

The Greeks set about making their preparations while Xerxes' army advanced south through Thessaly and Macedonia with the horde to end all hordes. There has been intense speculation and debate among historians as to just how large the Persian army was, with ancient accounts reporting that it drank rivers dry and stripped entire regions of their crops. Though Herodotus and the other Greek sources talk of a force numbering anything between a million and two and a half million fighting men, with equivalent numbers of support personnel, these figures are in all likelihood exaggerated, the product of either Greek propaganda or Persian misinformation. Modern scholars believe Xerxes' army was a more manageable but still extremely formidable 300,000-500,000 men, and the lowest modern estimates put the number at 100,000. Whatever the number, the Greeks would have their work cut out for them.

Indeed, the campaign might well be over before it had properly begun, for the timing of Xerxes' advance could not have been more unfortunate for the Greeks. As the Persians approached Thermopylae, the Spartans were engaged in celebrating the festival of Carneia, the traditional period of peacetime in Laekedaemon during which time no armies could march, on pain of offending the Gods in the gravest way possible. One of the two Spartan kings, Leonidas (the Spartans always had two monarchs, so that if one should fall in battle Sparta would still have a ruler), beseeched the Ephors, the Spartan high priests, for a special permission to dispatch a unit to Thermopylae. Given the extraordinary circumstances, the Ephors granted him the right to take the King's Bodyguard, a unit of three hundred men, to war.

Leonidas was sure he was marching to his death, since the renowned oracle at Delphi had predicted that Sparta must mourn a king in order to achieve victory. According to ancient accounts, the oracle foretold:

"For you, inhabitants of wide-wayed Sparta,

Either your great and glorious city must be wasted by Persian men,

Or if not that, then the bound of Lacedaemon must mourn a dead king, from Heracles' line.

The might of bulls or lions will not restrain him with opposing strength; for he has the might of Zeus.

I declare that he will not be restrained until he utterly tears apart one of these."

Seeking to fulfill the prophecy, Leonidas personally picked 300, all of which had living sons so their bloodlines would not be extinguished. According to Plutarch, when Leonidas was asked upon his departure by his wife Gorgo, Queen of Sparta, what she should do in his absence, he replied, "Marry a good man and bear good children."

Statue of Leonidas

The Spartans were willingly creating a suicide unit, but to the men who joined Leonidas it was undoubtedly a high honor to be selected. The ancient Roman historian Plutarch captured the essence of the Spartans' thinking and culture in recounting a story about one of the men who was not chosen, "When Paedaretus was not chosen to be one of the Three Hundred, an honor which ranked highest in the State, he departed cheerful and smiling, with the remark that he was glad if the State possessed three hundred citizens who were better than himself."

Thus, in the summer of 480 BC, Leonidas and his men marched towards Thermopylae. Alongside the vaunted 300 Spartans were a further 600 of the *perioikoi*, the Spartan "peers", which enjoyed similar rights to full-blooded Spartan citizens, and an equal number of helot servants and light infantrymen, for a total of 1,500. The Spartans were quickly joined along the march by another 3,000 hoplites from Corinth, Arcadia, Mantinea, Tegea and Mycenae, and more troops joined them as they progressed out of the Peloponnese and into Northern Greece. The Thespians sent 700 hoplites, the Thebans 400, and when the allied army reached Thermopylae the Phokians and Locrians, who inhabited the lands directly to the south of the pass, sent all 2,000 men they had, according to Herodotus. Thus, to bolster Leonidas' ranks, the Greeks either had around 6,000 men according to Herodotus or 7,500 according to ancient historian Diodorus Sicilus. Whatever the actual number, the Greeks were facing what even modern historians have estimated as being upwards of half a million men. Based on modern estimates, at best the Greeks were facing odds of 20-1, but it's more likely there were 50-80 Persians for every Greek.

Obviously the Greeks heading toward Thermopylae knew they were going to be outnumbered by an astounding amount ahead of time, so they were obviously determined to stand and fight there no matter how many men Xerxes had. As Plutarch so aptly put it, "The Spartans used to ask about the enemy, it was not important how many there are, but where the enemy was." But the Greeks weren't heading to Thermopylae simply to die a glorious death; they chose it because it was the best defensive ground.

Given the defensive advantages, the heavily outnumbered Greeks held the vast Persian army for several days at the mountain pass of Thermopylae before being overwhelmed by sheer numbers (Herodotus, The Histories, 210-34). Although the Greeks lost at Thermopylae, the bravery of the slain Leonidas and the Greeks who died with him became a rallying cry for the Greeks for the remainder of the Greco-Persian Wars.

Thermopylae was clearly an important battle in the Greco-Persian Wars, but a naval engagement between the Persian and Athenian fleets that took place at the same time near the city of Artemisium had an even greater impact on the Battle of Salamis. Herodotus' account states that the Greeks were vastly outnumbered by the Persian fleet, but that the battle was a draw (Herodotus, The Histories, VIII, 8-200). Plutarch's account reveals more details, particularly how the Greeks used their experiences at Artemisium at the subsequent Battle of Salamis. He wrote, "The battles which were fought at that time with the ships of the Barbarians in the narrows were not decisive of the main issue, it is true, but they were of the greatest service to the Hellenes in giving them experience, since they were thus taught by actual achievements in the face of danger that neither multitudes of ships." (Plutarch, Themistocles, VIII, 1).

Plutarch's passage reveals two important aspects of naval warfare that the Athenians learned at Artemisium and would later use at Salamis. First, the Athenians, due to their inferior numbers, fought in the narrows against the Persian fleet, where the Persians' numerical superiority mattered less since only a limited number of ships could fight at one time in the bottleneck created by the narrows. Furthermore, the Greeks learned that they could stand in the face of a numerically superior enemy, and the confidence the Athenians gained from the Battle of

Artemisium went a long way towards their victory at Salamis.

Chapter 3: The Persians Advance Through Attica

Despite the good showing of the Greek fleet at Artemisium, it only slowed the Persian advance temporarily and, if anything, provoked the wrath of Xerxes even more. When the Greek defense of Thermopylae failed, they fell back on their second defensive line, which spread across the Isthmus of Corinth on land, where the Peloponnesians (mainly Spartans) constructed a wall. The other end was at the Salamis strait (Hale 2009, 57). The Greeks yielded all land north of the line – essentially all of Attica – to Xerxes and the Persians.

Any Greeks who were unlucky enough to be caught north of the defensive line suffered greatly under the Persian army. Herodotus explained, "Along the valley of the Cephisus nothing was spared; Drymus, Charadra, Erochus, Tethronium, Amphicaea, Neon, Pedies, Trites, Elateia, Huampolis, Parapotamii – all these places were burnt to the ground, including Abae, where there was a temple of Apollo richly furnished with treasure and offerings of all kinds. There was an oracle there, as indeed there is today; the shrine belonging to it was plundered and burnt. A few Phocians were chased and caught near the mountains, and some women were raped successively by so many Persians that they died." (Herodotus, The Histories, VIII, 33).

Once the Persian army reached Panopes, it divided into two divisions; Xerxes led one division to Athens, while the other sacked the holy city of Delphi and its temple (Herodotus, The Histories, VIII, 34-5). When the Persians finally arrived in Athens, they found the city largely deserted except for a small force left to defend the Acropolis. After a successful siege, Xerxes leveled the final insult towards the Athenians by ordering the destruction of the Acropolis and its temples. Herodotus wrote, "But in the end the Persians solved their problem: a way of access to the Acropolis was found – for it was prophesied that all Athenian territory upon the continent of Greece must be overrun by the Persians. There is a place in front of the Acropolis, behind the way up to the gates, where the ascent is so steep that no guard was set, because it was not thought possible that any man would be able to climb it; here, by the shrine of Cercrops' daughter Aglaurus, some soldiers managed to scramble up the precipitous face of the cliff. . . Having left not one of them alive, they stripped the temple of its treasures and burnt everything on the Acropolis. Xerxes, now absolute master of Athens, dispatched a rider to Susa with news for Artabanus of his success." (Herodotus, The Histories, VIII, 53-54).

Chapter 4: Naval Warfare in the Ancient World

In order to understand how the Battle of Salamis was fought and why the Greeks won the battle, a basic understanding of maritime history during the 5th century BCE is needed. The Battle of Salamis may have established the Greeks, particularly the Athenians, as a naval power, but they were taming the waves of the Mediterranean Sea centuries before the Persian Wars. In the 8th century BCE, the Greeks began to expand and colonize islands and coastlines throughout the Mediterranean region from Italy to the Black Sea, and once trade between the Greek homeland and its many colonies became commonplace, ships were needed that could preserve perishable goods. With that, ships with closed galleys and two-level rows of oars were invented (Wallinga 1990, 137). In other words, it was trade and colonization, not war, which led to the evolution of the warship in the ancient Mediterranean, and it was the Phoenicians, not the Greeks, who invented the triremes that the Greeks used at Salamis. (Hale 2009, 17).

The trireme was a perfect battleship for its time, though it is difficult to compare it to any such vessel today. Triremes were long, fast wooden ships that could measure 120 feet from the nose of the ram at the bow to the curve of the stern (Hale 2009, xxiv), and while these ships could harness the power of the wind to propel them since most had a single sail, they were primarily moved by three rows of oars (thus the name trireme). Contrary to popular belief, the rowers were citizens, not slaves, and they each pulled fir wood oars, which could amount to 200 oars per ship with another 30 spares in reserve (Hale 2009, 24). Interestingly, unlike freight vessels of the period, triremes spent most of their lives on shore because the hulls needed to be constantly dried out to prevent rot caused by destructive shipworms (Hale 2009, xxv). While the crews of the Greek triremes at the Battle of Salamis were comprised of free citizens, the wealthiest of citizens served as trierarchs, or trireme captains (Hale 2009, xxx).

Perhaps the greatest impact that the invention of the trireme had on naval warfare was that the old method of marines fighting hand-to-hand on ships was replaced by maneuvers (Hale 2009, xxi), which meant that the Battle of Salamis was not won through brute force but by supreme strategies. The Greeks quickly learned that if they were to become the military masters of the sea, they needed something that mitigated their numerical inferiority, and they found it by adding rams to their already fast triremes. (Hale 2009, 19). The rams on Greeks triremes were not especially complex – metalworkers sheathed the beaks of the ships with bronze – but they proved to be highly effective, especially at the Battle of Salamis.

The Greeks also developed sophisticated maneuvers that were well suited to the sleek design of their triremes. The two most common naval maneuvers employed by the Greeks and some of their enemies, most notably the Phoenicians, were the diekplous and the periplous. The ancient Greek term diekplous is translated by modern philologists approximately as "breakthrough and encirclement," and it usually involved the fleet lining up abreast against its enemy and then performing the maneuver. The best preserved historical record of a diekplous maneuver being performed took place at the Battle of Arignusai in 406 BCE during the Peloponnesian War, where a smaller but faster fleet of 120 Peloponnesian triremes defeated a fleet of 150 Delian triremes (Wallinga 1990, 141). The ancient Greek historian, Xenophon, who fought in the Peloponnesian War, wrote about the engagement: "But all the vessels of the Lacedaemonians were arranged in a single line, with a view to breaking through the enemy and circling [diekplous] round him, inasmuch as they had superior seamen." (Xenophon, Hellenica, I, VI, 31).

The other maneuver that the Greeks often employed was the periplous, which is often translated as "freely moving around in the open water between and behind opposing lines." (Wallinga 1990, 145). At the Battle of Salamis the Greeks fought to prevent a Persian diekplous while using the periplous to destroy the Persian fleet.

Chapter 5: The Order of Battle

Satellite image of the straits at Salamis (center right)

The Battle of Salamis was fought in a narrow channel (much like the Battle of Artemisium) that separates the Attic peninsula from the island of Salamis. Despite the name Salamis being attributed to the island in modern times, there is some ambiguity in the ancient sources as to whether the reference was to the island or a town (Hammond 1956, 37).

The most detailed ancient source concerning the physical description and history of Salamis was written by the 1st century CE Greek geographer Pausanias, who wrote, "Salamis lies over against Eleusis, and stretches as far as the territory of Megara. It is said that the first to give this name to the island was Cychreus, who called it after his mother Salamis the daughter of Asopus, and afterwards it was colonised by the Aeginetans with Telamon. Philaeus, the son of Eurysaces, the son of Ajax, is said to have handed the island over to the Athenians, having been made an Athenian by them. Many years afterwards the Athenians drove out all the Salaminians, having discovered that they had been guilty of treachery in the war with Cassander." (Pausanias, Description of Greece, I, 35.1-2).

Obviously, since the battle was at sea, the exact positioning of the ships can only be implied from the historical sources, but two other notable landmarks from the Battle of Salamis can be located on land. Xerxes watched the entire battle from a throne on land (which will be discussed more thoroughly) below Mount Aegaleos, so modern scholars place his exact position opposite the island of Salamis and above the temple known as the Heracleum, which was the narrowest part of the channel (Hammond 1956, 38). The island of Pysttalia, which was the site of the limited land fighting during the Battle of Salamis, lies at the mouth of the channel (Morkot 1996, 76) in front of the town of Salamis (Hammond 1956, 38).

Perhaps one of the most fascinating aspects of the physical layout of the channel of Salamis is how so many triremes were able to fit into such a tightly confined area. The size of both fleets can be deduced by the accounts of Herodotus and Plutarch, along with Aeschylus' drama *The Persians*. In fact, Plutarch cites Aeschylus as his source for the size of the Persian fleet (Plutarch, Themistocles, XIV, 1), but he only gives the number of Attic (Athenian) ships in his account, which he placed at 180 (Plutarch, Themistocles, XIV, 1). Herodotus' account concurs, as he wrote that the Athenians numbered 180 triremes and accounted for half of the Greek fleet (Herodotus, The Histories, VIII, 44). The passage where Aeschylus noted the numbers of both fleets was a scene where a Persian messenger related the disaster of the battle to Xerxes' mother, Atossa. The scene states, "If number of ships might gain the fight, believe me, queen, the victory had been ours. The Greeks could tell but ten time thirty ships, with other ten, of most select equipment. Xerxes numbered a thousand ships, two hundred sail and seven of rapid wing beside." (Aeschylus The Persians, 312). Based on all three of the ancient accounts, the modern historian N.G.L. Hammond placed the total number of Persian vessels at 1,407 and the Greeks at 380, which included some Greek defectors from the Persian fleet who came over to join their countrymen after the Battle of Artemisium (Hammond 1956, 40).

Despite the discrepancy in numbers, many major battles have been won before the battle even started through supreme planning and strategy, and the Battle of Salamis was no different in this respect. One of the most vital aspects of any military strategy is determining where and when the battle will be fought; if a commander is able to pick the place and time to engage his enemy, then he already has two advantages in his favor. As the Persian fleet advanced towards Salamis and the Persian army neared the Greek wall across the Isthmus of Corinth, not all of the Greeks (especially the Spartans and other Peloponnesians) were convinced that Salamis was an ideal location to engage the Persians, but Themistocles, the wise commander of the Athenians, knew that Greek victory depended on holding the channel near Salamis. Once again, he relied on his excellent oratory skills to convince his countrymen to make a stand. According to Herodotus, Themistocles said, "Now for my plan: it will bring, if you adopt it, the following advantages: first, we shall be fighting in narrow waters, and there, with our inferior numbers, we shall win, provided things go as we may reasonably expect. Fighting in a confined space favours us but the open sea favours the enemy. Secondly, Salamis, where we have put our women and children, will be preserved; and thirdly – for you the most important point of all – you will be fighting in defence of the Peloponnese by remaining here just as much as by withdrawing to the Isthmus – nor, if you have the sense to follow my advice, will you draw the Persian army to the Peloponnese. If we beat them at sea, as I expect we shall, they will not advance to attack you on the Isthmus, or come any further than Attica; they will retreat in disorder, and we shall gain by the preservation of Megara, Aegina, and Salamis – where an oracle has already foretold our victory." (Herodotus, The Histories, VIII, 60).

Not only is Themistocles' intelligence and knowledge of military strategy related in this passage but also a deep understanding of the Greek psyche. After the Battle of Artemisium, Themistocles knew what his fleet was capable of and what it needed to do to win at Salamis; fighting in a narrow channel benefited the numerically inferior Greek fleet as it prevented the Persian fleet from maneuvering a diekplous and surrounding them. The Athenian general also appealed to the Greeks' emotional states by pointing out that the Persians would not stop until they were beaten, and that the oracle at Delphi predicted their wooden wall (of ships) would be the victors.

The Spartans and other Peloponnesians appear to have been placated by Themistocles' speech, but the wily Athenian commander had one last machination planned that would go a long way toward Greek victory at Salamis. Themistocles realized that if the Greek army had no way to retreat, they would fight more fiercely. As the two fleets assembled and faced each other in the Salamis channel, Themistocles believed that many of the men, especially the Peloponnesians, might desert in order to go back and defend their homes, so to prevent this, Themistocles devised a plan that utilized a combination of deception and guile. Herodotus explained, "At this point Themistocles, feeling that he would be outvoted by the Peloponnesians, slipped quietly away from the meeting and sent a man over in a boat to the Persian fleet, with instructions upon what to say when he got there. The man – Sicinnus – was one of Themistocles' slaves and used to attend upon his sons . . . Following his instructions, then, Sicinnus made his way to the Persian commanders and said: 'I am the bearer of a secret communication from the Athenian commander, who is a well-wisher to your king and hopes for a Persian victory. He has told me to report to you that the Greeks are afraid and are planning to slip away. Only prevent them from slipping through your fingers, and you have at this moment an opportunity of unparalleled success. They are at daggers drawn with each other, and will offer no opposition – on the contrary, you will see the pro-Persians amongst them fighting the rest.'" (Herodotus, The Histories, VIII, 75).

In the cover of darkness Themistocles had no way of knowing if his plan worked until his fellow Athenian (and occasional political rival) Aristides sailed quietly through the Persian fleet from the allied Greek state of Aegina. Despite the well documented conflicts between the two esteemed Athenians, Aristides offered to put aside all differences and defer to Themistocles. Plutarch wrote, "'O Themistocles,' he said, 'if we are wise, we shall at last lay aside our vain and puerile contention, and begin a salutary and honourable rivalry with one another in emulous struggles to save Hellas, thou as commanding general, I as assistant counsellor, since at the very outset I learn that thou art the only one who has adopted the best policy, urging as thous dost to fight a decisive sea-fight here in the narrows as soon as may be.'" (Plutarch, Aristides, VIII, 3).

A statue depicting Aristides

This was actually a crucial point for the Greeks before the battle even began because Aristides, who would prove to be indispensable in the land battle, joined the Greek fleet and saw the virtue in Themistocles' trick, which was successful. Herodotus recounted that not only was Themistocles' plan successful (since the Persian fleet encircled the Greeks), he was also so supremely confident that he didn't care how the Greeks would react if they found out he was behind it: "'It was I who was responsible for this move of the enemy; for as our men would not fight here of their own free will, it was necessary to make them, whether they wanted to do so or not. But take them the good news yourself; if I tell them, they will think I have invented it and will not believe me. Please, then, go in and make the report yourself. If they believe you, well and good; if they do not, it's all the same; for if we are surrounded, as you say we are, escape is no longer possible.'" (Herodotus, The Histories, VIII, 80).

Themistocles' ploy proved to be effective since it ensured the Greeks were forced to fight to the last ship, but he also demonstrated his qualities as a commander by choosing when the battle commenced, and the ancient sources agree that when the Battle of Salamis took place was almost as important as where it was fought. According to Plutarch, Themistocles chose a time that benefited the sleek, low to the water Greek triremes: "Themistocles is thought to have divined the best time for fighting with no less success than the best place, inasmuch as he took care not to send his triremes bow on against the Barbarian vessels until the hour of the day had come which always brought the breeze fresh from the sea and a swell rolling through the strait. This breeze wrought no harm to the Hellenic ships, since they lay low in the water and were rather small; but for the Barbarian ships, with their towering sterns and lofty decks and sluggish movements in getting under way, it was fatal, since it smote them and slewed them round broadside to the Hellenes." (Plutarch, Themistocles, XIV, 1-2).

Chapter 6: The Battle of Salamis

At dawn, before combat began, the leaders of both armies took their places. As mentioned above, Xerxes took a position of relative safety on the shore where he could observe the battle. According to Plutarch, "At break of day, Xerxes was seated on a high place and overlooking the disposition of his armament. This place was, according to Phanodemus, above the Heracleium, where only a narrow passage separates the island from Attica." (Plutarch, Themistocles, XIII, 1).

Xerxes stayed on his perch for the entire battle, never in danger, which stood in stark contrast to Themistocles, who took his place on a trireme amongst his men and roused them with his oratorical skills. Unfortunately, only a "compact version" (Zali 2013, 467) of the speech survives in Herodotus' account, and it is for the most part paraphrased. In the speech Themistocles used standard Greek rhetorical techniques (Zali 2013, 462) to exhort his men to demonstrate their better nature against their enemies, and despite the fact little of Themistocles's speech remains, it's easy to see how it fits into the overall picture of Greek victory at the Battle of Salamis. Themistocles – an expert at strategy and rhetoric – used all of his available skills to exhort the Greeks to fight fearlessly against overwhelming odds, and though the speech may not have been a decisive factor in the Greek victory at the Battle of Salamis, it was another plank in the "wooden wall" that the oracle prophesized.

One of the most interesting aspects of the Battle of Salamis, at least in terms of military maneuvers, is that no ancient source mentions a diekplous or an attempt at a diekplous by either navy (Wallinga 1990, 148). Some modern historians believe that the Phoenician ships that were at the rear ranks of the Persian fleet were expected to prevent a Greek diekplous (Hale 2009, 64), but one cannot say for sure based on the silence of the ancient sources.

The Greek fleet was drawn up in a single line against the Salamis shore, and while a careful look at the sources reveals that although the word diekplous was never used to describe maneuvers at Salamis, it was clearly on Themistocles' mind. It's apparent that the Athenian commander chose the narrow channel near Salamis, which was similar in topography to Artemisium, to prevent a Persian diekplous. It's possible that since the Greeks were successful at preventing one, the ancient sources simply never describe one when recounting the battle, but either way, the narrows clearly prevented the Persian fleet from performing the maneuver. For their part, the Greeks did not have the numbers to perform one.

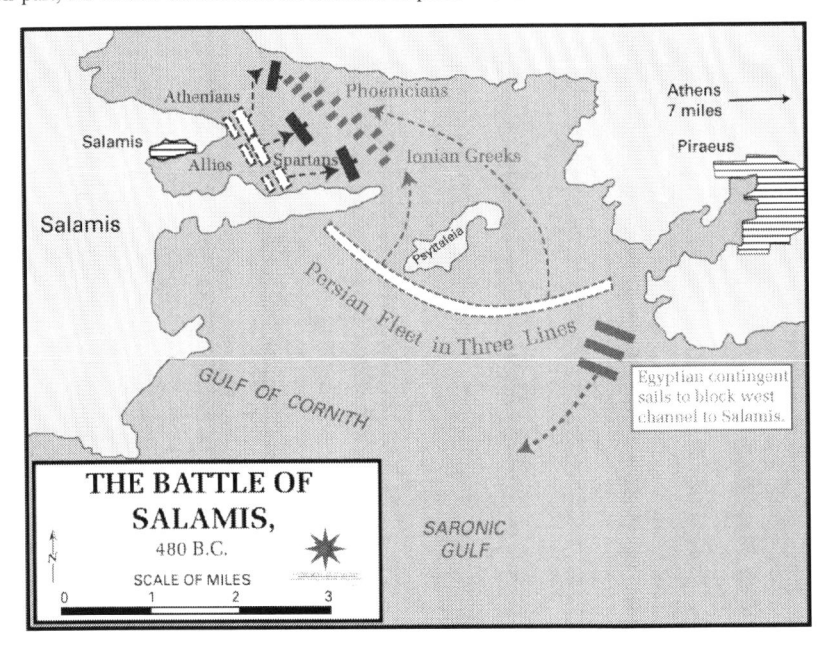

Map of the two navies' positions

The thin Greek line of triremes that faced the Persian fleet consisted of ships from Aegina on the right wing, Spartan ships in the middle, and the Athenian fleet on the left wing against the Phoenicians (Hale 2009, 65). As the Persian fleet moved forward to attack the Greeks, trumpets and war cries erupted from the Greek line. Aeschylus wrote, "Then the fierce trumpet's voice blazed o'er the main; and on the salt sea flood forthwith the oars, with measured plash, descended, and all their lines, with dexterous speed displayed, stood with opposing front. The right wing first, then the whole fleet bore down, and straight uprose a might shout. 'SONS OF THE GREEKS, ADVANCE! YOUR COUNTRY FREE, YOUR CHILDREN FREE, YOUR WIVES! THE ALTARS OF YOUR NATIVE GODS DELIVER, AND YOUR ANCESTRAL TOMBS – ALL'S NOW AT STAKE!'" (Aeschylus, The Persians, 313).

The Persians, who were perhaps overanxious and overaggressive due to their numerical superiority, moved toward the Greek line, but the line held and even back rowed in a feigned retreat in order to face the Persian ships with their rams (Hale 2009, 67). The Persian fleet was then at a serious disadvantage despite their numbers, as their broadsides were exposed to the deadly Greek rams (Hale 2009, 47). This early engagement was written about by both Herodotus and Plutarch, but the details in their accounts differ slightly. Herodotus wrote, "The whole fleet now got under way, and in a moment the Persians were on them. The Greeks checked their way and began to back astern; and they were on the point of running aground when Ameinias of Pallene, in command of an Athenian ship, drove ahead and rammed an enemy vessel. Seeing the two ships foul of one another and locked together, the rest of the Greek fleet hurried to Ameinias' assistance, and the general action began." (Herodotus, The Histories, VIII, 84).

Plutarch's account of the early fighting at the Battle of Salamis does not mention Ameinias, but it appears to be more revealing in terms of general strategy and maneuvers. Plutarch noted, "Now the first man to capture an enemy's ship was Lycomedes, an Athenian captain, who cut off its figure-head and dedicated it to Apollo the Laurel-bearer at Phlya. Then the rest, put on an equality in numbers with their foes, because the Barbarians had to attack them by detachments in the narrow strait and so ran afoul of one another, routed them, though they resisted till the evening drew on." (Plutarch, Themistocles, XV, 2).

Although Plutarch's account is much more concise – in fact, his total account of the actual fighting is just this short passage – it is also more revealing in terms of the successful strategies employed by the Greeks. Again, the narrow strait/channel between Attica and Salamis played a crucial role in this battle as it proved to mitigate the Persians' numerical superiority. By creating a bottleneck in the channel, the Greeks only had to fight the Persians as they came at them a few at a time, which also prevented the Persians from performing a diekplous maneuver.

It was not long after the initial fighting broke out that the battle moved into its second, crucial, phase. Due to frustration at not being able to encircle the Greek fleet, poor commanders, or a combination of both, the Persian fleet quickly demonstrated its lack of discipline and broke its line (Hale 2009, 69). Once the Persian line broke, the Battle of Salamis was decided as the only individual ships in the Persian fleet that were a match for the Greeks, one on one, were helmed by the Phoenicians. As the Persian line broke and each ship was left to its own devices, the Greeks held strong and picked their individual battles wisely. Herodotus explained, "The Persian fleet suffered severely in the battle, the Athenians and Aeginetans accounting for a great many of their ships. Since the Greek fleet worked together as a whole, while the Persians had lost formation and were no longer fighting on any plan, that was what was bound to happen." (Herodotus, The Histories, VIII, 86).

In ship to ship combat, the Persians were no match for the Greeks, who continued to use their rams to sink their enemy's ships. In the few instances where the method of boarding and then fighting on the desk of ships was used, the Persians fared well because they carried many archers and javelin men and their ships were higher off the sea (Hammond 1956, 48), but such instances were the exception at Salamis.

Early 20th century depiction of the Greek ships ramming Persian ships

Throughout the day, the Greeks continued to decimate the Persians one at a time using the ramming technique, but one commander in the Persian fleet stood out for her use of guile and intelligence. Since the Persians were so severely defeated at Salamis, none of their commanders are remembered very well except one: Artemisia of Halicarnassus. Artemisia was the queen of the city-state of Halicarnassus (ironically also the hometown of Herodotus), which was a part of the Caria satrapy in the Achaemenid Empire. By all accounts, Artemisia was a loyal subject of the Persians and even volunteered to lead a contingent from her city to follow Xerxes in his campaign against Greece in 480 BCE. Artemisia also fought against Themistocles and the Greeks at Artemisium, which is where she got her first taste of what the Persians were up against, but it was at Salamis where the queen became immortalized.

As fate would have it, Artemisia became famous for participating in a battle that she had advised the Persians against fighting. According to Herodotus, she said:

> "Tell the King to spare his ships and not do a naval battle because our enemies are much stronger than us in the sea, as men are to women. And why does he need to risk a naval battle? Athens for which he did undertake this expedition is his and the rest of Greece too. No man can stand against him and they who once resisted, were destroyed.
>
> If Xerxes chose not to rush into a naval encounter, but instead kept his ships close to the shore and either stayed there or moved them towards the Peloponnese, victory would be his. The Greeks can't hold out against him for very long. They will leave for their cities, because they don't have food in store on this island, as I have learned, and when our army will march against the Peloponnese they who have come from there will become worried and they will not stay here to fight to defend Athens.
>
> But if he hurries to engage I am afraid that the navy will be defeated and the land-forces will be weakened as well. In addition, he should also consider that he has certain untrustworthy allies, like the Egyptians, the Cyprians, the Kilikians and the Pamphylians, who are completely useless."

Interestingly, she gained her fame at the Battle of Salamis not through any excellent maneuvers or strategies but because of her cunning. After the Greeks broke the Persian line and it was everybody for themselves, Artemisia sprang into action. Herodotus explained, "I must however, mention Artemisia, on account of an exploit which still further increased her reputation with Xerxes . . . In this awkward situation she hit on a plan which turned out greatly to her advantage: with the Athenian close on her tail she drove ahead with all possible speed and rammed one of her friends . . . For the captain of the Athenian trireme, on seeing her ram an enemy, naturally supposed that her ship was a Greek one, or else a deserter which was fighting on the Greek side; so he abandoned the chase and turned to attack elsewhere." (Herodotus, The Histories, VIII, 87).

As the Battle of Salamis progressed and it became apparent to Xerxes that his navy had lost, the Great King tried one last ditch effort to win the day. Although he did not participate directly in the Battle of Salamis he watched the entire event from his perch, and the few Persian commanders that fought well were duly noted by Xerxes. Herodotus wrote, "Xerxes watched the course of the battle from the base of Mt Aegaleos, across the strait from Salamis; whenever he saw one of his officers behaving with distinction, he would find out his name, and his secretaries wrote it down, together with his city and parentage." (Herodotus, The Histories, VIII, 90). Indeed, it was from his mountain throne that he watched and was so impressed by Artemisia that he told one of his advisors "my men have turned into women, my women into men" (Herodotus, The Histories, VIII, 88).

While watching with anger as the Greeks annihilated his navy, Xerxes realized that he still had one card left to play: his immense land army. If Xerxes could somehow land his army on the island of Salamis, where all of the Athenian evacuees were located, then he could force the Athenians to terms, but he had few ships left to transport his army after the Greek fleet routed them, so he planned to bridge the channel. The narrow channel, which was an advantage for the Greeks, nearly turned into a disadvantage when Xerxes sent men to build a causeway across it. Plutarch explained, "After the sea-fight, Xerxes, sill furious at his failure, undertook to carry moles out into the sea on which he could lead his infantry across to Salamis against the Hellenes, damming up the intervening strait. (Plutarch, Themistocles, XVI, 1)

As clever as Xerxes' plan to bridge the strait of Salamis was, it never materialized as the few ships he had left quickly fell victim to Greek mop-up efforts. When it became obvious that they were defeated, the remaining Persian ships tried to sail for their original base at Phalerum on the Attic peninsula, near the mouth of the Salamis channel. The ancient sources reveal that few prisoners were taken, which suggests that among all the other strategies Themistocles planned, he told the Greeks to take no one alive. Thus, according to Herodotus, this phase of the battle was little more than a massacre: "When the Persian route began and they were trying to get back to Phalerum, the Aeginetan squadron, which was waiting to catch them in the narrows, did memorable service. The enemy was in hopeless confusion; such ships as offered resistance or tried to escape were cut to pieces by the Athenians, while the Aeginetans caught those which attempted to get clear, so that any ship which escaped the one enemy promptly fell amongst the other." (Herodotus, The Histories, VIII, 91).

Herodotus' account of the massacre of the Persian sailors by the Greeks can be corroborated by Aeschylus. The war veteran and dramatist wrote about the carnage from the perspective of a Persian: "Meanwhile the Greeks stroke after stroke dealt dexterous all around, till our ships showed their keels, and the blue sea was seen no more, with multitude of shops and corpses covered. All the shores were strewn, and the rough rocks, with dead; till, in the end, each ship in the barbaric host, that yet had oars, in most disordered flight rowed off. As men that fish for tunnies, so the Greeks, with broken booms, and fragments of the wreck, struck our snared men, and hacked them." (Aeschylus, The Persians, 313).

This phase of the Battle of Salamis may be the most difficult for people today to comprehend since the killing of prisoners of war is now deemed a war crime, and there is no doubt Themistocles was aware of and probably ordered the killing of all captured and fleeing Persians. In fact, this move may have been well thought out by the Athenian commander; after all, although most of the women and children of Attica were safely evacuated to Salamis, the Athenians who fought in the Battle of Salamis still faced uncertainties when they returned home. Would their homes and field still be intact? Would their sacred temples and shrines still be there when they wanted to give offerings? These were unknown to the Greeks when the battle commenced, but they could probably assume that the Persians devastated Attica.

The massacre also dealt with a logistical problem for the Greeks, who had nowhere and no way of caring for hundreds if not thousands of prisoners. Thus, just like they did at the Battle of Marathon, they simply killed any survivors.

While the Greeks were destroying the last of the Persian fleet, the last phase of the Battle of Salamis took place. As the day turned to night and Xerxes was trying to bridge the channel between Salamis and Attica, Persian transports ferried 400 of their elite soldiers to the island of Pysttaleia, and although somewhat peripheral to the eventual outcome of the Battle of Salamis, the island of Pysttaleia was important to both the Persians and Greeks and may have played a bigger role in the overall battle if the Persians would have been able to hold it. Pysttaleia is at the mouth of the channel of Salamis, which meant that if the Persians could have held the island, they may have been able to cross to Salamis and perhaps draw the Greeks onto land, where they would not have been so outclassed. At the same time, the island was important to the Greeks for spiritual reasons, as the Athenians believed it to be the sacred abode of the god Pan (Hale 2009, 63). The religious significance of the island should not be underestimated either, especially in the wake of the Persian destruction of so many Greek temples previously. After all, the Greeks had extra incentive to prevent them from defiling any more sacred spaces.

According to Plutarch, Aristides was the first Greek to notice Persians on Pysttaleia: "While the captains of the Hellenes were acting on this plan, Aristides noticed that Pysttaleia, a small island lying in the straits in front of Salamis, was full of the enemy. He therefore embarked in small boats the most ardent and the most warlike of the citizens, made a landing on Pysttaleia, joined battle with the Barbarians, and slew them all, save the few conspicuous men who were taken alive. Among these were three sons of the King's sister Sandaucé, whom he straightway sent to Themistocles, and it is said that, in obedience to some oracle or other, and at the bidding of Euphrantides the seer, they were sacrificed to Dionysus Carnivorous. Then Aristides lined the islet all round with his hoplites, and lay in wait for any who should be cast up there, that no friend might perish, and no foe escape." (Plutarch, Aristides, IX, 1-2).

With the fighting done, Herodotus wrote that there were not many Greek casualties, but he provided no numbers. He also wrote that the few Persians who survived the massacre drowned because they did not know how to swim (Herodotus, The Histories, VIII, 89). Among the multitude of Persians killed at the Battle of Salamis was Ariabinges, the son of Darius I and brother of Xerxes (Herodotus, The Histories, VIII, 89).

William Rainey's illustration depicting the death of Ariabinges

Meanwhile, having been massacred on both sea and land at Salamis, Xerxes and the Persian fleet quickly sailed back to Asia, but even still, the emperor had not abandoned his hopes for a conquest of Greece because the best of his army, under Mardonius, still remained in the field. However, the following year, in the summer of 479 BCE, the Persians faced a force of between 40,000 and 100,000 Greek infantry near the Boeotian city of Plataea. At the battle, the Greeks completely annihilated Mardonius' force of between 100,000-300,000 men, and Mardonius himself was killed. Around the same time, what remained of the Persian fleet was destroyed off Mycale. The Persian invasion was over, and no Persian army would ever set foot on Greek soil again.

Chapter 7: Why the Greeks Won at Salamis

When searching for reasons why the Greeks won the Battle of Salamis, a number of factors become apparent. To begin with, the Greeks had superior commanders and strategy. As soon as Xerxes and his army began their long march through Asia and Europe for Greece, the Greeks (especially the Athenians) prepared to meet their foe, and the Athenians made several moves before the arrival of the Persians that helped ensure their victory. For example, they used the surplus from their silver mines to create a brand new navy, appointed the bright and cunning Themistocles as their commander, and successfully evacuated their city and region so that the Persians had little to loot when they arrived.

The appointment of Themistocles to the high command proved to be the best move the Athenian made. Themistocles proved to be a supremely gifted commander before and during the Battle of Salamis. He used the Battle of Artemisium to successfully gauge the strengths and weaknesses of both his and his enemy's navy, and he then went on to pick the optimal location and time to engage the Persian fleet at Salamis, while his rousing oratory and rhetoric also gave his men an added incentive to fight. Themistocles even made sure none of his allies could leave the battle, and he was also farsighted enough to make amends with his old foe Aristides, who would be indispensable in the battle.

The supreme leadership abilities of Themistocles are sharply contrasted with the absence of any capable leader in the Persian navy; when the fighting began, disorder reigned on the Persian side. In fact, the Persians had no commander that even came close to the level of Aristides or any of the lesser Greek commanders.

Although Themistocles' speech before the Battle of Salamis helped to urge his men on, the Persians had already given them incentive to fight. When Xerxes invaded Greece and did not request earth and water from the Spartans and Athenians, he essentially indicated to them that he planned to wipe them out, which was confirmed when his army ravaged Attica. Xerxes' destruction of Attica must have evoked immense anger amongst the Greeks, especially when their holiest sites were destroyed. Revenge is a powerful emotion, and it no doubt played a large role in the fury with which the Greeks fought during the Battle of Salamis. The battle being fought in Greek waters also played a role in the Greek victory. Themistocles knew the best place to engage the Persian fleet, which of course came from an intimate knowledge of his homeland.

Perhaps the most obvious reason for the Greek victory lay not with any of their commanders, as good as they were, or a knowledge and love of their homeland, but with a psychological quality of Xerxes' that is aptly and ironically summed up in a Greek word: hubris. Xerxes' extreme arrogance was perhaps best exemplified by Herodotus when he wrote about the Great King's initial planning of the expedition. According to Herodotus, Xerxes said, "Have we anything to fear from them? The size of their army? Their wealth? The question is absurd; we know how they fight; we know how slender their resources are. People of their race we have already reduced to subjection – I mean the Greeks of Asia, Ionians, Aeolians, and Dorians." (Herodotus, The Histories, VII, 9).

Obviously, Xerxes severely misjudged the Greeks' abilities and willingness to fight, both on land and at sea. The Persian emperor believed that the immense size of his army and navy would be enough to subdue the Greeks, but he also rarely considered logistical problems of taking a force so large so far from home. Although Xerxes may never have considered these issues, Herodotus wrote that some of his advisors did. The historian wrote that some of the Persian emperor's advisors told him, "If you increase your forces, the two powers I have in mind will be even worse enemies to you than they are now. I will tell you what they are – the land and the sea. So far as I know there is not a harbour anywhere big enough to receive this fleet of ours and give it protection in the event of storms: and indeed there would have to be not merely on such harbour, but many – all along the coast by which you will sail. But there is not a single one; so I would have you realize, my lord, that men are at the mercy of circumstance, and not their master. Now let me tell you of your other great enemy, the land. If you meet with no opposition, the land itself will become more and more hostile to you the further you advance, drawn on and on; for men are never satisfied by success. What I mean is this – if nobody stops your advance, the land itself – the mere distance growing greater and greater as the days go by – will ultimately starve you." (Herodotus, The Histories, VII, 49).

In the end, since he considered himself the Great King of the Achaemenid Empire and descended from the gods, Xerxes felt compelled to listen to no man, no matter how good the counsel. As such, he was destined to be a slave to his own arrogance and emotions.

Chapter 8: Monuments and Trophies from the Battle of Salamis

Although the nature of a sea battle made it harder to construct monuments on the site of the fight, a number of trophies were taken and monuments were erected to commemorate the Greek victory at Salamis. Three intact Phoenician triremes that were captured by the Greeks served as trophies for their victory. One of the triremes was brought to the shrine of Poseidon on Cape Sunium, another went to the Poseidon Temple at the Isthmus, and the third was given as an offering to Ajax at Salamis (Hale 2009, 72). Another prize that the Greeks captured was the gold footstool of Xerxes, which was brought to the Acropolis of Athens and given as an offering to Athena (Hale 2009, 73).

The island of Salamis itself also had a trophy in honor of the Greek victory. Pausanias wrote, "In Salamis is a sanctuary of Artemis, and also a trophy erected in honour of the victory which Themistocles the son of Neocles won for the Greeks. There is also a sanctuary of Cyrchreus. When the Athenians were fighting the Persians at sea, a serpent is said to have appeared in the fleet, and the god in an oracle told the Athenians that it was Cychreus the hero. Before Salamis there is also an island called Psyttalea. Here they say that bout four hundred of the Persians landed, and when the fleet of Xerxes was defeated, these also were killed after the Greeks had crossed over to Psyttalea. The island has no artistic statue, only some roughly carved wooden images of Pan." Pausanias, Description of Greece, I, 36.1-2).

The victory at Salamis was obviously a proud moment for the Greeks, especially the Athenians, but the real rewards for Athens came in the succeeding years as the city became the pre-eminent force in the Greek world. Before the Persian Wars, Athens had no great traditions of philosophy, art, science, or historical writing, but after the Battle of Salamis, their culture began to flourish into what most moderns regard as the Golden Age of Athens (Hale 2009, xxv). The above opinion is not just confined to modern scholars; Plutarch also believed that it was Themistocles and his navy that brought Athens to greatness. He claimed, "But Themistocles did not, as Aristophanes, the comic poet says, 'knead the Pireus on to the city,' nay, he fastened the city of the Peraeus, and the land to the sea, And so it was that he increased the privileges of the common people as against the nobles, and filled them with boldness, since the controlling power came now into the hands of skippers and boastswins and pilots." (Plutarch, Themistocles, XIX, 3-4).

So it was that Themistocles and the Battle of Salamis transformed Athens. Previously a sleepy city-state that had just awoken from the nightmare of tyranny and was transitioning into early democracy, Athens subsequently became the world center of learning and culture. On the other hand, after the Battle of Salamis, Persia began a long decline. The Greeks began to become more entwined in the affairs of the Achaemenid Empire, which lasted until the Greek Macedonian king Alexander the Great conquered the Persians in 330 BCE (Briant 2002, 864).

A memorial commemorating the battle

Picture of a column dedicated to the Greek alliance to commemorate their victory in the war

Ironically, the Greeks' greatest war hero at Salamis could have become a character in a Greek tragedy. After the Battle of Salamis, Themistocles was honored by the Spartans for his bravery and guile, and although the Spartan commander Eurybiades received the first prize because he was a Spartan, Themistocles was given second prize for the tricks and maneuvers he employed before and during the battle (Jordan 1988, 551-53). However, Themistocles' place of honor among the Greeks was short lived; according to the ancient historian and veteran of the Peloponnesian War, Thucydides, Themistocles was accused of collaborating with the Persians and then ostracized and exiled: "As for the medism of Pausanias, the Lacedaemonians sent an embassy to Athens and accused Themistokles of involvement, which they discovered from the evidence about Pausanias, and demanded that they inflict the same punishment on him as well. They consented and – since he happened to be ostracized and was residing in Argos, frequenting the other parts of the Peloponnesos as well – sent men to accompany the Lacedaemonians, who were ready to help in the pursuit, with instructions to seize him wherever they found him. Themistokles detected this first and fled the Peloponnesos for Corcyra." (Thucydides, I, 135-136).

In response to the pressure that was brought against him, Themistocles sailed east to the Achaemenid Empire, made contact with Xerxes' successor, Artaxerxes I, and pled for mercy (Thucydides, I, 137). The ancient sources conflict somewhat on the end of his life; Thucydides claimed that he died of illness in exile, but Plutarch asserted that he committed suicide by drinking bull's blood. Either way, Themistocles probably had the greatest rise and most precipitous fall of any of the prominent Greek commanders involved in the Persian Wars.

Ironically, Themistocles' long-time rival, Aristides, fared much better. Although he never received the recognition and honors for his contributions at the Battle of Salamis that Themistocles did, Aristides went on to be a hero at and received much praise for his fighting at the Battle of Plataea in 479 BCE (Plutarch, Aristides, XI, 1-2). After that, Aristides lived a much longer and less controversial life than Themistocles, to the extent that the circumstances of his death were unrecorded by history. (Plutarch, Aristides, XXVI, 1-3).

The Battle of Cannae

Prelude to the Second Punic War

Carthage's loss in the First Punic War resulted in a complete dearth of money and resources across their empire, which was a serious problem because Carthage relied chiefly on mercenary armies. Thousands of mercenaries throughout the Carthaginian Empire were suddenly not getting their wages, and the result was inevitable: war. An all-out insurrection of mercenary contingents throughout the Punic Empire, including Iberia, Sardinia and Corsica, and a renewed attack from the subjugated Lybian tribes, followed. Suddenly, Carthage was fighting for her very life, and grudgingly accepting military and financial aid from her two old enemies, Syracuse and Rome.

The war dragged on for two years, but by 238 Carthage was once again secure, with order restored to her dominions. Still, the cost had been heavy; taking advantage of Carthage's desperate situation, Rome had conveniently seized both Sardinia and Corsica, which had been plunged into lawlessness by the mercenary uprising, and there was nothing Carthage could do about it. The mines of Iberia, with their vast amounts of as yet untapped wealth, were still secure, but control of them was dubious.

Crisis, as so often occurs, had brought political change in its wake, and the Barcid family, led by Hamilcar Barca, had risen to prominence during the Mercenary Wars. Hamilcar was a skilled general who rapidly rose to command all of the Carthaginian armies by ousting the competition of his rival, Hanno the Great. Hamilcar was populist and had the support of the common people, whereas Hanno was a scion of the old Carthaginian aristocracy, but their power was on the wane. Thus, it was Hamilcar and his son-in-law, Hasdrubal the Fair, who subdued the Iberian cities, but the loyalty of these new dominions was far from certain. Rather than owing allegiance to Carthage, the Iberian cities looked to Hamilcar exclusively for guidance, making Spain a virtual Barcid fief.

Hamilcar was killed in battle in 228, so Hasdrubal took over as his successor and began to look for a way to strike back at Rome in retaliation for the First Punic War and the blatant land grab in the chaos that followed. It appears likely that around 225, Hasdrubal began plotting with the Gauls of the Po Valley in the north of Italy (the only as yet unconquered area in the Italian Peninsula) to launch an attack on Rome with Carthaginian backing, but the Senate got wind of the plan and ordered a pre-emptive strike of their own, leading to a five-year war which eventually led to the annexation of the Po Valley. Hasdrubal himself was assassinated in 221, possibly with Roman collusion.

Rather than solve the Romans' problem, Hasdrubal's death brought about the rise of the most famous Carthaginian of all. Hasdrubal was succeeded by his brother-in-law and Hamilcar's son, Hannibal. In the history of war, only a select few men always make the list of greatest generals, and one of them is Hannibal, who has the distinction of being the only man who nearly brought Rome to its knees before its decline almost 700 years after his time.

A bust depicting Hannibal

For two years, Hannibal bided his time, consolidating his position in the Iberian peninsula and massing his forces, abiding by one of the greatest military truths and one which doubtless his tutors and his father, with their tales of Alexander and Alcibiades, had contributed to instill in him: numbers do not matter so much as concentration of force, i.e. what troops are available to fight in one single critical location, at any given time. Meanwhile, even as Hannibal was preparing to strike out against their very heart, the Romans seem to have grown unusually complacent; after all, Hannibal was new to overall command, and with both Hamilcar and Hasdrubal dead, they must have felt themselves secure. When in 218 Hannibal resurrected his brother-in-law's plan for a joint Gaulish and Carthaginian invasion of the Italian peninsula, the Romans were caught napping, something which they would live to regret in the following years.

Hannibal needed a *casus belli*, and in 219 BCE the Romans obliged him with one by forming an alliance with the powerful Iberian city of Saguntum, well south of the line drawn along the Ebro, and unilaterally declaring it a Roman protectorate. Hannibal took this for outright rebellion, and acted accordingly, investing the city and besieging it for eight months until it fell. He then protested to Carthage that Rome had broken the terms of their agreement with them, declaring that there could be only one feasible course of action: war. The Carthaginian rulers, having been burned once before, were wary of becoming embroiled in a new conflict with Rome, but such was Hannibal's popularity with the troops in the Iberian peninsula that, with the memory of the Mercenary Wars still fresh in their minds, they acceded to his demands rather than risk a full-blown mutiny.

Hannibal's Invasion of Italy

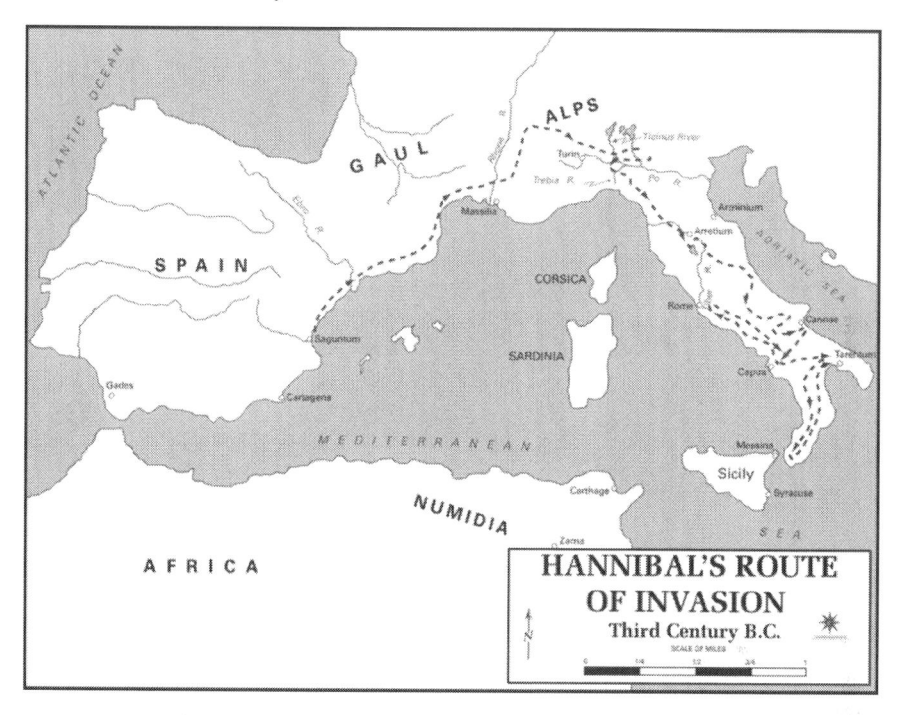

Estimated march of Hannibal's Invasion of Italy by the United States Military Academy

In the spring of 218 BCE, at the head of approximately 50,000 infantry, 15,000 cavalry, and 50 war elephants, Hannibal began marching northeast. His plan was breathtakingly ambitious; he would march through the Pyrenees, across southern Gaul, over the Alps and into Italy proper, thereby avoiding the heavily fortified border in the northwest of Italy. It was a route no general had ever taken before, let alone a general with so many animals (including elephants). His father Hamilcar had been defeated trying to invade southern Italy and attempting to outfight the Roman navy at sea; Hannibal would not make the same mistake.

Pushing aside with contemptuous ease the stiff resistance of the Pyrenean tribes, who contested every step of the way from their strongholds of the mountain passes, Hannibal pushed forwards with remarkable speed, leaving behind a detachment of some 10,000 Iberian soldiers to keep his lines of communication open and pacify the tumultuous region. He then marched on into southern Gaul, negotiating with the local chieftains and outfighting those who had a mind to contest his advance. His speed of maneuver, and his ability to move his army across rough terrain, proved unmatched in the ancient world since the time of Alexander the Great. By that point, his army, which now numbered some 40,000 infantry, 8,000 cavalry, and around 40 war elephants, danced up the valley of the Rhone to evade a Roman force sent to bar his passage southwards through the strategically vital gap in the mountains where the Alps meet the Mediterranean. With that route closed to him, Hannibal, undaunted, struck south and east across the Alps themselves.

Exactly what route he took is still the subject of hotly contested debate today, and even Roman scholars writing shortly after his prodigious feat seem to have no clear idea of where precisely he made his passage, but one thing is certain: it was one of the most remarkable maneuvers in military history. There were no roads greater than a goat-track across the Alps, none of them continuous, and the high passes were smothered by snow, often year-round, with drifts dozens of feet deep. Moreover, those passes included other hazards, such as potential rockfalls, and the barren terrain offered limited supplies. To top it all off, these passes were crawling with bellicose tribesmen who lived by banditry and hid in impregnable fortresses perched atop sheer crags. To Hannibal's army, most of them Iberians from the sun-baked plains of southern Spain or Carthaginians from the hot deserts of Northern Africa, the Alps must have looked like an icy Hell.

Hannibal's passage of the Alps remains the most famous event of his life and legend, and even though the location of his crossing matters little compared to the fact that he ultimately did get across, it has nonetheless been the most compelling mystery of his life for over 2,000 years. Even ancient historians were intrigued and tried to figure out the answer. The well known ancient Greek historian Polybius mentioned that Hannibal's men came into conflict with a Celtic tribe, the Allobroges, which was situated near the northern part of the range along the banks of the river Isère. The famous Roman historian Livy, writing over 150 years after Polybius, claimed Hannibal took a southerly route.

It is believed that both historians used the same source, a soldier in Hannibal's army, Sosylus of Lacedaemon, who wrote a history of the Second Punic War. Geographers and historians have pointed to the 6 most likely mountain passes that could have actually been used and then tried to narrow it down by finding one that seems to match the descriptions of both Livy and Polybius. A handful of historians used those accounts to theorize that Hannibal crossed the Alps at the Col du Montgenèvre pass, which would have been in the southern part of the range near northwest Italy. That also happened to be one of the better known road passes in the ancient world, and it was used often for diplomacy.

Wherever the crossing, and despite the innumerable difficulties, Hannibal got across. He reached the rolling foothills of Northern Italy several months later, at the head of 20,000 infantry, 4,000 cavalry, and a mere handful of war elephants (the great beasts having fared none too well, as was to be expected, in the mountain passes). If figures relating to his troop numbers before and after his celebrated crossing are to be believed, only half of the men Hannibal marched into the Alps marched back out again, and Hannibal must have known that no supply convoys could ever hope to cross where his army had passed. Nor, with the Roman navy's supremacy in the Mediterranean, could he have much hope of resupply or retreat by sea. Like Caesar would do nearly 170 years later crossing the Rubicon, Hannibal had cast the die. He and his men were left with no choice but victory or death.

Costly as it was, Hannibal's choice to cross the Alps was not done so for vainglorious reasons. By appearing suddenly in Northern Italy, crossing terrain that was reckoned to be impassable, Hannibal took the Romans completely by surprise, and the main Roman army that had been mobilized to fight Hannibal was caught completely wrong-footed. When news of Hannibal's appearance reached its commander, Publius Scipio (father of the redoubtable Scipio Africanus, who would cross swords with Hannibal himself in the years to come), he was in the process of pushing his men across the Pyrenees and into Iberia. He quickly loaded his rearguard onto ships, sailed across to Italy, and hurried to intercept Hannibal by forced march.

Scipio engaged Hannibal's forces at Ticinus, but he could only hope to fight a delaying action with the limited troops at his disposal. Hannibal's celebrated Numidian cavalry routed Scipio's forces, and would have killed Scipio himself had it not been for Scipio Africanus' timely rescue. Emboldened by this Roman defeat, the Gauls of the Po valley rose in revolt, sending a large force (around 20,000 men) to join Hannibal's army. Hannibal then marched his force south of Scipio's main base at Placentia, on the Trebia river, cutting him off from the support of Consul Sempronius Longus, who was marching up from southern Italy to come to his aid and bring Hannibal to battle. However, when the provisions promised to his army by the Cisalpine Gauls failed to materialize, Hannibal was forced to abandon his tactically superior position to capture the supply depots at Clastidium, allowing Longus and Scipio to join their forces near the Trebia.

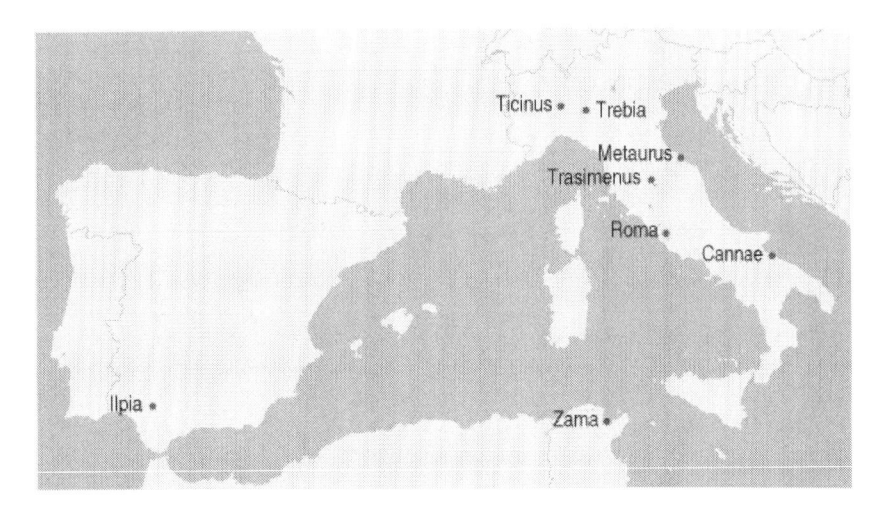

Although the Roman Senate was now hurriedly raising legions in Rome, and two powerful Roman armies had joined together, Hannibal apparently remained unfazed. He promptly marched on the Roman camp on the Trebia, making a show of force and inviting Scipio and Longus to attack him. The two Roman generals obliged, throwing their celebrated infantry across the Trebia in order to attack Hannibal's forces, arrayed on the bluffs above the river. Exhausted by their river crossing, the Roman troops became entangled in a bloody melee with Hannibal's infantry, fighting each other to a standstill until Hannibal unveiled his master stroke. Concealed from the Roman infantry by the terrain until the last moment, his light infantry and cavalry stormed into the Roman flanks, enveloped the entire force and, trapping the legions with their backs to the river, annihilated them. It was a crushing victory for Hannibal, and a disaster for Rome. It would be the first of many.

THE BATTLE OF TREBIA
218 B.C.

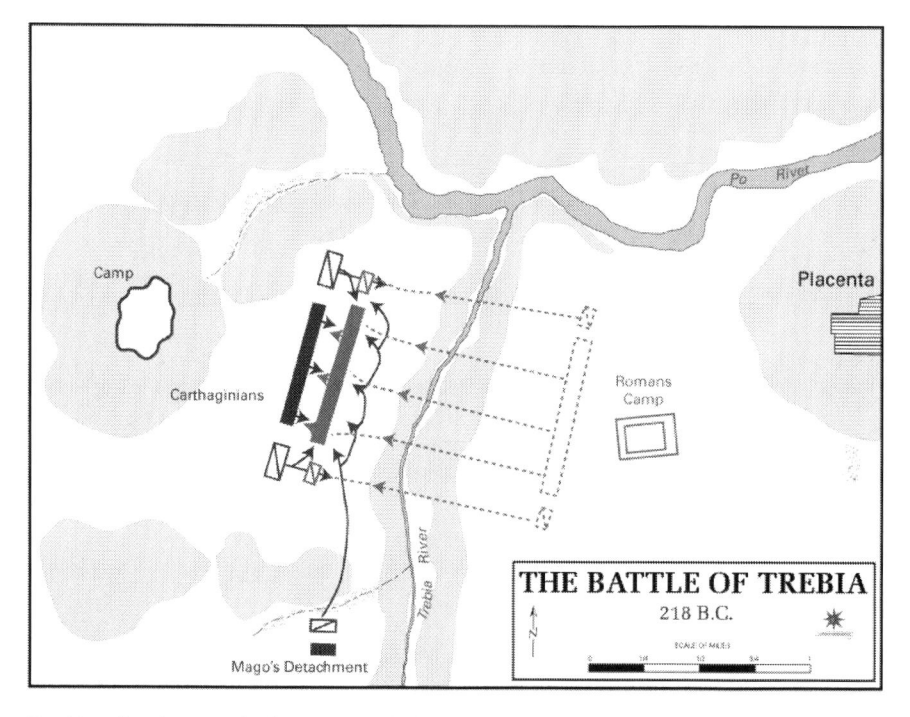

By this point, the campaigning season, which traditionally stopped during the winter months, was virtually over. Hannibal decided to winter his troops in Cisalpine Gaul, but he quickly wore out his welcome there. Possibly because the Gauls were displeased at how Hannibal had used their levies to grind down the Roman forces, the supplies they provided were stilted and ungenerous. In early spring, Hannibal decided to find himself a more secure base and made ready to carry the war into Italy proper. However, despite the winter lull, the Romans had not been idle. Two consular armies, under consuls Servilius and Flaminius, had marched at the beginning of the new year to block Hannibal's routes to the south and east, fortifying their positions there and effectively immuring him within northern Italy. A normal general would have thought himself trapped. Hannibal, however, had a plan. To the south lay the Apennines Mountains and the huge swampy delta of the Arno river, in modern Tuscany, an area reckoned impassable by any army.

Hannibal must have reckoned that after what he had faced in the Alps, he and his men were ready for any challenge. After a brief pause for consideration, he ordered his army to march for the Arno. The Apennines were less of a challenge than the Alps had been, and Hannibal's forces made decent enough time as they crossed through them, but Hannibal himself suffered a debilitating injury, losing an eye to a virulent infection (believed to be conjunctivitis) that kept him bedridden for a spell. His army then descended into the basin of the Arno, but the going was far harder than even Hannibal could have anticipated. The entire region was a festering swamp, with not a single scrap of dry, solid land for his men and horses to sleep on. Hannibal quickly realized he had marched his men into a death-trap. With no choice but to push on, he and his men marched uninterruptedly for four days and three nights, in water and mud that often came up to their waists, with no rest except what they could snatch on their feet. Hundreds, perhaps thousands of Hannibal's men perished on the march. Some were drowned, others were swallowed by quicksand, others contracted malaria or dysentery from drinking the swampy water, and still more simply died of exhaustion. By the end of the march, Hannibal had lost the last of his war elephants, as well as virtually all of his supplies and wheeled transport, but he was now in Etruria, Roman heartland, with both Flaminius and Servilius to the north of him.

As Polybius noted in his account, Hannibal had reached an important crossroad in his campaign. As Polybius wrote, "[Hannibal] calculated that, if he passed the camp and made a descent into the district beyond, Flaminius (partly for fear of popular reproach and partly of personal irritation) would be unable to endure watching passively the devastation of the country but would spontaneously follow him…and give him opportunities for attack." Hannibal needed to bring Flaminius to battle, to avoid the danger of having a large enemy force to his rear, but he found Flaminius too passive to give him the battle he sought.

In order to persuade the Consul – who had a healthy fear of his abilities – to take to the field against him, Hannibal set about ravaging the surrounding Etrurian countryside, sacking towns, burning markets and generally wreaking havoc in the hope that Flaminius would become so incensed that he would be forced to defend the Italian heartland, or that a direct order should arrive from Rome ordering him to do so. Hannibal, though his military strategy was sound, was not as strong in his political choices as he was in battle: by devastating Etruria, he lost support among the local people, whom he might otherwise have been able to lure away from their alliance to Rome. Moreover, despite Hannibal's best efforts, Flaminius stubbornly stayed put in his defensive position. Frustrated by the Roman general's supineness, Hannibal marched around Flaminius's flank and cut him off from Rome, the kind of turning movement in warfare that was rarely used in the ancient world but became standard fare (and often the ultimate strategic goal) over the next 2,000 years. Even with such a massive threat to his lines of supply and communication, Flaminius still refused to march, so Hannibal turned and marched southwards. This time, with the Senate demanding what exactly he was playing at, Flaminius had no choice but to chase him.

Flaminius marched his 30,000 men after Hannibal, but the Carthaginian forces outstripped him. Desperate to bring the enemy to battle, Flaminius pushed recklessly onwards without scouting his line of advance, a mistake which was to cost him dear. On the northern edge of Lake Trasimene, Flaminius marched his army through a narrow defile and onto a small plain that was ringed by wooded mountains, through which his trackers reported Hannibal had marched some time previously. It was only when the last of the Roman forces had marched through the defile that Hannibal swung the jaws of his trap shut: his cavalry rushed forward from concealed positions to close the only gap through which Flaminius's force could retreat, and then his entire army poured howling out of the woods and fell onto the Romans before they had the chance to take up battle positions. In the ensuing desperate melee, virtually the entire Roman army was wiped out: 15,000 or more, including Flaminius himself, were killed, cut down in the melee or drowned in the lake trying to swim to safety. Around 5,000 more Roman soldiers were captured, and the remainder scattered into the hills. In one masterful stroke, Hannibal had disposed of the last field army in Northern Italy, successfully executing antiquity's greatest ambush. Rome herself was now at his mercy.

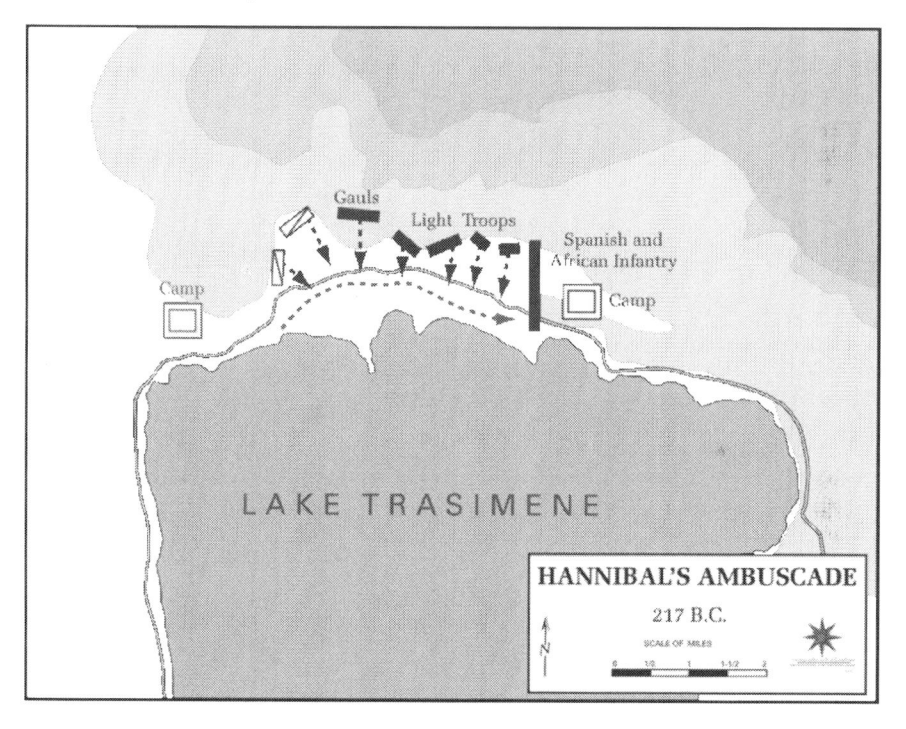

![Map of Hannibal's Ambuscade at Lake Trasimene, 217 B.C., showing positions of Gauls, Light Troops, Spanish and African Infantry, and two Camps around the northern shore of Lake Trasimene.]

HANNIBAL'S AMBUSCADE
217 B.C.

Hannibal was now in an ideal position to strike at Rome, but he chose not to do so. If he ever had any siege artillery in his baggage train (no mention is made of it in the original sources) then he lost it in the Alps or in the swamps of the Arno, because he had none available to invest Rome, nor, apparently, the engineering expertise either among his Carthaginian troops or his Gaulish levies to manufacture any. Without siege engines, he could still have chosen to ring the city with earthworks and lay siege to it, but instead he decided to march into Southern Italy, where he hoped to incite revolt among Rome's subject states.

Statue of Fabius Maximus

The Romans, desperate for something, anything, to rid themselves of this Carthaginian nemesis, appointed General Fabius Maximus as Dictator, an extraordinary measure which was only undertaken in times of the greatest crisis. Maximus, who had a healthy respect for Hannibal's generalship and was painfully aware of what had befallen Roman armies in pitched battles against him, now developed the "Fabian Strategy", which focused on indirect, attritional warfare. This strategy called for relying on skirmishes, ambushes, and dilatory tactics to harass, undermine and frighten Hannibal's forces, avoiding pitched battle which would almost certainly have proven ruinous. Though Maximus' tactics were effective, this indirect mode of warfare was considered dishonorable, even cowardly, by many Romans, who derisively nicknamed him "Cunctator" ("The Delayer").

Frustrated by Maximus' tactics, Hannibal took out his spite by ravaging the country estates and cities of the Apulian region before making his way into Campania, one of the most important agrarian regions in Italy because of its vast fertile plains that produced harvests crucial to feeding the great masses of Rome. Even the threat to the Campanian exports failed to draw Maximus into open battle, but Hannibal was so overzealous in his harrowing of Campania that, he soon realized, come the winter his army would have nothing to live off. Accordingly, he decided to march back to Apulia, but found his path blocked by a number of different Roman contingents that Maximus had placed at crucial passes to bar his way back. Hannibal responded with customary brilliance, by feinting his entire army at a thickly wooded hill, suggesting he was going to march through the forest and ignore the pass, and when the Roman army repositioned to attempt to bar his way, promptly marched his men about and through the pass they had so obligingly left unguarded, a tactical master-stroke which so damaged Maximus' already tarnished reputation as a commander that he was forced to step down as Dictator. As British historian Adrian Goldsworthy noted, the maneuver was "a classic of ancient generalship, finding its way into nearly every historical narrative of the war and being used by later military manuals".

Opposing Forces

Fabius Maximus was quite content with striking at Hannibal's army and its few lines of logistical support with small raiding forces. In this way, he could keep Hannibal's thinly stretched out support lines under constant tension and nervous. Maximus' countrymen, however, disagreed with his careful and length approach to the Carthaginian problem. The Roman Republic wanted a Roman army to meet Hannibal's army on the field of battle, the people of Rome wanted that Roman army to drive Hannibal from the Italian Peninsula. The Roman people were still angry over the defeats that their armies had suffered at the battle of Trebia and the battle of Lake Trasimene. The Roman Republic wanted to avenge those dead legions and the only way in which that could be done, they believed, was through strength of arms and not through cunning or being skilled in the art of deception.

In addition to the sting of not one but two severe losses, the Roman people were also upset about the fact that Hannibal and his troops were marching at will through the peninsula. Fabius Maximus, it seemed to the people, was allowing Hannibal time to gather his far-flung troops. This gathering of soldiers would create an even larger Carthaginian army, which in turn would require an even greater number of Roman and allied troops to beat him. And finally, like so many other people throughout history, the Roman people wanted a quick victory. They had no desire to witness – or to be held hostage by – a long and protracted campaign which would give them nothing but small victories.

The people of Rome didn't want to see a hungry Hannibal Barca slipping away from the grip of Roman justice; they wanted to see the bulk of Hannibal's army dead upon the field of battle, with the others running for their lives or prisoners in the hands of the Roman legions. They wanted the backbone of the Carthaginian army broken, and they wanted Hannibal himself to be marched through the streets of Rome in chains, part of a Roman general's triumphant return to the city.

Having fallen out of favor with both the Roman people and the Roman government, Fabius Maximus found that his services as dictator were no longer needed. Instead, the Roman government set up the tried and true process of electing officials who would, in their capacities as Roman generals, bring the war to Hannibal Barca and attempt to remove him from the Italian Peninsula. The Roman Republic had certain unique cultural and societal requirements placed upon any male citizen who sought to move upwards in society or have a successful career in politics. The most important of these requirements, and the one which could not be avoided, was for that individual to have served for at least some period of time in the military. Thus, no Roman citizen who had any sort of political aspirations could honestly expect to be able to achieve his goals if he did not spend a minimum of at least two years in the service of a legion. That way, when it came time for the elected officials of Rome to take the command of a legion, the politicians in question had at least a rudimentary understanding of military matters, engineering, logistics, and tactics.

Following the destruction of the Roman legions at the Battle of Trebia and the Battle of Lake Trasimene, Rome spent significant time and resources raising new legions to replace those that were lost. The Roman government was confident that the Republic could levy new legions from within the borders of the Italian Peninsula, and the creation of new legions, which was to be done solely from Romans and Rome's Italian allies, showed Hannibal exactly what the Roman government thought of him. The Romans knew Hannibal and his Carthaginians and his army could fight, but they had no intent of interrupting campaigns being carried out in other provinces or territories.

While various legion commanders out in the far-flung reaches of the growing Roman Republic offered to return to hunt down and drive out Hannibal and his army, the Roman government told these generals to focus solely upon the campaigns that their legions were actively engaged in. In other words, the citizens back in Rome would settle the problem of Hannibal Barca themselves.

Of course, since Rome was intent on having their existing legions continue to wage wars in other provinces and territories, new legions had to be formed, and this required several steps. Gathering new recruits wasn't difficult since service in the military was a requirement for social advancement, but the new soldiers had to be trained to fight as heavy infantry and work together. For these men to be trained properly, however, they needed to have equipment, including swords, shields, javelins, helmets and assorted armor. In addition to this, the new recruits had to be clothed, fed and paid. Finally, commanders for the newly established legions were going to have to be found.

The senators of Rome clamored to be given the right to command cohorts within the new legions, but the right to command the legions themselves would fall upon the shoulders of former consuls, and overall command of the massive army that was being created would be given to the two current consuls.

With the abandonment of Fabius Maximus' strategic plan to starve Hannibal and his force off of the Italian Peninsula by striking at the few supply lines that the Carthaginian general had, and also by denying him the ability to live off of the land, the Roman government devised a new battle plan. This plan was extremely simple and direct, and it spoke quite frankly to the Roman desire to resolve the current conflict with Carthage through strength of arms. The Roman Republic and her allies on the Italian Peninsula would gather an army together that would dwarf Hannibal's force.

The rationale behind this strategy was that if Hannibal could defeat Roman forces that were of an equal size, or one which was slightly larger, then surely if the Romans had numbers on their side they would be victorious. The Romans understandably believed that the tactical abilities of Hannibal and the skills of his veteran troops could be negated by an overwhelmingly superior force of trained legionaries; after all, it's not as though the Romans didn't know how to fight.

With that, the Roman Republic and her Italian allies – the Etruscans and the Samnites – set about the long process of building a grand army. By using those few veterans who had survived the battles of both Trebia and Lake Trasimene as core elements, and also by using a training program that had served the legions well for decades, the Romans and their allies were able to build entirely new legions in order to fight Hannibal and the Carthaginian army. The Etruscans and the Samnites, who modeled their own legions upon those of Rome's, set about the task of building and preparing their own new legions as well.

In a relatively short amount of time, the Roman Republic, with her allies beside her, had assembled the largest army that they had ever put into the field. While there are, of course, widely varying accounts and estimates as to the actual size of the Roman and allied combined force, most historians believe Polybius' account, which claimed the forces reached a combined total of an estimated 86,000 troops. Rome, of course, brought with her the lion's share of the men with a full 8 legions, each legion at full strength with 5,000 men per legion. In addition to this, the Roman legions were accompanied by an estimated 2,000 of their own Roman cavalry. The Etruscans and the Samnites combined to create a total of 8 legions as well, as well as an additional 4,000 cavalry.

Since this new Roman army was essentially the combination of two separate armies, both of the Roman consuls were in joint command of the new army. This was in stark contrast to the usual system, which dictated that only one consul retained control of the entire force. In this case, both consuls, being equals in the Roman government, would share the responsibilities of commanding such a tremendous force, and when the army was in the field, the two consuls would alternate days on which they commanded.

The two consuls who commanded this newly formed Roman army were Lucius Aemilius Paullus and Gaius Terentius Varro. Varro would be the scapegoat for the Roman massacre at Cannae for over two millennia, though this stigma is not due to anything he did or failed to do at the battle. Instead, the fact the blame was laid at the feet of Varro is a result of two specific factors. The first was that Varro had the "bad luck" of surviving the massacre at Cannae; in accordance with Roman expectations, Rome would have fully have supported any decision he made that resulted in suicide. The second significant factor was Varro's actual position in Roman society, notably the fact that his family was not well to do. While his family was of an aristocratic line, they lacked the financial ability to defend Varro's name and character following the battle.

This was not the case for Lucius Aemilius Paullus' family, and Paullus died while attempting to escape the massive trap devised by Hannibal at Cannae. Since Paullus' family was significantly wealthy, they were able to set the blame for the Roman defeat squarely upon the shoulders upon Varro, and his descendants were able to conduct a successful propaganda campaign over the centuries. The family consistently painted Varro as a rash coward and a fool, and they also called into question his military abilities. Implicit in the criticism was Varro's low place on the aristocratic social scale. Paullus, on the other hand, was portrayed as an ideal Roman citizen who did his duty and was betrayed by the ineptitude of a colleague. Furthermore, the Paullus family had great assistance in their efforts to demonize Varro because the ancient historian Polybius owed a great deal to his patron, Lucius Aemilius Paullus' grandfather.

Of course, all that was in the future. The Roman generals alternated the command of the combined force from day to day, and they had a vastly different tactical approach to the situations that they came upon. Paullus has been described as a man who was the most conservative of the two consuls, one who chose his actions carefully and thus planned accordingly for any engagement. Varro, however, has been described as a man who was both reckless and heedless of danger, and unheeding of advice offered to him. According to Polybius and other contemporaries, Varro ignored advice offered up by Paullus on the day of the battle, August 2, 216 BCE. They claimed Paullus cautioned Varro against marching the army out to meet Hannibal and the Carthaginian army at Cannae.

Unlike the massive army the Roman Republic and her allies had assembled and were marching through Italy looking for Hannibal, the Carthaginian army was not a homogeneous force. Carthage had relied upon naval power to make its fortune and spread its power and position throughout the Mediterranean, and in order for Carthage to continue to do these things, and in order for the merchants to continue turning a profit, the city elders had hired mercenaries when fighting on land was necessary. The hiring of mercenary forces for land battles also had a tremendous impact on the Carthaginian navy; while a small unit of Carthaginian men would also be part of the army, the ships of the Carthaginian navy were manned by Carthaginian sailors. These ships, in turn, would then be used to transport the mercenaries whom the city had hired to the necessary battlefields.

Throughout most of its history, the armies Carthage sent to the field were commanded by Carthaginians who had served in the infantry and cavalry. The one exception shortly before the Second Punic War had occurred during the First Punic War when Carthage had hired a Spartan general to drive the Romans away from Carthage.

While the army itself was commanded by a Carthaginian, the mercenary units making up the bulk of the army were commanded and officered by their own men. Thus, the Numidian cavalry would have a Numidian officer commanding them, and a Gallic infantry unit would have their own Gallic commander. It was the responsibility of the Carthaginian general to ensure that all of the various units of the army were able to function together as a single entity.

Some Carthaginian generals carried out this task better than others, of course, but none were as skilled or successful as Hannibal. One of the ways which Hannibal used his charisma was to combine it with other aspects of his personality, such as his personal bravery. Hannibal could often be found fighting beside his men in the thick of a battle, leading them from the front and by his own example. He harbored no fear of death and trusted in the strength and battle prowess of the men under his command. His willingness to place his own fate into their hands made them admire him, and in turn they were inspired by him.

At the same time, the mercenary army Hannibal had helped to create and which he commanded was possibly the finest army the city of Carthage had ever put into the field. Like all of the Carthaginian armies prior to the Second Punic War, Hannibal's force was an amalgamation of mercenary units, and these individual units operated as part of the whole. They had been chosen from countries that were either strictly mercenary in their dealing with the Roman Republic, or they consisted of people who had no love for the Romans. The various mercenary units which made up Hannibal's army had also been chosen for their specialties, such as cavalry, light infantry, heavy infantry, and spearmen. Some of the units, such as the Numidians, fought strictly for coin and out of no particular animosity towards the Roman Republic. The Gallic forces, however, had been fighting on and off with the Roman Republic for nearly two centuries prior to the battle of Cannae.

Thus it was that the force Hannibal Barca commanded at Cannae had a vast array of mercenaries, consisting of Spanish, Gallic, Libyans, Iberians, Numidians and small units of professional Carthaginian soldiers.

The Numidians excelled in the art of war from horseback and were frighteningly skillful cavalrymen. The ancient historians recorded that the Numidians rode from their earliest youth and that they had the disturbing ability to throw a spear effectively from the back of a galloping horse.

The Libyans that fought for Hannibal did so as heavy infantry at the battle, and these Libyans were equipped with the armor and weapons of Roman legionaries who had been killed in previous engagements with Hannibal's army. With this armor, as well as their own short spears and captured Roman short swords, the Libyans fought in a phalanx formation. This particular formation had served the Libyans well when battling Macedonian units, and it would serve them well again as they fought against the densely packed formation of the Roman legions.

The Spanish and Gallic forces Hannibal had hired and integrated into the Carthaginian army were not nearly as disciplined or organized. These two particular groups were wild and could not be counted upon in difficult situations, and their specific fighting style had them trained to withdraw when too much pressure was placed upon them. However, the fact they couldn't stand up against the Romans on open ground also meant Hannibal knew how to utilize them. Indeed, he made certain that he would remain with the Spanish and Gallic troops when his trap was sprung upon the Roman army marching towards him.

Preparing the Trap at Cannae

Hannibal understood the temperament of the Roman people and the Roman Republic itself, and he was also well aware that the tremendous size of the army the Romans and their allies had assembled meant that the Romans were anxious to finish the war. Thus, he could rightly assume the Roman commanders would be seeking a single decisive battle.

Armed with this knowledge, as well as with his intimate knowledge of the tactics of the Roman legions, Hannibal balanced the weight of his knowledge against what he knew of his own army. Most of the forces under his command were exceptionally skilled veterans, and they had survived the deadly march through the Pyrenees and over the Alps. In addition to their combat skills and their abilities as soldiers, the men of the Carthaginian army were fiercely loyal to Hannibal.

As such, Hannibal prepared a trap which he believed the Romans would march into. The maneuver would be simple, but it would also be done on a massive scale. He would use a double enveloping move with his forces, which would not require any sort of trickery or a grand ruse but tight coordination on both wings of the Carthaginian army. Hannibal's job would be made easier by the Romans' impatience and desire to win a decisive victory, which ensured they would push forward and put in all their men.

Planning for the battle to come, and with the Romans refusing to fight on the first day – as Hannibal had known they would since Lucius Aemilius Paullus had been in command on that day – Hannibal was able to select the field of battle at Cannae. The battlefield of Cannae is located in the southeastern portion of the Italian Peninsula, and the Aufidus River serves as both a barrier and the border of the battlefield. When Hannibal originally chose Cannae and marched his army into it, he did so for three specific reasons. The first reason was that Cannae was equipped with a large storehouse, which contained a vast amount of supplies that would serve his army. The constant lack of logistical support from Carthage and a continuous lack of necessary supplies made Cannae an excellent choice for resupply. The second reason was the land itself; by seizing Cannae, Hannibal gained not only the supplies but also a commanding position of a large area. This commanding position would enable him to strike out against a large array of

Roman and allied targets, and the Carthaginians would have exceptional mobility at Cannae, allowing Hannibal to use cavalry raids against Roman foragers and water gatherers. The third and final reason that Hannibal seized the area of Cannae was because he could count on a strong Roman response. Hannibal knew the Romans would react as quickly as possible because there was a large amount of supplies at Cannae and the position granted the Carthaginians access to large swaths of Roman territory. Hannibal rightly figured his position at Cannae would be far too much for Lucius Aemilius Paullus and Gaius Terentius Varro to ignore.

Sure enough, the two consuls rapidly marched the army to Cannae, and within two days' march, Varro and Paullus discovered Hannibal's army camped on the left side of the Aufidus River. With this discovery, the Roman generals made the decision to encamp as well.

Unlike Hannibal's camp, however, the Roman encampment consisted of two separate sites. The first and larger of the two camps was also pitched upon the left side of the Aufidus, just 6 miles away from the Carthaginian camp. Both Varro and Paullus were in the larger camp since the majority of the Roman and allied forces were established there, while the second and smaller of the two camps (which consisted of an estimated 10,000 troops) was established to ensure the protection of the foraging and water bearing parties sent forth from the main camp. These supply parties would need to provide sufficient water for nearly 80,000 men. In addition to protecting these important supply parties, the legionaries in the smaller camp were also supposed to harass any supply parties that might issue forth from the Carthaginian camp.

By this time, Hannibal had plenty of experience operating within the dangerous confines of an enemy country. Knowing full well that his own supply parties would need protection, and that the Roman supply parties would need the same, Hannibal took appropriate steps to protect his own while destroying the enemy's. Varro and Paullus dispatched small cavalry and infantry units to carry out the necessary tasks of protection and harassment, but Hannibal dispatched elements of his superior cavalry to disrupt the Romans. Thanks to these efforts, the Roman foragers and water bearers could not bring enough supplies and water into the rest of the Roman army. This lack of water would prove to be a factor in the massacre that followed.

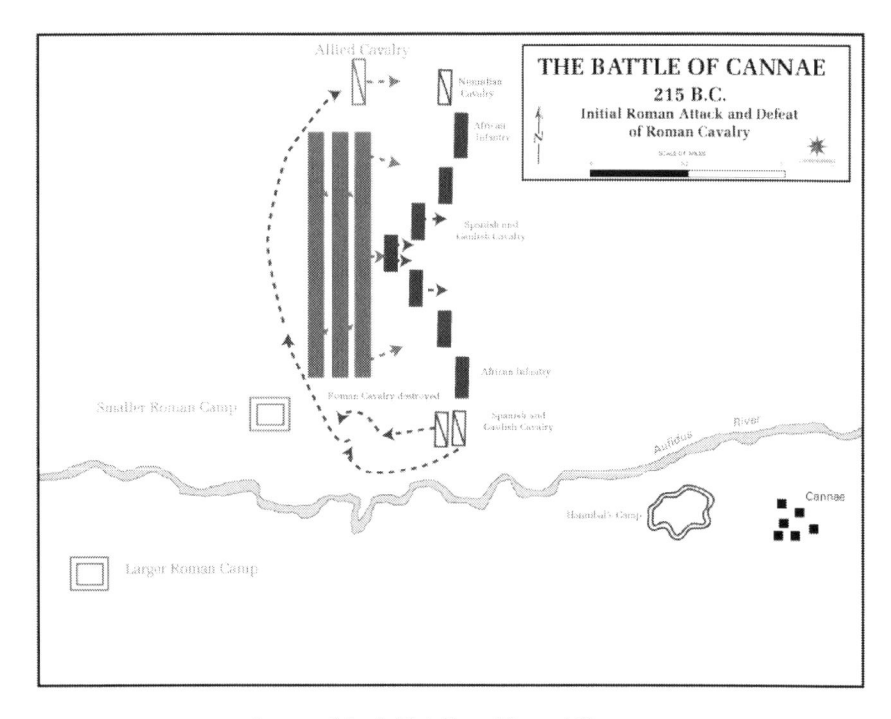

A map of the initial dispositions at Cannae

On August 1, 216 BCE, acting on information about the Roman army, Hannibal rode out and offered battle to the Romans. He did this because the information indicated Paullus was in command of the army that day. Hannibal judged that Paullus would not want to engage immediately in battle, and he was right, as Paullus refused to take the field. Paullus wanted to avoid fighting Hannibal in open ground, despite the significant advantage in manpower.

While that may have been wise, Hannibal knew that the consuls were alternating command of the Roman army and that he would be facing Varro on the following day. He also knew that Varro, unlike Paullus, tended to be both rash and impulsive, and he counted upon the Roman commander's infamous impatience. Hannibal also assumed Paullus' refusal to fight would make Varro even more impatient to fight on August 2.

The Battle Plans

On the morning of the battle, Varro believed he had managed to pin down Hannibal and the Carthaginian army in one place, and with the Carthaginians at Cannae, the Roman army would finally be able to bring Hannibal and his army to the decisive battle that all of Rome was seeking. Indeed, it appeared to the Romans that the Carthaginian general had finally trapped himself. The Roman force was nearly twice the size of the Carthaginians, and the battlefield had a wide plain which could ensure not only that the Romans could put their entire force in the field but that Hannibal couldn't hide any reserves. The Romans were painfully aware that Hannibal had used subterfuge to bring about reserves at critical junctures and surprise his opponents.

Perhaps most crucially, Varro thought Hannibal made a critical error by positioning his army with its back to the Aufidus River. The Aufidus River ran along the rear of the Carthaginian army and along its left flank as well, so Varro believed that it would prevent the Carthaginians from running when pressed. Combined with his numerical advantage, the Carthaginians would be unable to cut their way out to escape as well, and the right flank itself would be closed off as a route of escape for the Carthaginians by the presence of Roman cavalry.

At the Battle of Trebia, the Roman infantry had succeeded in breaking through the center of the Carthaginian infantry, but Hannibal had hidden Carthaginian troops as reinforcements. The Roman general hoped, then, to recreate this breaking of the Carthaginian infantry at the battle of Cannae. Varro sought, however, to do it on a much larger scale than had been done at Trebia by increasing the depth of his infantry and stacking it. This meant that rather than spreading his tens of thousands of infantry out on a wide front that might push the Carthaginian army back into the Aufidus River, Varro wished solely to break the Carthaginian line. He would do this to show the strength of Rome's legions and for the psychological effect it would have upon the Carthaginian army forced to watch as Varro split the line in two. With the army thus separated, the Roman and allied infantry would crush the Carthaginians, destroying the various mercenary units piecemeal.

The Roman cavalry, which Varro would deploy on his own flanks, were to destroy the Carthaginian cavalry. Through the destruction of the Carthaginian cavalry, and by driving those that survived back into the flanks of the Carthaginian infantry, Varro would have the remnants of the Carthaginian cavalry and infantry trapped.

Once the Carthaginian army was separated, Varro would have the Roman infantry attack the right flank and center of the Carthaginians on the left (in an attempt to outflank them). The Roman cavalry, in turn, would then be used to attack that section's left flank. For the right section of the divided Carthaginian army, the opposite would be true; the Roman infantry would thus be on the Carthaginians' left and center, with the right flank of that section being hemmed in by the Roman cavalry. The Aufidus River would run behind both segments of the Carthaginian army, forming a final wall which the Carthaginians would not be able to breach without a great loss of life.

To Varro, the fears of his co-commander were unfounded. By the end of the day, Varro was certain that the Carthaginian army would cease to exist as a functional military unit, and with any luck, Hannibal Barca would either be dead upon the battlefield or a prisoner whom Varro could proudly march through the streets of Rome.

Of course, Hannibal had far different ideas. He knew Varro would deploy his army in a formation with the infantry in the center of the line and cavalry on either flank. This formation was the traditional deployment of nearly all of the armies of that time period, and Hannibal would be deploying his own Carthaginian troops in the same fashion, but Hannibal deployed his troops according to the strengths and weaknesses of the various units.

Hannibal would create his line by starting on either flank and positioning his cavalry. While his army overall was significantly smaller than the Roman army (perhaps around 50,000 men compared to Varro's nearly 85,000), the Carthaginian cavalry numbered nearly 10,000, which was 4,000 more than the Roman cavalry. Moreover, these cavalry were more skilled than those that made up Varro's cavalry. The Roman legions relied primarily upon the strength of the heavily armed infantry working in conjunction to win their battles, while the Roman cavalry would be used to turn an enemy's flank by slashing into their unprotected sides and help chase and hunt down fleeing enemy troops. This, however, was not the case with the Carthaginian cavalry, which Hannibal divided into three separate groups. The first two groups were from Hispanic and Celtic tribes respectively. They fought in a brutal and vicious fashion, making up in ferocity what they lacked in grace. The third group consisted of the Numidians.

Hannibal was also fully aware of each infantry unit's individual strengths and weaknesses. With these aspects of his infantry clearly in mind, Hannibal prepared an infantry line that would support his plan and give it the best possible chance of success against the overwhelmingly large force which the Romans, Etruscans, and Samnites had assembled. On the left and right flanks of his infantry line, Hannibal positioned his cavalry to counteract and defeat the Roman cavalry. Then, working in from both the left and the right sides, Hannibal stationed his Iberian heavy infantry units. These were men who were armed and equipped with the gear and weapons of the Roman legionaries whom Hannibal's Carthaginians had already defeated. The Iberians were skilled soldiers and battle-hardened veterans, which meant they were also disciplined. These men would stand, and they would fight.

Meanwhile, the center of the Carthaginian line of battle was made up of men from both Spain and Gaul. While these men were fierce warriors, they were not heavy infantry and were uncomfortable with large set battles. The style of combat with which these men were most familiar was one where they could rapidly strike and then break away. Hannibal had no doubts concerning the courage of these men, but he needed them to be a cohesive force for his plan of double envelopment to work against the Roman army, and with the desire and habit of the Spanish and Gallic warriors to slip away fully in mind, Hannibal set up the Spanish and Gallic units in an alternating fashion. Thus, there would be a Spanish or Gallic unit alongside an Iberian unit, but the Spaniards and Gauls would never be stationed alongside their own compatriots, which Hannibal hoped would ensure no unit could compel nearby countrymen to panic and run. Moreover, the Spanish troops and Gallic troops would feel compelled to outperform one another in order to show that they were the better fighters.

Just as importantly, Hannibal knew that his own presence in the midst of his skittish Spanish and Gallic infantry would serve as a catalyst. Not only would the men seek to outperform one another for the sake of their own honor, they would want to impress their general with their personal bravery and prowess. Hannibal knew this about the men, and thus he sought to act upon it. In addition to his own presence, Hannibal also helped to keep his infantry firm by making sure that he would be able to position his army first upon the field at Cannae. This simple act of arriving first at the scene of the fight to come enabled him to utilize the pros and cons of the ground at Cannae so that they would be beneficial to his tactical goals.

While Varro believed that the position of Hannibal's infantry with the Aufidus River at the rear of the Carthaginian army was a catastrophic mistake, Hannibal obviously did not. Instead, Hannibal knew that his position in front of the river would serve two important purposes that could well give him victory in the battle to come. The first of these purposes was that the Aufidus River's mere presence would serve as a further bulwark to the courage of his Spanish and Gallic infantry. After all, these men knew that if they did break and run, they would eventually be forced to attempt to cross the river, which would put them in extremely vulnerable positions. The Roman legionaries, armed with the pilum (a short javelin), would be able to cut down the fleeing Spanish and Gallic troops at their leisure. Moreover, in addition to strengthening the resolve of the men in the center of his infantry line, Hannibal believed that the position of the Aufidus River at his rear protected him. The Roman troops and cavalry would be unable to attack the rear of his infantry from that position since there were no bridges or easy fords for the Romans to utilize.

What Varro also failed to realize was that the Carthaginian army, by arriving first upon Cannae and being able to choose its position, had tremendous benefits with its back to the Aufidus River. By establishing his force in front of the river, Hannibal ensured the Roman army had a hill at its back. This, in turn, would make any sort of orderly withdrawal from the battlefield difficult should they attempt to do so up the hill. A legionary climbing the hill in full armor and unable to maintain discipline or unit cohesion could be easily killed by Carthaginian cavalry and light infantry. In addition to having the hill behind them, the Romans also had the Aufidus River on their right flank. This hemmed the Roman legions in just as much as Varro believed that the river was trapping the Carthaginians.

Furthermore, Hannibal had stationed his troops in such a way that they stood with the sun behind their backs. With the sun rising behind the Carthaginians, the Roman legions would find that they had to march into the sun's glare, shining not only from the sky but being reflected and magnified by the armor and the weapons of the Carthaginians. The position of the sun, then, partially blinded the approaching Roman infantry and cavalry.

Lastly, Hannibal had noticed that the winds on the day of the battle were blowing in a southeasterly direction. While this fact would potentially mean little to the first few ranks of

Varro's compressed and stacked up legions advancing upon the Carthaginians, it would be misery to others. The following 30-50 rows of Roman legionaries would be forced to deal with the dust and the sand that was stirred up by tens of thousands of marching feet.

Thus, the river, the sun, and the wind all seemed to favor Hannibal and the Carthaginian army at the beginning of that fateful August day.

The Battle of Cannae

According to the ancient historian Polybius, both sides were forced to begin the battle on a minimum of sleep. This fatigue was a direct result of both the Romans and the Carthaginians having traveled a good distance from their camps to the site of the battle. The Carthaginian army had left their camp earlier than the Romans had so Hannibal could be certain that he and his men would be able to seize the ground that he both wanted and needed, while the Roman legions and their allies had to deal with thirst. The raids by the Carthaginian cavalry on the Roman foragers and water bearers had effectively limited the amount of water available, and this thirst was exacerbated by the dust and sand kicked up by the combatants and subsequently driven steadily into the Roman ranks by the southeasterly wind.

The opening movements of the Battle of Cannae gave no suggestion that it would be one of the most decisive battles in history, but unbeknownst to the Romans, it fit the pattern that Hannibal needed in order to pull off a double envelopment that would crash down upon the Roman line from both flanks and make escape all but impossible. Polybius described the beginning of the fighting: "The battle was begun by an engagement between the advanced guard of the two armies; and at first the affair between these light-armed troops was indecisive. But as soon as the Iberian and Celtic cavalry got at the Romans, the battle began in earnest, and in the true barbaric fashion: for there was none of the usual formal advance and retreat; but when they once got to close quarters, they grappled man to man, and, dismounting from their horses, fought on foot. But when the Carthaginians had got the upper hand in this encounter and killed most of their opponents on the ground,— because the Romans all maintained the fight with spirit and determination,—and began chasing the remainder along the river, slaying as they went and giving no quarter; then the legionaries took the place of the light-armed and closed with the enemy."

With the Roman and allied legions advancing steadily towards the Carthaginian lines, Hannibal placed himself directly in the front and center of his Spanish and Gallic troops. He made sure that all of the men could see him, and from that exposed position he led his Spanish and Gallic units forward while the Iberian heavy infantry – which stood on either flank of the advancing light infantry – remained rooted in place. The Iberians were to serve as walls on either side of the double envelopment that Hannibal was seeking to use, and the steadfast position of these heavy infantrymen would ensure that the Roman legions remained focused upon the center of the Carthaginian line.

As Hannibal and the Spanish and Gallic troops advanced, the far edges of the center remained connected at their junctions with the Iberians. These Spanish and Gallic units remained in place so that as Hannibal and the other units advanced the Carthaginian line started to create a crescent formation. This crescent curved out towards the advancing Roman legionaries so that within a short time only Hannibal and a small portion of the Carthaginian troops with him met the brunt of the initial attack by Varro's legions.

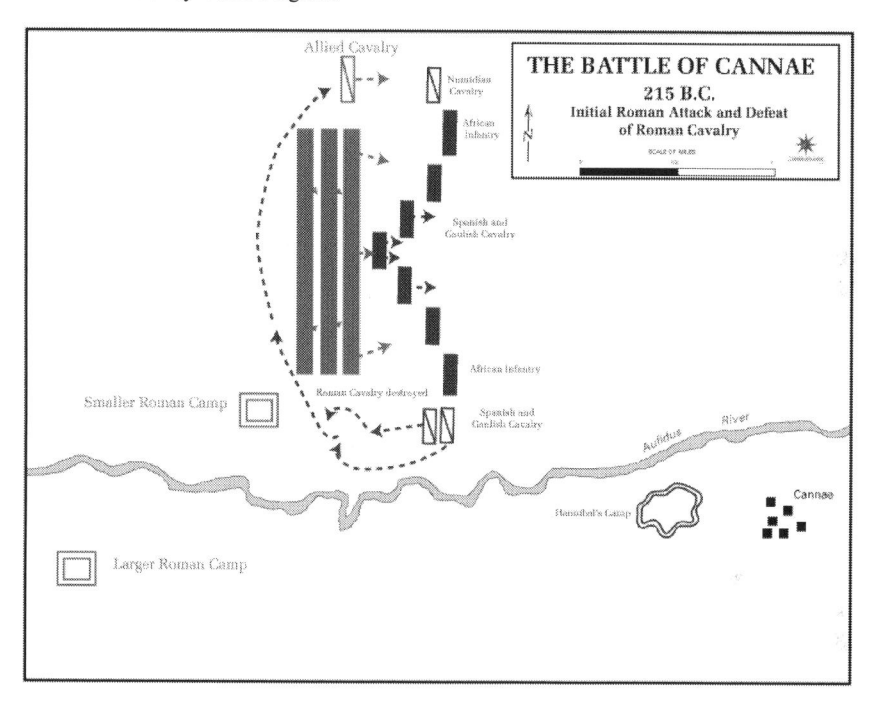

The opening movements at Cannae

Hannibal stayed with his men as the battle ensued, keeping them in a tight formation and encouraging them as they all fell slowly back. None of his Spanish or Gallic troops broke or ran; as Hannibal hoped, they stood beside him and fought even as the Roman legions pushed them backward.

While Hannibal and the Spanish and the Gallic troops steadily fell back, the cavalry of both sides continued to engage one another in combat. On the left flank, nearly 6,500 Hispanic and Celtic cavalry slammed into the Roman and allied cavalry on that flank. Both the Hispanic and the Celtic horsemen dismounted and went about the business of cutting down the legion's cavalry on the left flank. The Carthaginians were ruthless and gave no quarter to the legionaries.

The Numidian cavalry had been positioned on the right flank of the line by Hannibal, and the task of these feared cavalrymen was to keep the Roman cavalry occupied and thus pinned in one place. The Numidians did this by slipping in and out of the Roman cavalry formations, keeping the Romans turned around so that they weren't quite aware of what was going on across the rest of the field.

Shortly after the Hispanic and Celtic cavalry had dispatched the first set, they rode up to the rear of the Roman cavalry, and within a matter of minutes, the Roman cavalry found themselves fighting for their lives on two fronts. The Carthaginian cavalry was attempting to squeeze the Roman cavalry out of existence, and the Roman cavalry quickly fled from the field of Cannae. Polybius described the clash between the cavalry: "Though he had been from the first on the right wing, and had taken part in the cavalry engagement, Lucius Aemilius [Paullus] still survived. Determined to act up to his own exhortatory speech, and seeing that the decision of the battle rested mainly on the legionaries, riding up to the centre of the line he led the charge himself, and personally grappled with the enemy, at the same time cheering on and exhorting his soldiers to the charge. Hannibal, on the other side, did the same, for he too had taken his place on the centre from the commencement. The Numidian horse on the Carthaginian right were meanwhile charging the cavalry on the Roman left; and though, from the peculiar nature of their mode of fighting, they neither inflicted nor received much harm, they yet rendered the enemy's horse useless by keeping them occupied, and charging them first on one side and then on another. But when Hasdrubal, after all but annihilating the cavalry by the river, came from the left to the support of the Numidians, the Roman allied cavalry, seeing his charge approaching, broke and fled."

By the time the Roman cavalry decided that discretion was the better part of valor, Hannibal and his Spanish and the Gallic troops had reversed the crescent. The shape of the center of the Carthaginian line now bowed in, arcing towards the Aufidus River, while the Iberian heavy infantry on either wing still remained steadfast and unengaged. Naturally, the Roman legions, who were stacked up as deeply as 50 men in some places, continued to push and fight forward. Their momentum was impressive, with the men kept in motion by the thousands of men pushing forward from the rear, but as Polybius explained, they were marching right into Hannibal's trap, and when the last ranks of the Roman legions were finally abreast of the Iberians, Hannibal's heavy infantry were in position to execute the pincer on both flanks of the Roman line. "For a short time the Iberian and Celtic lines stood their ground and fought gallantly; but; presently overpowered by the weight of the heavy-armed lines, they gave way and retired to the rear, thus breaking up the crescent. The Roman maniples followed with spirit, and easily cut their way through the enemy's line; since the Celts had been drawn up in a thin line, while the Romans had closed up from the wings towards the centre and the point of danger. For the two wings did not come into action at the same time as the centre: but the centre was first engaged, because the

Gauls, having been stationed on the arc of the crescent, had come into contact with the enemy long before the wings, the convex of the crescent being towards the enemy. The Romans, however, going in pursuit of these troops, and hastily closing in towards the centre and the part of the enemy which was giving ground, advanced so far, that the Libyan heavy-armed troops on either wing got on their flanks. Those on the right, facing to the left, charged from the right upon the Roman flank; while those who were on the left wing faced to the right, and, dressing by the left, charged their right flank,1 the exigency of the moment suggesting to them what they ought to do. Thus it came about, as Hannibal had planned, that the Romans were caught between two hostile lines of Libyans—thanks to their impetuous pursuit of the Celts."

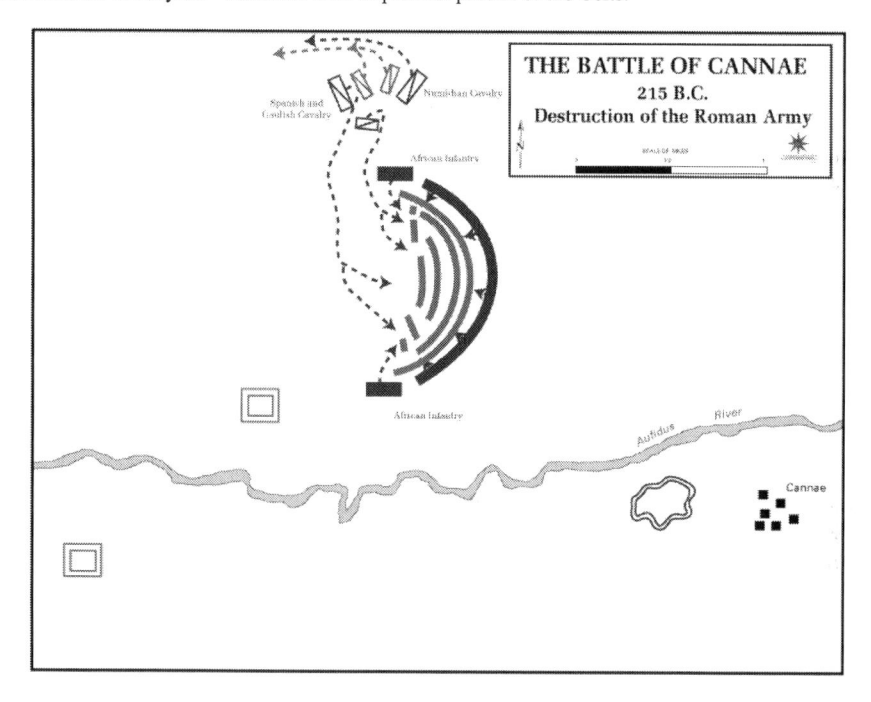

A map depicting the flight of the Roman cavalry and the successful pincer

The Iberian units smashed into each of the unprotected flanks of the massive Roman army, and the tightly packed Roman legionaries could not quickly turn their large, heavy shields in time to protect their lightly armored and nearly unprotected sides. In addition to this sudden attack by the Iberians, the fog of war had already settled upon Cannae, in some cases literally. In addition to the heat of the day and the growing dehydration of the Roman legionaries, the din of battle ensured that the Romans couldn't see what was going on ahead of them thanks to the sand and dust.

Due to these factors, the Roman legionaries would have been completely confused by the sudden presence and sight of the Iberians. As Hannibal's heavy infantry, the Iberians wore the armor and the accouterments of the legionaries themselves, so it would have seemed for at least a moment to the Roman legionaries that they were being attacked by other Romans. Fear would also have been rampant because Varro had arrayed his forces so that the veterans of previous battles and campaigns spearheaded the attack, which left the rear ranks populated with a large number of raw recruits. These men would have been easy for the Iberians to break, especially when the Carthaginian cavalry arrived and effectively sealed off any escape from the rear.

Hannibal and the Spanish and Gallic troops were able to hold the center, and when the Iberians attacked, the forward momentum of Varro's legions was stopped. At this point, the legionaries were still being pressed and pushed forward by the men moving up from their rear, while Hannibal and his men started to push back from the center, the Iberians crashed down on the flanks, and the Carthaginian cavalry swooped in from behind.

The Romans were trapped, their much larger force completely surrounded by a significantly smaller one, and what followed was a complete massacre. Livy captured the desperate straits the Romans had unwittingly put themselves in: "The Carthaginians were driven back and began to withdraw nervously, while the Romans pressed on forward, maintaining the impetus of their attack and driving through the enemy line, which was now in headlong and panic stricken flight. This brought the Romans up against the centre of the Carthaginian position, and then, finding little resistance, against the African reserves. These troops were positioned on both wings, which were drawn back somewhat from the projecting central wedge held by the Gauls and Spanish soldiers. As the wedge was driven back it came level with the main lines of the Carthaginians central position. As they continued to withdraw, the centre of their line became concave, while the African troops on the two wings formed a pair of projecting horns, as it were, gradually enclosing the Roman troops as they charged unthinkingly on against the centre. The Carthaginians rapidly extended their wings and closed in on their opponents from behind. The Romans were now in trouble: their initially successful first assault on the fleeing Gauls and Spaniards had to be abandoned, as they turned to face a new wave of attacks from the Africans behind them. The battle became an unequal struggle for them; they were totally surrounded, and though exhausted, were now compelled to face fresh and vigorous opponents."

According to Polybius, Paullus fell as the Carthaginian cavalry closed in from behind: "At that point Hasdrubal appears to have acted with great skill and discretion. Seeing the Numidians to be strong in numbers, and more effective and formidable to troops that had once been forced from their ground, he left the pursuit [of the Roman cavalry] to them; while he himself hastened to the part of the field where the infantry were engaged, and brought his men up to support the Libyans. Then, by charging the Roman legions on the rear, and harassing them by hurling squadron after squadron upon them at many points at once, he raised the spirits of the Libyans, and dismayed and depressed those of the Romans. It was at this point that Lucius Aemilius fell, in the thick of the fight, covered with wounds: a man who did his duty to his country at that last hour of his life, as he had throughout its previous years, if any man ever did."

Livy gave an even more heroic account of Paullus' death, a clear attempt to create a martyr out of the disaster: "A military tribune called Gnaeus Lentulus was riding past, when he saw the bloodstained consul sitting on a rock. 'Lucius Aemilius Paullus,' he cried, 'you are the only one whom the gods in heaven will hold blameless for today's disaster. Come, take my horse, while there is strength left in your body and I am here to act as your companion, supporter, and defender. Do not desecrate this dreadful battle further with a consul's death. We have cause enough for tears of grief without that.' The consul replied, 'You are a brave man, Gnaeus Cornelius, and a good one. Bless you for it. But you have very little time to escape the enemy's clutches; don't waste it in futile acts of pity. Hurry! Tell the Senate to see to Rome's defences and strengthen them before the victorious enemy arrives. And have a quiet word for me in private with Quintus Fabius. Tell him that as long as I lived and even as I died, I never forgot his words of wisdom. Now leave me here to breathe my last among my slaughtered soldiers. I have no desire to stand trial once again for my consulship, still less to denounce a colleague in the hope that I might protect my own good name by accusing someone else of failure.' As they spoke, a crowd of fugitives raced by, with the enemy in hot pursuit. Without even knowing who he was, they hacked the consul to death, while Lentulus' horse carried him off in the general confusion."

John Trumbull's painting depicting the death of Paullus

Polybius described the end of the battle and the resulting rout:

> "As long as the Romans could keep an unbroken front, to turn first in one direction and then in another to meet the assaults of the enemy, they held out; but the outer files of the circle continually falling, and the circle becoming more and more contracted, they at last were all killed on the field; and among them Marcus Atilius and Gnaeus Servilius, the Consuls of the previous year, who had shown themselves brave men and worthy of Rome in the battle. While this struggle and carnage were going on, the Numidian horse were pursuing the fugitives, most of whom they cut down or hurled from their horses; but some few escaped into Venusia, among whom was Gaius Terentius, the Consul, who thus sought a flight, as disgraceful to himself, as his conduct in office had been disastrous to his country.

> "Such was the end of the battle of Cannae, in which both sides fought with the most conspicuous gallantry, the conquered no less than the conquerors. This is proved by the fact that, out of six thousand horse, only seventy escaped with Gaius Terentius to Venusia, and about three hundred of the allied cavalry to various towns in the neighbourhood. Of the infantry ten thousand were taken prisoners in fair

fight, but were not actually engaged in the battle: of those who were actually engaged only about three thousand perhaps escaped to the towns of the surrounding district; all the rest died nobly, to the number of seventy thousand, the Carthaginians being on this occasion, as on previous ones, mainly indebted for their victory to their superiority in cavalry: a lesson to posterity that in actual war it is better to have half the number of infantry, and the superiority in cavalry, than to engage your enemy with an equality in both. On the side of Hannibal there fell four thousand Celts, fifteen hundred Iberians and Libyans, and about two hundred horse.

"The ten thousand Romans who were captured had not, as I said, been engaged in the actual battle; and the reason was this. Lucius Aemilius left ten thousand infantry in his camp that, in case Hannibal should disregard the safety of his own camp, and take his whole army on to the field, they might seize the opportunity, while the battle was going on, of forcing their way in and capturing the enemy's baggage; or if, on the other hand, Hannibal should, in view of this contingency, leave a guard in his camp, the number of the enemy in the field might thereby be diminished. These men were captured in the following circumstances. Hannibal, as a matter of fact, did leave a sufficient guard in his camp; and as soon as the battle began, the Romans, according to their instructions, assaulted and tried to take those thus left by Hannibal. At first they held their own: but just as they were beginning to waver, Hannibal, who was by this time gaining a victory all along the line, came to their relief, and routing the Romans, shut them up in their own camp; killed two thousand of them; and took all the rest prisoners. In like manner the Numidian horse brought in all those who had taken refuge in the various strongholds about the district, amounting to two thousand of the routed cavalry."

Some historians have estimated that nearly 600 Romans were killed each minute from the beginning of the battle until its end at nightfall. Of the nearly 85,000 Roman and allied troops that fought at Cannae, only an estimated 14,000 of them managed to escape the deft trap Hannibal had sprung. Those 14,000 survivors managed to live by cutting their way out of the trap and making their way to the safe city of Canusium. The rest of the men who did not escape the slaughter remained to fight until they were cut down.

Only darkness brought an end to the killing, but with the coming of daybreak, the Carthaginian soldiers were once more among the Romans. Livy vividly depicted the scene on the field the day after the battle: "Thousands of Roman soldiers lay there, infantry and cavalry scattered everywhere, united in a death which the blind chances of battle or flight had brought upon them. A few, whose wounds had been staunched by the morning frosts, even rose from among the heaps of dead all covered in blood – only to be slaughtered there and then by their enemies. Others were discovered, still alive, but lying there with their knees or hamstrings sliced apart, baring their necks or throats and begging their enemies to drain the rest of their blood. Some were even found with their heads buried in the ground, having dug small pits for themselves and buried their faces in the earth, and then simply smothered themselves to death. The most spectacular sight of all was a Numidian soldier, still alive but lying beneath a dead Roman, with his nose and ears torn to shreds. The Roman had fought to his final breath, and when his hands could no longer hold his weapon, his anger turned to madness, and he died tearing his enemy to pieces with his teeth..."

Most of the Roman wounded were executed, and an estimated 10,000 legionaries were taken prisoner. When the killing of the wounded was finished, nearly 70,000 Roman, Etruscan and Samnite legionaries had been killed at the battle, while Hannibal had lost just 6,000.

Hannibal allowed his victorious men to move amongst the dead, stripping the fallen of everything of use, including weapons, armor, clothing, and rings. Polybius stated that scores of Roman noblemen had fallen in the battle, and all of these men wore the golden rings which marked their status in Roman society. Other rings indicated who among the fallen had been senators. When Hannibal's men were finished stripping rings from the dead, Polybius recorded that the Carthaginians had a bushel full of hundreds of rings.

A statue of Hannibal, with the rings of the Roman nobles he had killed in the battle of Cannae, resting on a Roman standard.

The Aftermath

A medieval depiction of Cannae

The Battle of Cannae was an unqualified disaster for Rome, unprecedented in the annals of the city, and one with consequences which echoed around the Mediterranean. The Syracusans and Macedonians, now believing that Rome's star was on the wane, abandoned their alliances with the Republic and sided instead with Hannibal. With yet another Roman army decimated, Rome was again at Hannibal's mercy, as Livy noted: "Never before, while the City itself was still safe, had there been such excitement and panic within its walls. I shall not attempt to describe it, nor will I weaken the reality by going into details... it was not wound upon wound but multiplied disaster that was now announced. For according to the reports two consular armies and two consuls were lost; there was no longer any Roman camp, any general, any single soldier in existence; Apulia, Samnium, almost the whole of Italy lay at Hannibal's feet. Certainly there is no other nation that would not have succumbed beneath such a weight of calamity."

In just 20 months, Hannibal had destroyed 3 Roman armies, totaling about 16 legions and upwards of 150,000-200,000 men, and it is estimated that Rome had lost 20% of its adult men. Once again, however, Hannibal inexplicably wavered and opted not to attack Rome itself.

Though he still lacked siege equipment, there would almost certainly have been someone among his allies with expertise in siege warfare, but Hannibal refused to march north, choosing instead to stay in southern Italy. Much of the blame for Hannibal's supineness, in this case, remains with the Carthaginian oligarchy, who once again refused to provide him with money, reinforcements, or the siege equipment he so vitally needed. According to legend, after Cannae, the Numidian cavalry commander Maharbal suggested that Hannibal march on Rome. When Hannibal resisted, Maharbal was alleged to have said, "Truly the Gods have not bestowed all things upon the same person. Thou knowest indeed, Hannibal, how to conquer, but thou knowest not how to make use of your victory." Livy also criticized the great Carthaginian commander for not marching on Rome: "In his moment of victory Hannibal was surrounded by his staff, crowding round to congratulate him and urge him after such a massive success to spend the remainder of the day and the following night resting himself, and giving his exhausted soldiers time to recover. But Maharbal, his cavalry commander would have none of it, urging him not to waste a moment. 'I'll tell you what this battle has really achieved,' he declared, 'when in five days time you are feasting on the Capitol. Follow up quickly. I'll go ahead with the cavalry, and before they even realise we are coming, the Romans will discover we've arrived.' For Hannibal it all seemed far too optimistic, an almost inconceivable possibility. He commended Maharbal for his imaginative idea, but said he needed time to think it through…That single day's delay, by common consent, proved the salvation of Rome and her empire."

Whether Hannibal made the right decision or not, he could certainly have exerted himself a little more. In the event, he chose to capture several cities in southern Italy, and established his headquarters in Capua, one of the richest cities in Southern Italy, which had defected to his side after Cannae, as had much of the southern part of the Italian Peninsula. Hannibal's lassitude during this period, referred to by classical scholars as the "lazings of Capua", is uncharacteristic, but it allowed the Romans to rally. Hannibal contented himself to send a peace delegation to negotiate terms with Rome, but the Senate still refused to deal with Hannibal. Instead, Rome re-dedicated itself to raising more armies and fighting Hannibal.

In the wake of the catastrophe at Cannae, the Roman ruling elite re-evaluated Fabius Maximus' strategy, and began to use his tactics to harass, delay, and whittle down Hannibal's forces in the field, studiously avoiding open battle whenever they could. For years they harried Hannibal's armies, and while there were blunders that allowed Hannibal to lash out (three Roman armies were destroyed in the period between 215 and 212 BCE) the victories were minor and ultimately meaningless. After almost half a decade of continuous warfare, Apulia was a scorched desert incapable of sustaining an army in the field, and Hannibal was getting no supplies either from his allies or from Carthage. Moreover, his allies were proving to be hopelessly ineffective in the field, meaning he either had to lead the force himself or risk losing one of his field armies. Whenever Hannibal did take command, the results were often devastating for Rome, but decisive victory eluded him. Rome could raise far more troops than Hannibal, unsupported, could ever hope to obtain, and a war of attrition was destined to favor them in the end. The tide was finally turning against Hannibal.

   In 211, Hannibal received a massive blow as, while his army was in the field, the Romans besieged and captured, with great loss, his base at Capua. Still reeling from this news, his woes were compounded when he discovered that his Syracusan allies had also been crushed, with Sicily fallen to the Romans, and Philip, the king of Macedon, also defeated and driven out of the Roman dominions. Hannibal himself continued to prove himself a great general, inflicting several notable defeats upon all the armies sent against him, but they were, in the long term, meaningless. He fought on, but continued to lose territories throughout 210 and 209 BCE, and between 208 and 207 BCE he was pushed ever southwards, finally being forced to retire to Apulia, where he anxiously awaited reinforcements under the command of his brother, Hasdrubal. At the eleventh hour, these reinforcements might have turned the tide, for once he had the troops at his command Hannibal planned to march upon Rome once and for all. However, Hasdrubal never reached Hannibal. He got himself entangled in a battle with the Romans on the Metaurus, and his army was defeated and he himself killed. Hannibal, knowing his situation in Apulia was untenable, was forced to retreat into Bruttium, the southernmost tip of the Italian peninsula, where he was also forced to endure the horror of having his brother's severed head tossed over the walls and into his camp.

   For all intents and purposes, Hannibal's campaign in Italy was over. He succeeded in holding on in Bruttium for a further four years, but was never able to push northward and his army was fast dwindling to nothing, with his veterans being killed off and his mercenaries melting away. In 206 BCE, it was reported to him that Roman armies had occupied the entirety of Iberia, driving the Carthaginian forces from the peninsula, a victory obtained by his old enemy Scipio Africanus, who had utterly crushed the Carthaginians at Ilipa. Finally, in 203 BCE, he was peremptorily recalled to Carthage, 15 years and scores of victories after he had first entered Italy in arms. The reason for his recall was simple: Rome was on the march. A massive army, under the command of Scipio "Africanus", the General whose bravery had saved his eponymous father's life at the beginning of Hannibal's Italian campaign, was preparing to attack and destroy Carthage. Rome wanted revenge.

   While Hannibal had been in Italy, it had been relatively easy for the Carthaginian oligarchy, particularly the Hundred and Four, a federation of powerful traders, and Hannibal's chief political rival, Hanno the Great, to marginalize him. For years his political party, the Barcids, had struggled to obtain even a token amount of funds and troops for his enterprise, but Hannibal's arrival on the scene changed all that. Even his rivals could not deny the simple fact that, all else aside, the man could fight a battle like no other general alive. With Rome threatening invasion, Hannibal was suddenly the necessary hero of the hour. Bolstering his Italian mercenaries with levies from Africa and Carthage, the Carthaginian ruling elite desperately invested the money that Hannibal had begged for throughout the last decade in order to assemble a scratch force capable of at least presenting an appearance of force against Scipio Africanus' army.

Hannibal can hardly have been thrilled to see the amount of trouble the Carthaginians went to in order to assemble an army that, had he had his way years before, might well have been completely unnecessary. Certainly it appears that he prepared to take the field with less than his customary ardor. At 45, he was still far from old, but ever since he had first left Carthage he had spent virtually all of his adult life fighting, and the strain was beginning to tell. By all accounts he was in poor health, and prone to sickness. Indeed, rather than seek to bring Scipio Africanus to battle, in 202 BCE Hannibal met the Roman general and attempted to talk peace. The army the Carthaginians had succeeded in gathering, not to mention the presence of Hannibal himself, convinced Scipio that he might be well-advised to seek a diplomatic solution, and the two began negotiations, which were helped by the fact that both generals recognized a kindred spirit in the other. Through negotiations, Carthage was forced to give up much, especially considering Hannibal's roster of victories, but Rome's star was on the rise once again, and Hannibal knew he could not hope to win a protracted war.

Hannibal agreed to Scipio's terms: Carthage would lose possession of Iberia and the Mediterranean islands, renouncing all claims to overseas territories but maintaining its heartland and African possessions, with the exception of the Numidian kingdom of Masinissa, who had declared for Rome. Reparations would be made, Scipio demanded, to Rome itself and to the countless families which Carthage's wars had decimated, and the Carthaginian army and fleet must both be reduced in numbers, in order for them to never again threaten Rome's supremacy. Hannibal, who recognized these terms, though harsh, as probably the best deal Carthage was likely to achieve, acceded to them, but the proposed peace between he and Scipio never happened. While the negotiations were going on, a Roman fleet which had gotten itself stranded upon the coast of Tunisia was seized by the Carthaginian navy and ransacked of all its supplies and equipment. When Scipio heard of this, he furiously demanded reparations, but, unaccountably, the Carthaginian oligarchy high-handedly turned him down. Perhaps they felt secure enough with Hannibal at the head of an army on Carthaginian soil to defy Rome, or perhaps the terms of the treaty stung their pride. Whatever their reasons, they could not have committed a bigger diplomatic error if they had gone out of their way to do so. Scipio departed the negotiations in a rage. There would be no terms.

Engraving of the Battle of Zama

On October 19th, 202 BC, on the plain of Zama, in modern Tunisia, battle was joined. Scipio Africanus led 34,000 Roman legionary infantry, including veteran survivors of Cannae, who had a score to settle with Hannibal, and 9,000 crack Numidian cavalry (the same heavy horse which Hannibal's general Maharbal had used to such devastating effect against the Romans for two decades). Hannibal himself marched to stop him with 45,000 Italian, Iberian, Gaulish and North African infantry (both mercenary and levied), 4,000 cavalry, and around 80 war elephants. For the first time in one of the battles of the Second Punic War, Hannibal had the infantry advantage and Rome had the cavalry advantage.

Battle of Zama

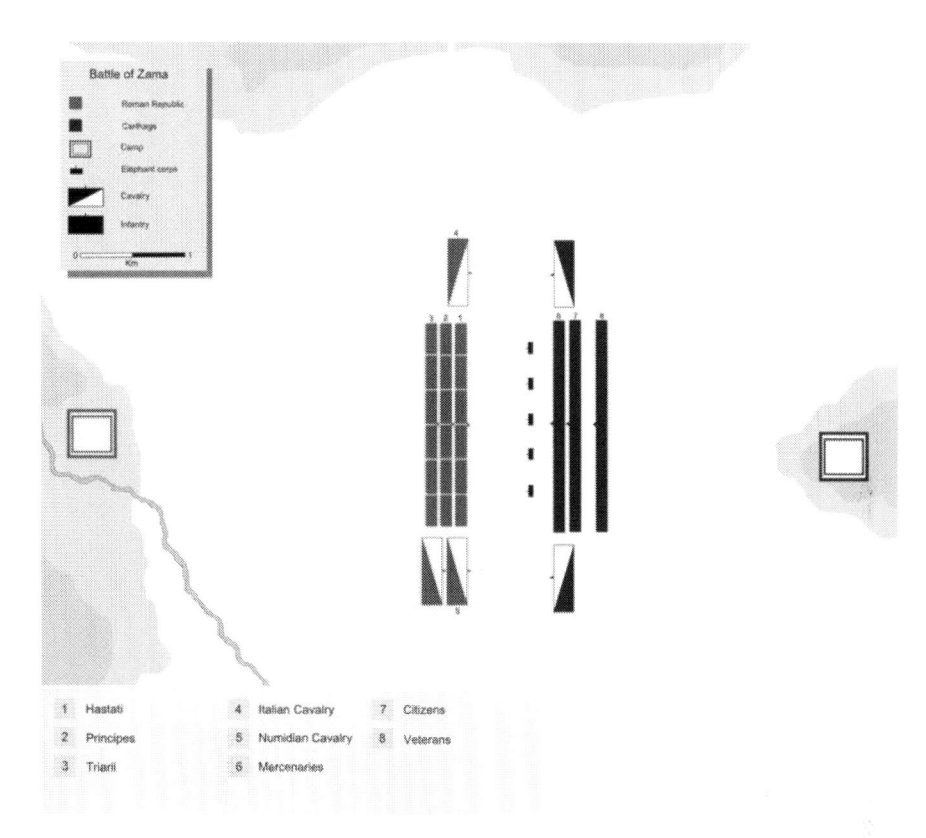

- ■ Roman Republic
- ■ Carthage
- ☐ Camp
- ■ Elephant corps
- ◤ Cavalry
- ■ Infantry

0 — 1 Km

1	Hastati	4	Italian Cavalry	7	Citizens
2	Principes	5	Numidian Cavalry	8	Veterans
3	Triarii	6	Mercenaries		

    Hannibal deployed his cavalry on the wings, then placed three lines of infantry, with his Italian veterans in reserve, behind his war elephants, which were to be his secret weapon. Scipio countered by placing his own infantry in three lines, with his veteran heavy infantry in reserve and his own cavalry, which outnumbered Hannibal's by more than two to one, on the flanks. Hannibal opened the battle by pushing forward his war elephants and light infantry, but Scipio checked their advance before they could smash into his battle-lines by unleashing a cloud of skirmishers who harried the elephants with storms of arrows and javelins, while the Roman cavalry blew trumpets to confuse and frighten the elephants, several of which turned the way they had come and charged into the Carthaginian left flank, creating chaos there. Scipio also intentionally opened gaps in his own line for the elephants to drive through harmlessly. Masinissa took advantage of this to charge home against the cavalry on that flank and drive it from the field, but he found himself embroiled in a chase orchestrated on the fly by Hannibal as the Carthaginian cavalry lured him away from the main battle.

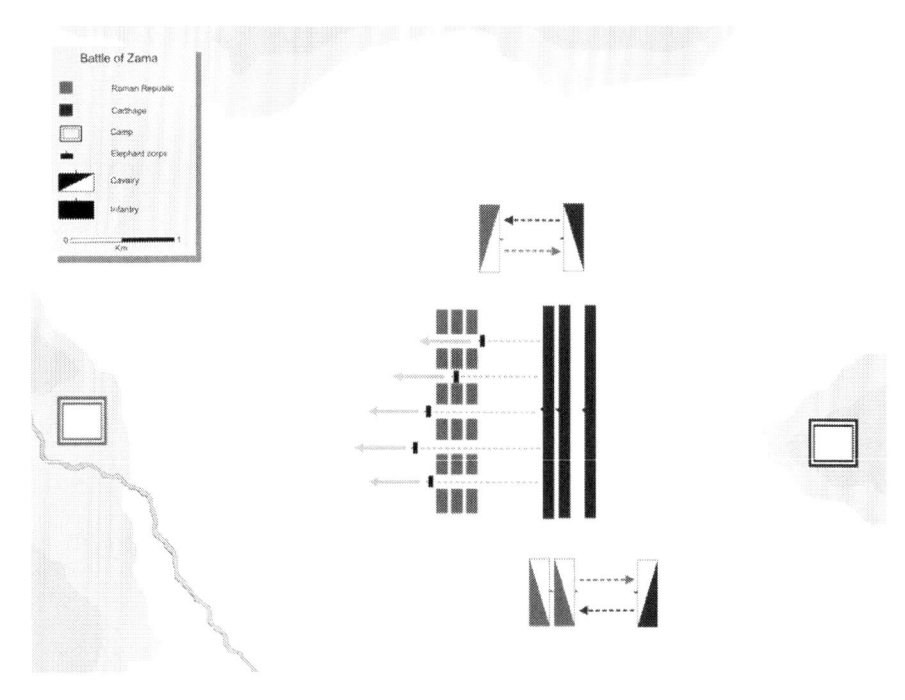

Meanwhile, the Roman and Carthaginian infantry were hammering each other in the center of the battle-line, with both sides momentarily gaining the advantage, only to be driven back in turn. The battle raged for hours, with neither side able to gain the upper hand, but eventually Masinissa, who had chased the Carthaginian cavalry clean off the field with his superior numbers, returned and charged the Carthaginian forces from behind, enveloping them. Scipio rallied his faltering and exhausted troops to one last great effort and they fell upon the Carthaginian troops, which were trapped and unable to maneuver.

Like Hannibal's masterpiece at Cannae, but this time with the roles inverted, the encircled force had nowhere to run. Thousands were cut down where they stood, with only around a tenth of Hannibal's original force, including Hannibal himself, succeeding in breaking free and escaping. For Carthage, the battle was an utter catastrophe, with over 20,000 dead and 20,000 taken prisoner, most of which were grievously wounded. Hannibal's first defeat was so dire that he lost all credibility in Carthage, and his enemies used it to blacken his reputation and forced him to surrender his generalship. With no army in the field, Carthage sued for peace, at far more costly terms than those which they could have accepted with no further loss of life.

Now that Carthage had surrendered virtually all military ambition, Hannibal himself devoted himself to politics. He secured his election to chief magistrate through the support of the Barcid party and introduced highly successful political and financial reforms, much to the chagrin of his rivals. Hannibal was so successful as a politician that Carthage, despite still being hampered by a heavy war indemnity, prospered to the point that the Romans demanded he step down as magistrate. Rather than do so, Hannibal voluntarily went into exile, worried he might expose Carthage to new Roman reprisals.

For the next eight years he was received as a mercenary commander at many middle-eastern courts, particularly at the court of Antiochus of Syria, in Ephesus, who was preparing for an invasion of Italy. Hannibal, ever conscious of his oath to his father, offered to take command of Antiochus's troops, but Antiochus declined the offer and was soundly beaten the following year. Antiochus, seeking a scapegoat, blamed Hannibal and proposed to sell him to the Romans, prompting him to move yet again. Strabo and Plutarch both wrote that Hannibal spent some time at the court of Artaxias I, and he eventually made his way back to Asia Minor and fought with Prusias I of Bithynia against King Eumenes II of Pergamon, a Roman ally. It was said that during one naval battle, Hannibal devised the idea of filling large pots with venomous snakes and throwing them onto the enemies' ships, wreaking havoc. After Hannibal defeated Eumenes in a couple of land battles, Rome demanded that Bythinia surrender Hannibal to them. The frightened Prusias complied, but Hannibal was determined not to let himself be taken alive and poisoned himself at Lybissa, in Asia Minor, in 183 BCE Roman historians speculated he had long carried the poison in a ring in case he needed to use it in battle, but poison kept that long might very well no longer be effective. In any case, Hannibal left a letter behind which dryly remarked that his death should provide some comfort to the Romans by relieving them of the fear they had felt for so long, since they apparently could not abide waiting patiently for an old man to die. "Let us relieve the Romans from the anxiety they have so long experienced, since they think it tries their patience too much to wait for an old man's death."

Despite Hannibal's incredible success in Italy, Carthage was on the brink of death by the end of the Second Punic War, but it swiftly proved once again that it was nothing if not resourceful. Despite having been humbled and reduced virtually to city-state status, Carthage quickly recovered economically by taking advantage of the privileged trading position which had been the backbone of her wealth since her foundation. Interestingly, the ruthless demilitarization imposed by the Romans upon the Carthaginians actually aided the city's economic redevelopment; since Carthage no longer had to pay to maintain vast mercenary armies at home or abroad, their defense budget was virtually nonexistent.

Over the next five decades, Carthage slowly rebuilt her economy and even prospered, causing much annoyance and some alarm in Rome. However, ever since the defeat at Cannae, Massinissa's Numidians had raided across the new Carthaginian border with impunity, and since Carthage lacked a standing army she was forced to bring any grievances she might have before the Roman Senate, where Punic complaints were generally overruled as a matter of principle.

Carthage eventually responded by refusing to pay the annual tribute to Rome and raising an army, which they launched in a retaliatory raid against Massinissa, only to promptly be defeated by the Numidians.

This behavior alarmed much of the Roman political establishment, including the famous orator Cato the Elder, who began to end all of his speeches, regardless of their subject matter, by urging the destruction of Carthage. In his biography of Cato the Elder, Plutarch wrote:

> "Some will have the overthrow of Carthage to have been one of his last acts of state; when, indeed, Scipio the younger did by his velour give it the last blow, but the war, chiefly by the counsel and advice of Cato, was undertaken on the following occasion. Cato was sent to the Carthaginians and Masinissa, King of Numidia, who were at war with one another, to know the cause of their difference. He, it seems, had been a friend of the Romans from the beginning; and they, too, since they were conquered by Scipio, were of the Roman confederacy, having been shorn of their power by loss of territory and a heavy tax. Finding Carthage, not (as the Romans thought) low and in an ill condition, but well manned, full of riches and all sorts of arms and ammunition, and perceiving the Carthaginians carry it high, he conceived that it was not a time for the Romans to adjust affairs between them and Masinissa; but rather that they themselves would fall into danger, unless they should find means to check this rapid new growth of Rome's ancient irreconcilable enemy. Therefore, returning quickly to Rome, he acquainted the senate that the former defeats and blows given to the Carthaginians had not so much diminished their strength, as it had abated their imprudence and folly; that they were not become weaker, but more experienced in war, and did only skirmish with the Numidians to exercise themselves the better to cope with the Romans: that the peace and league they had made was but a kind of suspension of war which awaited a fairer opportunity to break out again.
>
> Moreover, they say that, shaking his gown, he took occasion to let drop some African figs before the senate. And on their admiring the size and beauty of them, he presently added, that the place that bore them was but three days' sail from Rome. Nay, he never after this gave his opinion, but at the end he would be sure to come out with this sentence, 'ALSO, CARTHAGE, METHINKS, OUGHT UTTERLY TO BE Destroyed.' But Publius Scipio Nasica would always declare his opinion to the contrary, in these words, 'It seems requisite to me that Carthage should still stand.' For seeing his countrymen to be grown wanton and insolent, and the people made, by their prosperity, obstinate and disobedient to the senate, and drawing the whole city, whither they would, after them, he would have had the fear of Carthage to serve as a bit to hold the

contumacy of the multitude; and he looked upon the Carthaginians as too weak to overcome the Romans, and too great to be despised by them. On the other side, it seemed a perilous thing to Cato that a city which had been always great, and was now grown sober and wise, by reason of its former calamities, should still lie, as it were, in wait for the follies and dangerous excesses of the overpowerful Roman people; so that he thought it the wisest course to have all outward dangers removed, when they had so many inward ones among themselves.

Thus Cato, they say, stirred up the third and last war against the Carthaginians: but no sooner was the said war begun, than he died, prophesying of the person that should put an end to it who was then only a young man"

Ancient bust of Cato the Elder

Matters ultimately did come to a head in 149 BCE, when Rome, tired of Carthaginian resurgence and seeking a pretext for invasion, first demanded that hundreds of children from Carthaginian noble families be handed over as hostages. When it seemed as though the

Carthaginians might actually accede to this condition, the Romans ordered Carthage to be demolished and the entire city rebuilt inland away from the coast. The Carthaginians, unsurprisingly, told the Senate this was unacceptable, after which Rome promptly declared war.

A Roman fleet carrying 80,000 infantry and 4,000 cavalry landed in North Africa, depositing the troops near the Carthaginian city of Utica. This Roman force represented 20 legions of disciplined Roman legionaries, and they were camped only 10 miles from the city of Carthage. The presence of this force, combined with the failure of the Romans to control the Numidians and the Roman Senate's harsh demands, ensured a change in the Carthaginian government; the party which had so long sought to appease Rome following the end of the Second Punic War was replaced and a government which sought to fight the Romans and retain their Carthaginian pride came into power following the Roman demand that Carthage be abandoned.

The Roman army and fleet did not attack the Carthaginians immediately after Carthage's refusal to comply to the last demand to abandon the city, and this waiting period proved to be exceptionally costly for the Roman legions. The legions were struck down with disease, after which the combat ready legionaries were so few in number that the Roman command was unable to launch any sort of attack against the city of Carthage.

While the Roman army sough to heal itself and prepare for a vigorous campaign against Carthage, the Carthaginians were seemingly trapped within the walls of Carthage. The Romans had underestimated the tenacity of the Carthaginians, however. With 20 Roman legions a mere 10 miles from them, the Carthaginian people transformed their temples into workshops for the fabrication of weapons and armor. It was said that the Carthaginian women even went so far as to cut short their hair, and the shorn locks were twisted into cord for use as bowstrings. Thus, while the Romans sought to bring their legions back up to their peak physical condition, the Carthaginians proposed to defend themselves from the inevitable siege and gathered food and supplies.

After the passing of several months the Romans were ready to begin what they believed would be a short and successful siege. The Roman legions were divided into two commands. The first section was commanded by consul Manius Manilius, whose command consisted of the greater portion of the infantry and cavalry. His plan of attack was to cross an isthmus which separated the cities of Utica and Carthage, and upon crossing the isthmus, he would have the legions fill in the protective ditch surrounding the city of Carthage. With this impediment taken care of, he would have his legions move on to the first of two walls. The first was a low parapet which his legions would easily be able to climb, and the second was the high wall which protected the city itself. Siege engines and scaling equipment would be used to breach the high wall and attack the unprotected city.

The second wing of the Roman attack would come in the form of an attack by sea, which would be led by consul Lucius Marcius Censorinus. Censorinus would sail the Roman fleet up to the unprotected sea wall of Carthage. Some of his troops would disembark, and together the ground troops and seaborne troops would assault the city. The landed infantry and the seaborne troops would both use scaling ladders to assault the wall in conjunction with Manilius' assault on the city's front.

Once the plan of attack was agreed upon and in place, both Manius Manilius and Lucius Marcius Censorinus launched their attacks on the city. Neither of the consuls expected there to be any sort of resistance from the Carthaginians, as both men knew that the city had been unable to send out for arms, armor and assistance. Of course, both of the consuls had failed to take into consideration the fact that the Carthaginians might well have found a way to defend themselves against a Roman attack they knew was coming.

When the combined attack occurred, the consuls were horrified by the fierce, desperate resistance of the Carthaginians to the Roman attack. Confused and disorientated, the legions fell back; their first assault on Carthage had been an unequivocal failure. Having been disabused of the notion that the conquest would be easy, the consuls fell back and regrouped their forces. The consuls struck at the city once more, but again the Romans were repelled by the Carthaginians and had to fall back well away from the city.

At this point the Roman consuls became worried. Carthage would not simply surrender itself to Rome, and they were worried about forces under the Carthaginian commander Hasdrubal, who had positioned himself behind the Romans on the opposite side of a lake. He fortified his positions and looked for opportunities to strike at the Roman legions, and one came when engineers attached to Censorinus' command entered the woods around the lake. The task that they sought to accomplish was the harvesting of wood to build larger siege engines for a renewed assault upon Carthage, but while the engineers were directing the gathering of wood, a small force of Carthaginians under the command of Himilco Phameas fell upon them.

Despite the attack, the engineers, while suffering a large loss of men, were still able to gather enough wood for the siege engines, and with this wood, Censorinus and Manilius constructed new engines and ladders for a third assault upon the city of Carthage. This attack took place with both groups of legions operating in conjunction with the other, but this third attempt was still beaten back.

After this failure, Manilius focused on the fortifications in the front of the city, but even here the Carthaginians were able to successfully beat back the Roman assaults. Eventually, Manilius became despondent and lacked any belief that the Roman legions would ever succeed in breaking through the walls of Carthage.

While Manilius suffered from a lack of faith, Lucius Marius Censorinus did not. Rather than bemoaning the fate of the legions in front of Carthage, Censorinus prepared for another attempt to break into the city. Using Roman perseverance, Censorinus had his legions fill in a portion of the lake next to Carthage, and when that was done, he had a wider space with which he could assault the Carthaginian walls. Using two large battering rams, his troops finally succeeded in breaking the wall, but when they attempted to make use of the breach and gain the city, they were beaten back by the Carthaginians. When night descended, the Carthaginians started to rebuild the wall.

Although they repaired the wall, the Carthaginians also realized that the work would be insufficient to stop the Roman battering rams. What followed was an example of Carthaginian heroism and determination. Under the cover of darkness, a group of Carthaginians attacked the Romans through the breach in the city wall in order to destroy the battering rams. The lightly armed forces were rapidly beaten back by the Roman forces, but not before disabling the battering rams and rendering them useless until the Romans could repair them.

When day dawned, the Roman legionaries saw that the Carthaginians, armed solely with clubs and stones, stood in the small courtyard open to the breach. The Carthaginians lined the courtyard, the roofs, and the walls and waited for the legionaries. The commander of the Roman troops at the breach was a young tribune by the name of Publius Cornelius Scipio Aemilianus. Instead of having his troops rush headlong into the breach, he stationed groups of men along either side of the breach and then ordered a unit of legionaries into the city.

The Carthaginians were ferocious in their defense of the city, and once again the legionaries were driven back and out of the breach. Had Aemilianus not stationed troops on either side of the breach, the Carthaginians may have succeeded in annihilating the Roman forces altogether, and as a result, Aemilianus' actions came to the attention of the commanders.

Shortly after this, before the Roman consuls could prepare the legions for another assault on Carthage, widespread illnesses began to sweep the ranks once more. With the troops sick, Censorinus took his command post out of the fleet, which sat off of the port side of Carthage, and began to plot his next move. The Carthaginians, however, had already began to act upon theirs. Since the winds were blowing towards the Roman fleet, people within the city prepared a large group of fire boats. These vessels were filled with tinder and flammables before being carried through the city to a corner of the city wall which protruded into the sea. With the wall serving as a shield from Roman eyes, the Carthaginians lowered the boats into the water and raised the sails, and as the wind started to drive the boats around the wall and towards the Roman fleet, the Carthaginians poured both pitch and brimstone onto the boats from atop the walls and lit them. The wind drove the boats furiously into the Roman ships, lighting them on fire, and the tactic proved so effective that Rome lost nearly the entire fleet anchored off of Carthage's walls.

After the loss of the fleet, Censorinus returned to Rome, both to report on the status of the war and to take care of the political necessity of conducting an election to retain his position as consul. Meanwhile, Manilius stayed within his camp outside of the city. The Carthaginians, however, did not remain within the city. Shortly after Censorius' departure for Rome the

Carthaginians made a night assault upon the Roman camp. Mostly unarmed, the Carthaginian troops carried wooden planks with which to cross the ditch which surrounded the Roman camp, and after crossing the trench the Carthaginians attempted to destroy the Roman fortifications.

As the Carthaginians assaulted the front of the encampment, Aemilianus exited the camp via the rear upon his horse and charged the Carthaginians from the flank. Due to the inevitable confusion of night combat, the Carthaginians believed that the young tribune was at the head of a larger force and retreated to the sanctuary of Carthage. As the war progressed Aemilianus' name gained more recognition and renown.

Aemilianus continued making a good name for himself, and in addition to his bravery, he was known for his ability to use subterfuge and trickery when necessary. Such an incident occurred when the Carthaginians launched another attack upon Manilius' camp, this time from the sea at night. While Manilius chose to keep his troops within the walls, Aemilianus led a large group of cavalry out onto the field where the Carthaginians were gathered and assaulting the fortifications. By ordering his cavalry to carry only lit torches and to not engage the Carthaginians, and by having the cavalry ride around the enemy yelling and waving their torches, Aemilianus was able to force the Carthaginian to withdraw in confusion.

While the Carthaginians continued to hold out against the Roman siege, Manilius left his encampment with two legions to seek an engagement with a roving Carthaginian force commanded by Hasdrubal. However, Manilius' timidity and lack of tactical knowledge led him to make several poor decisions which Aemilianus attempted to turn the consul from. Undeterred, Manilius proceeded into a narrow valley, allowing Hasdrubal to ambush the two legions, but in the fighting that followed, Aemilianus took command of a large group of cavalry and effectively enabled the defeated legions to withdraw. When it was later discovered that four cohorts of the legions had been left behind, dug in yet surrounded, Aemilianus again took the initiative and with his cavalry achieved what was believed to be impossible by breaking the hold of Hasdrubal's forces around the four cohorts, driving the Carthaginians from the field, and rescuing the trapped legionaries.

Shortly after this incident, Aemilianus returned to Rome and sought out a consul seat. Many of the men with whom he had served in North Africa wrote home that Aemilianus alone could destroy Carthage. Even the consul Manilius, shortly before being replaced, sent word to Rome that Aemilianus should return to North Africa, not as a tribune but as consul, in order to bring an end to the Carthaginians.

By December of 148 BCE, the citizens of Rome had grown tired of the war already. They had also heard of Aemilianus' exploits in North Africa, so when the time to vote came, he was awarded a consul position. In addition to this, he was given North Africa as his province so that he might command the legions. The Roman public also gave him the right to conscript men into service to replace those who had already been lost in the war.

Thus, in the spring of 147 BCE, Aemilianus gathered his troops and sailed for the Carthaginian city of Utica. Meanwhile, the Romans in North Africa continued to push against the Carthaginian defenses. From the spring of 147 to the spring of 146, Aemilianus drove his forces through the Carthaginian territories, restoring discipline to the legions, capturing Carthaginian positions of strength, and stopping supplies from reaching Carthage.

Finally, as the spring of 146 neared its end, Aemilianus attacked the city of Carthage. The Carthaginians, weak from nearly three years of siege warfare, disease, and lack of supplies, were unable to defend their walls when the Romans attacked. As the legionaries poured into the city, a brutal form of fighting began from street to street and house to house. For seven days, the Romans and Carthaginians engaged in brutal urban warfare, but Rome was victorious in the end. Only 50,000 of Carthage's citizens survived, and these people were sold into slavery. For 17 days the Romans burned the city to the ground, and those buildings that remained were torn down by hand so that nothing of the city remained.

A picture of the excavated ruins of Ancient Carthage

The Third Punic War marked the end of Carthage as any sort of city or people, and it allowed Rome to continue its rise to power within the Mediterranean. Rome's ability to soundly defeat an enemy regardless of its location was a factor for new enemies and possible challengers alike to consider.

The Battle of the Teutoburg Forest

Varus

A statue of Varus near the battlefield

To analyze the Battle of the Teutoburg Forest, it is necessary to gain an understanding of the Roman rule of Lex Provincia, and how that affected the two commanders who represented the two sides in the battle.

For the Roman Empire, it was a middle-aged man, Publius Quinctilius Varus, who needed to enforce Lex Provincia. Lex Provincia was a template that the Roman Empire had created for the order and rule of conquered territories, and it was used by the conquering Roman general with the assistance of 10 legates. These politicians and the general would look at the issues presented by the conquered populace, the number of towns, and the estimated population, amongst other factors. The Lex Provincia would, therefore, be a set of laws for the appointed governor to rule properly and collect taxes. It would be this set of laws that Varus was attempting to enforce in a province that he didn't fully understand. This lack of understanding, as well as the fact that Rome had conquered the territory, was one of the primary reasons that Arminius rose up against Roman rule in Germania.

According to ancient Roman historians, Publius Quinctilius Varus was born into an aristocratic family in 49 BCE. His family, though noble by birth, was noble in name only; the family had become nearly destitute due to poor political alliances which Varus' father (Sextus Quinctilius Varus) had made well prior to his birth. Sextus decided to place his support and his fortune with the Senatorial Party in the Roman Civil War. The Roman Civil War, also known as the Great Civil War or Caesar's Civil War, was fought between Caesar's supporters and supporters of Pompey the Great and the Senate from 49-45 BCE. Caesar's victory in this civil war would eventually lead to the dissolution of the Roman Republic and see the creation of the Roman Empire some years after Caesar's assassination.

Unfortunately for Varus, his father had chosen to fight against Caesar and his allies. While Sextus managed to survive the Civil War, he committed suicide in 42 BCE. Thus, he left Varus both fatherless and destitute with nothing save a family name which was linked to betrayal in the society of the new Roman Empire.

Nonetheless, Varus rose above these difficulties which he had inherited. As a young man, he did not follow in his father's footsteps regarding political allegiances. Instead, Varus became a strong and steady supporter of the Emperor, Augustus, the chosen heir of Julius Caesar who had finished Caesar's work of ending the Roman Republic and then became the Empire's first true leader. In 13 BCE, Varus was able to gain the support of the populace of Rome and was elected consul (the other consul elected at this time alongside Varus was Tiberius, the stepson and eventual successor of Augustus).

A coin depicting Varus

Varus' political power and popularity continued to rise, as evidenced by the events surrounding the death of Marcus Vipsanius Agrippa in 12 BCE. Upon Agrippa's death, it was Varus who was asked to deliver the man's eulogy at the funeral, a mark of respect in Roman society.

Agrippa

As Varus' political power continued to grow, so too did his familiarity and friendship with the Emperor's family and allies. This familiarity and friendship with the Emperor's family had begun in 14 BCE when Varus became bound not only by loyalty to Augustus but through marriage as well. This familial connection to the Emperor, in addition to his political savvy and abilities, made Varus an excellent candidate for governor of Roman provinces. For the Emperor, the decision to employ Varus as a governor was an easy one considering the man's loyalty, family connections, and proven political skills.

The first province which the Emperor sent Varus to was Africa, and after the successful governorship of that province, Varus was then moved to Syria, which included the rebellious country of Judea. The Jewish people had long been difficult to control, and Varus was an unpopular governor while he was in control of the Syrian province. His rule was marked by harsh and unforgiving punishments which were compounded by the fact that he set the Roman taxes upon the locals at what were considered to be exceptionally high rates.

When a rebellion amongst the Jewish population rose up in Judea in 4 BCE, Varus set off with the Roman legions under his control, and they rapidly marched into Judea and occupied the city of Jerusalem. It was in Jerusalem that Varus truly made his mark as a harsh governor, reacting swiftly and decisively to put down the rebellion. While occupying the city, Varus captured an estimated 2,000 Jewish rebels, and rather than keeping these men as prisoners or selling them off as slaves, Varus crucified them all, an act which restored order and instilled fear in the population. The Jewish people would protest this in a ban on purchasing Roman goods, but they did not rise up again while Varus was the Syrian province's governor.

That said, the ancient historian Paterculus was critical of Varus, not only as a man but for his governorship of Syria: "Varus Quintilius, descended from a famous rather than a high-born family, was a man of mild character and of a quiet disposition, somewhat slow in mind as he was in body, and more accustomed to the leisure of the camp than to actual service in war. That he was no despiser of money is demonstrated by his governorship of Syria: he entered the rich province a poor man, but left it a rich man and the province poor."

When his time in the province of Syria had finished, Varus once more returned to Rome. For several years, he remained in the city and little information about him survives. When Varus appears in the historical record once again, it is for political reasons, as Augustus chose to call upon Varus once more to serve as governor of the province of Germania. Thus it was in 6 CE that Varus left Rome and went to take control of Germania, his primary purpose being to rule the province in the name of Rome and ensure proper taxation and Romanization of the people.

Given his past actions, when the German commander Arminius informed Varus of a revolt in the northern part of Germania in 9 CE, it should come as no surprise that Varus took his legions north to quell the growing rebellion. Not only was a sudden show of strength and an overwhelming use of force generally standard procedure for Roman governors, it was also in keeping with Varus' character. He had stopped an uprising in Judea with his legions, and he intended to do the same in Germania with the three legions and their auxiliary forces that were under his command.

Arminius

"Arminius, without doubt Germania's liberator, who challenged the Roman people not in its beginnings like other kings and leaders, but in the peak of its empire; in battles with changing success, undefeated in the war." – Tacitus

For the Germanic tribes at the Battle of the Teutoburg Forest, the commander was a young man in his early 20s named Arminius. It was Arminius who orchestrated an alliance with a small coalition of Germanic tribes, and once he had gathered these various tribes together, he took control of the preparations to attempt to drive the Romans out of Germania in 9 CE.

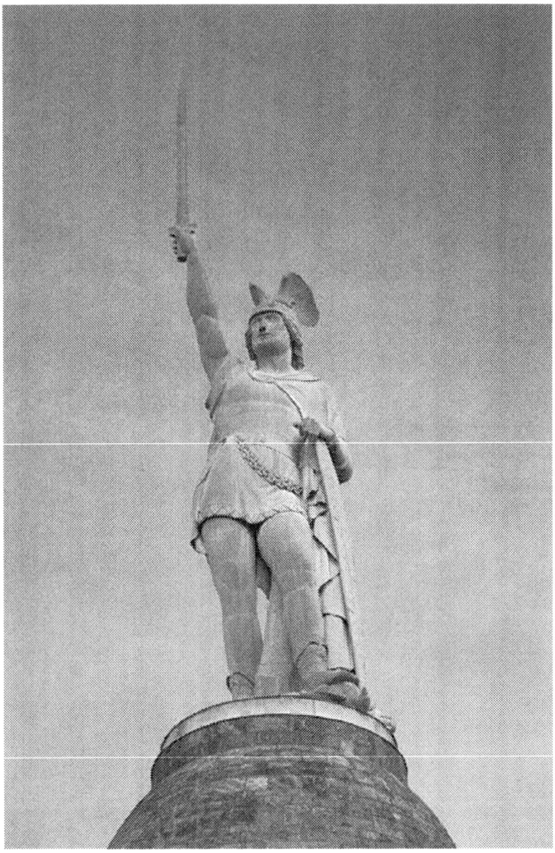

Pictures of a monument to Arminius near the battlefield

Arminius, it is believed, was the son of a chief named Sigimirus who led the Cherusci tribe. Born in either 18 or 17 BCE in Magna Germania (Greater Germany), Arminius was eventually seized as a hostage by the Romans. In an effort to ensure the compliance of his father, Arminius was removed from Germania and sent to live in the city of Rome. There, Arminius was far enough removed from his father to effectively ensure that his father – and, therefore, the Cherusci tribe – would remain loyal and continue to live up to their obligations to Rome.

While in Rome, Arminius was sent to live with a Roman family of some aristocratic rank, and under the guidance of that family, Arminius was trained in the Roman art of war. He was given a thorough military education by the finest strategic and tactical minds of the ancient times. In addition to his military training to command Roman legionaries in the future, Arminius was granted Roman citizenship, a coveted position in the ancient world, especially by those who were under the control of the Roman Empire. By the time Arminius was ready to lead troops as a commander in a Roman legion, he had achieved the social rank of "equestrian," which meant that he was essentially a petty noble in Roman society.

An ancient bust believed to depict Arminius

Thus, it was with some sense of security that the Roman government sent Arminius out to the Balkan Peninsula in the year 4 CE. There, on the Balkan Peninsula, Arminius was given command of an auxiliary detachment made up of Cheruscan troops, members of his own tribe. Once on the Balkan Peninsula Arminius commanded his troops and led them in the Pannonian Wars, a series of conflicts fought between the Roman Empire and some of the Illyrian tribes from 6-9 CE. Arminius led his troops against the Illyrian warriors for over a year at least before he was sent to Germania in either 7 or 8 CE in order to assist the governor of the province with controlling the rebellious elements of the Germanic tribes. By the time Arminius returned, the Roman Empire had secured large swaths of Germanic territory, thus establishing a strong position for themselves from which the Roman legions could launch military expeditions in order to continuously expand Roman territory.

It was at this time that Arminius first came into contact with the governor of the Roman controlled territory, Publius Quinctilius Varus. With the knowledge that the Roman Empire would seek to continue its expansion within the province of Germania, and thus to completely control the Germanic territories, Arminius made the decision to return fully to his Germanic roots by beginning to plot against Rome. Undoubtedly, Arminius must have believed that given his knowledge of military strategy and tactics, he would be the one most likely to step into the political vacuum created by the hoped for the expulsion of the Romans from Germania. The Germanic tribes followed leaders who had proven themselves through the strength of arms and valor in combat, and Arminius was well known for both, so should he succeed in leading a revolt against the Roman Empire, he would be the most suitable of all for the ultimate position of authority, the first among the warrior peers of the Germanic tribes.

While many of the ancient authors and historians have labeled Arminius as a traitor to Rome, this should not be viewed as a true statement. The fact Arminius was raised and educated in Rome after he was taken as a hostage from his family and his culture hardly made him a Roman. At the same time, the fact Arminius was considered to be a member of the Roman nobility did not mean that he viewed himself as Roman, or that he felt beholden to them for the education, training, and citizenship which he received. It is more than likely that Arminius harbored a deep resentment towards the Roman Empire, and that he sought to make the best of a bad situation when he was a hostage. Perhaps he raised up a rebellion against Rome in the hopes of exacting some sort of vengeance against the Roman Empire for its domination of Germania, or perhaps he simply sought power.

Regardless of his reasons, Arminius started to plot against Rome shortly after his arrival in Germania. He sought out members of the other Germanic tribes and attempted to create an alliance between the various tribes. The Germanic people at this point in history were divided into nearly fifty separate tribal groups at that time, and Arminius succeeded in unifying five of them. These five tribes, and his own tribe the Cherusci as well would form the nucleus of the rebellion. While individual warriors from other tribal groups would join the effort, the small alliance Arminius had managed to forge would be the central players in the attack against the Roman military elements which were stationed in the Germanic territory.

Before the Ambush

"The Romans were holding portions of it - not entire regions, but merely such districts as happened to have been subdued, so that no record has been made of the fact- and soldiers of theirs were wintering there and cities were being founded. The barbarians were adapting themselves to Roman ways, were becoming accustomed to hold markets, and were meeting in peaceful assemblages. They had not, however, forgotten their ancestral habits, their native manners, their old life of independence, or the power derived from arms." – Cassius Dio

In the fall of 9 CE, once Arminius had gathered his forces and planned an ambush to destroy the Roman forces in Germania, he brought news to Varus that a small revolt was taking place in the north of Roman held Germania. Cassius Dio explained the background that led up to Arminius's message to Varus: "[W]hen Quinctilius Varus became governor of the province of Germania, and in the discharge of his official duties was administering the affairs of these peoples also, he strove to change them more rapidly. Besides issuing orders to them as if they were actually slaves of the Romans, he exacted money as he would from subject nations. To this they were in no mood to submit, for the leaders longed for their former ascendancy and the masses preferred their accustomed condition to foreign domination. Now they did not openly revolt, since they saw that there were many Roman troops near the Rhine and many within their own borders. Instead, they received Varus, pretending that they would do all he demanded of them, and thus they drew him far away from the Rhine into the land of the Cherusci, toward the Visurgis, and there by behaving in a most peaceful and friendly manner led him to believe that they would live submissively without the presence of soldiers. Consequently he did not keep his legions together, as was proper in a hostile country, but distributed many of the soldiers to helpless communities, which asked for them for the alleged purpose of guarding various points, arresting robbers, or escorting provision trains. Among those deepest in the conspiracy and leaders of the plot and of the war were Arminius and Segimer, who were his constant companions and often shared his mess. He accordingly became confident, and expecting no harm, not only refused to believe all those who suspected what was going on and advised him to be on his guard, but actually rebuked them for being needlessly excited and slandering his friends."

Given his actions and the time he spent with the young German, it made sense that Varus listened to Arminius and trusted him. After all, not only was Arminius a commander of Varus' own auxiliary troops, he was also a Roman citizen. Moreover, in addition to his military stature and his citizenship, Arminius was German, so Varus could rely on the fact Arminius knew the people and thus what would be best for keeping discipline.

In the few years that Varus and Arminius had known one another, Varus had come to trust and to rely upon the young man. Varus also believed Arminius was not only sympathetic to the Roman cause in Germania, but that Arminius identified more as a Roman – due to his upbringing, noble status and his citizenship – rather than the barbarians who had birthed and raised him prior to his being taken as a hostage.

Varus, therefore, had no reason to distrust any information which Arminius brought to him regarding a revolt in the north, nor did Varus have any reason to suspect Arminius of preparing to betray Rome, or of planning an attack upon the Roman legions under Varus' command.

Of course, Varus' faith and trust in young Arminius would prove to be a fatal mistake, and it would mark the beginning of what many historians have labeled the Roman military's greatest defeat. Paterculus summed this up in the course of a rather glowing description of Arminius: "Thereupon appeared a young man of noble birth, brave in action and alert in mind, possessing an intelligence quite beyond the ordinary barbarian; he was, namely, Arminius, the son of Segimer, a prince of that nation, and he showed in his countenance and in his eyes the fire of the mind within. He had been associated with us constantly on private campaigns, and had even attained the dignity of equestrian rank. This young man made use of the negligence of the general as an opportunity for treachery, sagaciously seeing that no one could be more quickly overpowered than the man who feared nothing, and that the most common beginning of disaster was a sense of security."

Moreover, Varus was warned about the possibility that Arminius was being treacherous. A German named Segestes, a high standing member of Arminius' own tribe, warned Varus that Arminius and his men were treacherous and were planning to commit some sort of offense against Rome. Segestes told Varus that he should not trust Arminius and that he should be on his guard at all times. In the end, Varus did not heed Segestes' advice, probably dismissing it as a petty intratribal rivalry brought on by Segestes' baser desires and instincts. Segestes, however, was a German who was loyal to the Roman government, and his warnings were given in an effort to maintain the status quo.

Since Varus trusted Arminius and thus trusted the information that Arminius brought to him at face value, Varus also listened to the young man's military advice regarding the rebellious Germans. Arminius was, after all, a decorated soldier, so Varus accepted the man's advice when he suggested that all three of the legions under his command should participate in the show of force that Varus intended to make. Such a large force, accompanied by Germanic auxiliaries, might certainly bring the rambunctious and disobedient northern tribe to heel. Furthermore, since Varus was preparing to march his legions to their winter quarters, and since he believed that a show of force would be enough to silence the budding revolt, Varus gave permission for the camp followers to march along with the legions rather than having the camp followers wait until the short campaign had ended. These camp followers consisted of the legionaries' families, as well as the numerous hangers-on that tended to cling to the fringes of every military encampment.

Fully convinced that his legions were in no real danger from the Germans, Varus kept his legions in a long column formation (which also consisted of the camp followers) as he marched towards the north. Believing that the only danger lay ahead to the north, Varus did not even bother with scouts or flankers along the column as it prepared to enter the Teutoburg Forest. Arminius, who had been riding at the fore of the column with his auxiliary troops, rode back to the center to suggest to Varus that he should ride ahead to scout the way. It is said that he offered to make sure that the road was safe, and that he would see if there were any loyal Germans in the area who might be able to assist the Roman legions against the northern tribe.

Varus readily agreed and was given permission to take the whole of his cavalry auxiliary and scout forward.

Thus it was that Varus marched his ill-prepared and unsuspecting legions into an ambush laid within the Teutoburg Forest.

The Teutoburg Forest and the Opposing Forces

"The mountains had an uneven surface broken by ravines, and the trees grew close together and very high. Hence the Romans, even before the enemy assailed them, were having a hard time of it felling trees, building roads, and bridging places that required it. They had with them many wagons and many beasts of burden as in time of peace; moreover, not a few women and children and a large retinue of servants were following them - one more reason for their advancing in scattered groups. Meanwhile a violent rain and wind came up that separated them still further, while the ground, that had become slippery around the roots and logs, made walking very treacherous for them, and the tops of the trees kept breaking off and falling down, causing much confusion." – Cassius Dio

To understand any battle completely, it is necessary to be familiar with the environment and terrain, and this is especially true of the Battle of the Teutoburg Forest, for Arminius' excellent use of the terrain was a large contributor to the horrendous defeat the Romans suffered.

In order for Varus' legions to reach the area where the theoretical revolt was taking place, he had to march them through the Teutoburg Forest. The forest covers nearly 1,622 square miles and is primarily made up of low, forested hills. Today the Teutoburg Forest (in German it can be found on maps under the name Teutoburger Wald) is split roughly into two separate national parks. The forest is also in two separate German states, that of North Rhine-Westphalia and Lower Saxony.

The forest is primarily a deciduous forest, meaning that it has four distinct seasons including a changing of the leaves. Indeed, the forest is much the same as it was when the battle took place between the Germanic tribes under the command of Arminius and the Roman legions under the command of Varus, thick with ancient trees and heavy ground foliage. In addition to the heavy terrain, there are two primary ridges which run through the forest: the northeastern and the southwestern ridges. There are also long valleys which run between these two ridges, and many of the valleys have exits which break the continuity of the ridges.

Altogether the terrain of the Teutoburg Forest was as much an enemy to the Roman legionaries as it was an ally to the Germanic warriors. Arminius would use the terrain, and adapt it where necessary, to achieve his goal of destroying the three Roman legions marching their way northward.

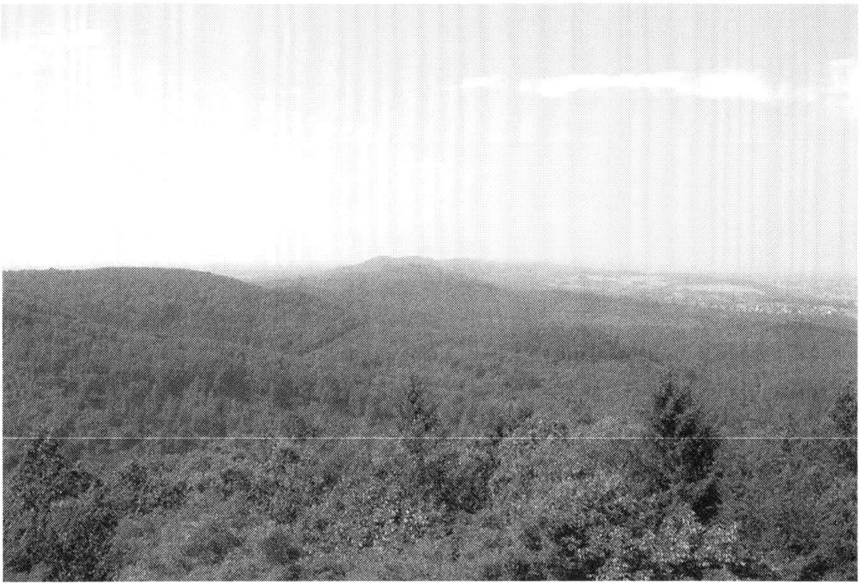

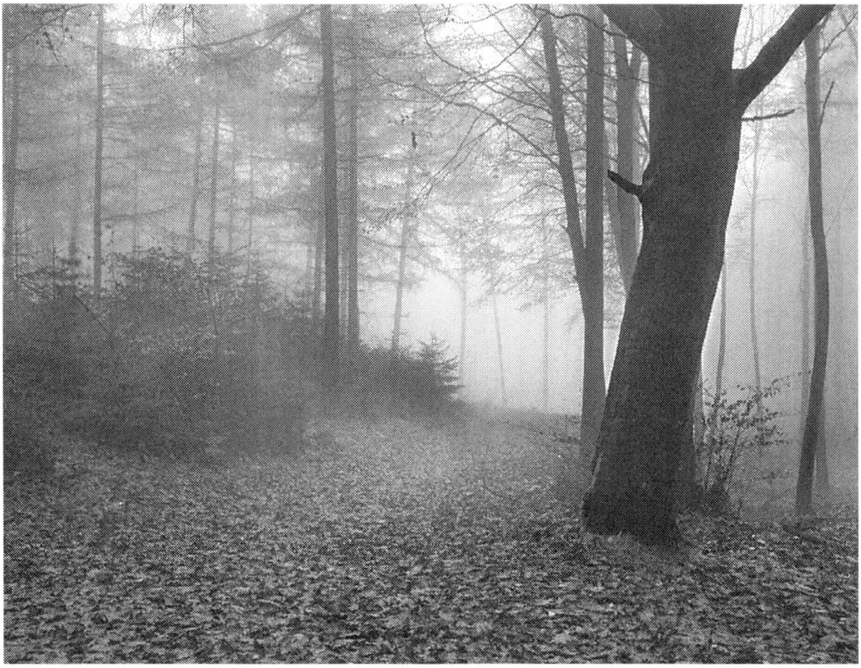

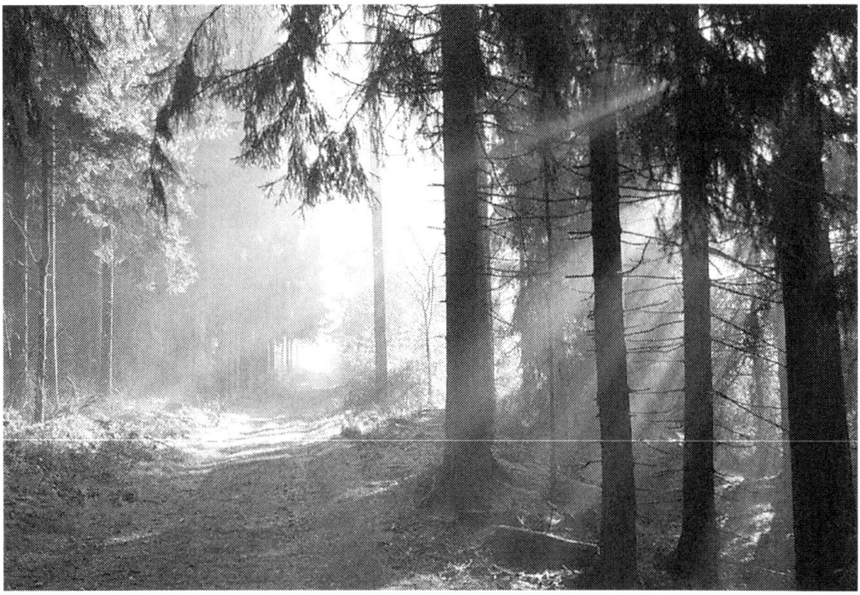

Pictures of the Teutoburg Forest

The Germanic Tribes

When the time came to convince Varus that there was a revolt that needed quelling, Arminius had convinced five of an estimated 50 Germanic tribes to form an alliance. These five tribes – the Chatti, the Marsi, the Sugambri, the Bructeri, and the Chauci – joined with the Cherusci to ready themselves for a battle. With the military assets of these five tribes joined together, Arminius began to prepare an ambush for the well trained and feared Roman legions.

Caesar's writings on his Gallic Wars included the names of some of the most noteworthy tribes. Arminius' own tribe, the Cherusci, was one of the most powerful in Germania, and Arminius himself was considered to be a prince amongst them. More important than his family's social standing in Germanic society, however, was Arminius' prowess as a warrior. In addition to his combat skills and his royal status amongst his own tribe, Arminius was also a charismatic leader and a man who had led his men to victory in battle.

Since Rome's invasion of the Germanic territories decades earlier, many of the Germanic tribes had put up a fierce resistance to Roman rule. While there were certainly elements of the German hierarchy that wished to be absorbed into the Roman Empire – either through an acceptance of what they believed to be Rome's invincibility upon the field of battle, or because they sought to obtain the promised benefits of being a full citizen of Rome – there were still thousands of Germanic warriors who wished to be free of the yoke of Roman control.

These warriors were both familiar and also proficient with Roman weapons, and the reason for their familiarity and skill with these weapons was a simple one: many of them had served (or were currently serving) in the Roman military as auxiliary troops. Their service with the Roman legions made these men familiar not only with Roman weaponry but also Roman infantry and cavalry tactics as well. Arminius would have been extremely adept at employing his countrymen against the Roman legions. For Arminius and his troops, there would be no surprises in regard to the tactics, weapons or skills that the Roman legionaries could bring to the field of battle.

One of the reasons Varus may have been lulled into a false sense of security was the size of this force. He had three legions and corresponding auxiliary forces, giving him a force of nearly 20,000 troops. Varus assumed that it would take a significantly larger number of Germanic warriors to defeat his legions in open combat, and he also knew there would be no easy way for a Germanic force of such size to be gathered due to the village and town structure of Germanic society. Most Germans lived in villages which usually numbered no more than 20-30 families, of which only a portion of the men would be available for military service. Considering the fact that the Germans lived in such small communities, which were usually separated by an average of half a mile, gathering a significant number of Germanic warriors for any large-scale military exercise would have been incredibly difficult, or so Varus believed. Varus also believed, as did most Romans, that the Germanic tribes were men in appearance only; put simply, the Romans did not think the Germans had any sort of society or culture worthy of comparison to a civilized society like their own.

This elitist and the ethnocentric view did not allow for the Romans to see the Germans as a people, nor did it allow for the Romans to believe that there was any sort of real or regular communications between the villages or – more importantly – between the tribes. This, however, was a far cry from the truth. The Germanic villages and various communities kept up regular trade and interacted with one another on a regular basis. There was intermarriage between the communities, and various craftsmen in different villages would often have customers that came from long distances to purchase their wares. While the Romans often ridiculed the Germanic people for lacking what the Romans considered to be basic necessities, such as paved roads, it did not mean that the Germans did not have roads connecting the communities together. The roads were simply unsophisticated in comparison.

As it would turn out, these Germanic roads and communications were put to excellent use by Arminius and his men when they were planning for the ambush. For Arminius, there was no need to rush while setting things into motion. By understanding that time was neither for nor against him, Arminius used the connections between the Germanic communities to seek out allies. These allies were not simply entire tribes, but individual warriors who would join him in his cause, or villages of unallied tribes who were sympathetic to the cause as well. As he gathered these like-minded warriors to him, Arminius and his men began the long process of ensuring that the army he was building would be prepared for war.

While a great many of the Germanic warriors would come to the battle fully armed, Arminius knew full well that there would be others who would need some – if not all – of the accouterments of war. By using the same roads he had traveled to gain allies, Arminius started the process of preparing the men for war. Weapons production was increased amongst the blacksmiths in loyal villages so that all of the warriors who joined would be fully armed. This process of readying the men for war would be long, and it would require patience as the Germanic settlements were spread out and small, especially in the north where Arminius needed to spread the word in order to gather as many warriors as possible.

When Arminius' troops were gathered and prepared for the battle, Arminius knew that his troops would have several distinct advantages over their Roman foes. The first of these would be the familiarity that most of his men would have with both Roman tactics and Roman weapons. The second advantage would be their own armor and weaponry. The Germanic warriors would be wearing light armor and wielding several different types of weapons, and these weapons, ranging from short swords to spears, could be used more effectively in the close confines of the Teutoburg Forest, unlike the weapons and armor of the Roman legionaries. Finally, and most importantly, the Germanic warriors would be employing infantry and cavalry tactics designed and perfected for the environment in which they lived.

Many Roman historians of the time proclaimed the inferiority of the Germanic warriors. Roman legion commanders, however, expressed their frustrations with their inability to crush the Germanic tribes and to bring the German warriors to open battle. The Germanic troops were known for lightning fast attacks and then withdrawing in what the Roman commanders viewed as complete disarray. The Romans, used to massive set battles, bitterly complained about the Germans refusing to engage them in battle in a way in which they were familiar. Of course, the Romans would hardly be the first or last great empire whose military struggled to deal with such guerrilla tactics.

While the Germanic tribes were ridiculed for their particular method of warfare, the tactics they employed were undeniably successful. As Roman legionaries attempted to defend themselves from German attacks, they would invariably open themselves up to individual attacks that could separate a legionary from his group, leaving him open to attack from multiple sides. When the Roman forces would attempt to press an attack against assaulting Germanic troops, the German attack would stop and the warriors would slip away. These tactics – while they were unable to stem the tide of Roman conquest in Germania – would prove to be devastating against Varus' legions on their march through the Teutoburg Forest.

The Roman Legions

Varus has long been either vilified as wildly incompetent or painted as a noble sacrifice to the equally noble goals of Roman expansion and imperialism, but of course, he was neither one of those completely. Some historians, especially those who were his contemporaries, attempted to present to their readers an image of Varus as an incompetent governor, a man who never should have been given the reins in such a troubled province as Germania. These historians believed that a stronger man of better family and character should have been handed the task, for someone as weak-willed and from such a poor familial background as Varus was obviously a poor choice regardless of his ties to the Emperor. Other historians have stated that the sole reason that Varus was even presented with the opportunities to rule in the name of Rome was because of his familial bond and political connections to the Emperor. These detractors ignored his previously successful positions in other fairly wild provinces, and they ignored his basic political savvy and skills as well.

That said, when Varus was placed in control of the province of Germania, he was woefully unprepared for the political, social and cultural situation in which he found himself. Germania was unlike any of the other provinces in the Roman Empire, and the Germanic peoples were, after all, less than human in the eyes of the Roman populace. Most of the Germans were barely fit to be slaves let alone be allowed to attempt to achieve the status of a Roman citizen. An exceptionally small amount of the German people, including men such as Arminius, who had been raised in Rome, could honestly be considered civilized and worthy of the status.

In addition to his trust in Arminius, and thus the men whose respect and loyalty which Arminius commanded, Varus had confidence in his righteousness through the strength of the Roman Empire's legions. In Germania, Varus had command of three full legions, the Seventeenth, the Eighteenth and the Nineteenth legions. Along with these three legions, Varus also had a large number of supporting auxiliary troops raised up from the local Germanic tribes. The total troop strength which was afforded to Varus at that time was estimated to be at almost 20,000 men, and these three legions were highly trained, well-disciplined and extremely motivated soldiers. The basic Roman legionary enlisted for a minimum of 25 years at this point in the Empire's history, and war was the sole profession of these soldiers. Due to the influence of Augustus, the Roman military at this time became the first military organization loyal completely and utterly to the Empire itself.

The legions that Varus commanded were veteran troops, men who had seen a significant amount of fighting, and these legionaries were fully aware of the capabilities of the Germanic troops on the battlefield. The Roman legionaries of 9 CE were also the recipients of centuries of military experience gathered from some of the most brutal warfare fought in the ancient world.

The Roman legions had been perfecting the art of war, and each successive generation of legionaries was equipped with the finest weapons and equipment available.

One of the key ingredients to this success and perfection was the Roman military's complete willingness to incorporate discovered technologies. If a different weapon, type of armor, or basic equipment or artillery worked better than what they were using, the Romans were not afraid to adopt that piece of military hardware for their own uses. Thus, the Romans marching into the forest were using the finest military equipment in the world, all of which had long since proven effective on the field of battle.

In this battle, however, the legions' training and equipment would be major contributors to the disaster.

Laying the Trap

Otto Albert Koch's painting of German warriors attacking the Romans

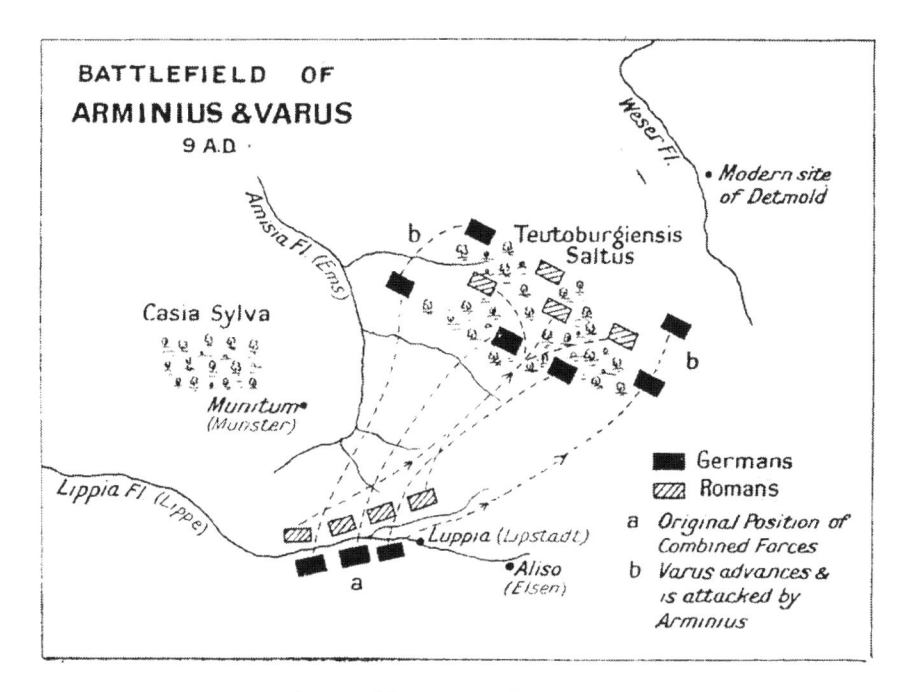

A map of the trap and the ambush

"They escorted him as he set out, and then begged to be excused from further attendance, in order, as they claimed, to assemble their allied forces, after which they would quietly come to his aid. Then they took charge of their troops, which were already in waiting somewhere, and after the men in each community had put to death the detachments of soldiers for which they had previously asked, they came upon Varus in the midst of forests by this time almost impenetrable. And there, at the very moment of revealing themselves as enemies instead of subjects, they wrought great and dire havoc." – Cassius Dio

At the time of the battle of the Teutoburg Forest, the Roman legions represented the pinnacle in military training and technology. Under the leadership of commanders such as Julius Caesar, the legions had decimated populations, torn down cities, and brought down entire countries.

For the Germanic warriors serving under Arminius' command to be successful against the Roman legions, the technological advantages the Romans enjoyed needed to be neutralized. In order to do that, Arminius and his officers needed to be the ones who would choose the place of the battle, and they needed the element of surprise as well since the Roman legions were historically known to not perform well when attacked suddenly and without warning. The battlefield which Arminius choose would, in turn, need to negate the various strengths of the Roman legionaries.

By negating these strengths, the Germanic warriors would be able to maximize their own particular strengths and skills. Arminius knew that the Roman legions were nearly invincible upon the open battlefield, due not only to their superior weapons and technology but also because of the discipline and training of the Roman legionaries. These men were trained to fight together in small to large units with plenty of space around them to maneuver. In addition to this, the discipline which the Roman legions exacted for even the smallest of infractions was frightening. Desertion or even poor performance in a battle could result in what was known as a decimation. In a decimation, one man out of every 10 in a unit was randomly selected and executed by his comrades. The shamed legions were then forced to camp outside of the protective encampment of the rest of the legions until they redeemed themselves in battle. This type of discipline ensured the best performance from the legionaries, as to do anything else might be akin to a death sentence.

With his intimate knowledge of Roman training, tactics, strategies and basic discipline, Arminius knew that he needed to choose a place that would confine the Romans in such a way as to negate their ability to form into even the smallest of units. With this aspect of their tactics taken away, the Roman legionaries would be helpless due to the fact that they were heavy infantry, carrying an average of 70 pounds of equipment, armor, and weapons. Thus burdened, they would be unable to match the Germanic light infantry. Arminius also knew that his Germanic tribesmen were not only equal in bravery to the Roman legionaries but that the Germanic troops were exceptionally skilled in light infantry tactics and fighting. The light armor that the Germans wore, and their confidence in their own ability to attack either singly or in small groups was also a significant factor. And of course, many of the Germanic warriors had hunted and fought for years in the dense, thick confines of the Teutoburg Forest.

Thus, it was in the Teutoburg Forest that Arminius and his commanders chose a stretch of narrow passage running between what was known as the Great Bog and Kalkriese Hill. This narrow passage was used on a regular basis for Germans traveling through the village. While this particular stretch of road was an acceptable way to travel for small groups of people, it was not a wise choice for large groups, and it was an especially difficult passageway for the size of Varus' command. Arminius and his men selected this stretch of passageway between the Great Bog and Kalkriese Hill because of the difficulties which it would naturally produce for the Roman legions, their auxiliaries, their baggage, and their camp followers to try and navigate. In addition to the natural obstacles presented by the passageway and the forest, Arminius and his men constructed their own impediments meant to slow down and to trap the approaching legions.

Some historians believe that the primary obstacle which the Germans constructed was a wall which ran along one side of the passageway the Roman legions were traveling. This wall was estimated to have been nearly a mile in length, the base of it consisting of sod that had been cut out of the passageway itself. The removal of the sod was done in order to narrow the width of the passageway, slimming the distance down to a mere fifteen feet from the base of Kalkriese Hill to the Great Bog. This width ran the entire length of the one-mile wall, essentially creating a massive chokepoint for the Roman legions. Here at this wall, where the passageway curved to the west to follow the natural curve of Kalkriese Hill, was where Arminius chose to launch his ambush against Varus' column.

The wall which was constructed is believed to have had a base of some 15 feet. Successive levels of sod and turf were placed upon the 15 foot wide base, with each level a little narrower than its predecessor, and this continued until the wall reached a height of roughly 5 feet. With the completion of the wall, the Germanic warriors hid it by cutting branches and brush and placing it in thick levels in front of the wall. This presented the illusion of a natural barrier, one that also would afford the Germanic warriors a protected place to launch their initial missile attacks as the Romans marched past.

A picture of reconstructed fortifications in the Teutoburg Forest to approximate the Germanic tribes' wall

On the opposite side of the passageway, running parallel to that wall and Kalkriese Hill, was the Great Bog. The part directly across the wall was also known as the Kalkriese Depression, an area thick with water, sinkholes and a wide array of natural obstacles that would prevent any massive exodus from the roadside by the Roman legions when the ambush was launched. The Kalkriese Depression would ensure that the Roman legionaries remained pinned to the road while they marched. With the trap sprung, the Romans would remain on the road not only due to the Kalkriese Depression but also because they would have had the fear of decimation or some other form of punishment in their minds should they fail to acquit themselves admirably in battle.

This wall constructed by Arminius' troops would prove to be a significant factor in the ambush. The Germans, having built the wall and hidden it, also ensured that the Romans would march along it by destroying a second passageway that traveled farther up to the north around the Great Bog before turning west. The Germans achieved this by digging out a section of the passageway from where it deviated from the main path. The removed section quickly flooded, and an additional pile of brush in front of the second passageway hid it from the Romans. When the Romans came marching along the passageway and it branched off to the left, they had no choice but to follow it since it looked as though there was no second passageway which they could follow. Thus, Arminius ensured the Roman legions would have no choice but to march into the trap.

Varus, as befitting a Roman governor, was marching with his legions through the Teutoburg Forest. While the Romans would have been familiar with certain sections of the massive forest due primarily to previous campaigns and traveling from winter to summer quarters and vice versa, the section the legions were traveling through to quell the revolt in the north were new to them. It is estimated that due to the size of Varus' column, it ran for perhaps two and a quarter miles in length.

During the early part of the first century CE, the Roman legions marched in a specific order designed to optimize the legions performance and ability while marching and preparing – at the end of the march – to construct their base camp for the evening. This specific order dictated that auxiliaries brought up the rear of the column while Roman and auxiliary cavalry were at the front. Between these two sections of auxiliaries marched the Seventeenth, Eighteenth and Nineteenth legions. Each legion's baggage train, artillery and camp followers would have been attached to it as well for the march. Varus, in turn, would have ridden in the column's center accompanied by his commanders, specifically the generals of each legion and possibly additional legates who controlled various sections of each legion.

The normal Roman marching order also called for an average front of nine men across for the column. This frontage would adapt to the terrain and the width of the road upon which the column was traveling, but due to the narrowness of the passageway in the Teutoburg Forest, the frontage dropped to six men according to some of the Roman survivors of the ambush. Then, when the column reached the section of the passageway that ran parallel to the wall which Arminius' troops had built, it is believed that the frontage was narrowed down once more to a mere four men. The incredibly small frontage would have been disconcerting to the Roman legionaries since they knew they were marching through unfamiliar territory and that the Germanic troops were known to launch small surprise attacks on Roman units regardless of size or strength. Though Varus believed that the area through which they traveled was peaceful and that it had been successfully pacified, many of his legionaries were well aware that the Germans didn't care if an area was pacified or not; the Germanic warriors would attack anywhere at any time they wished.

Varus, however, did not share the same worries and fears of his legionaries. He was concerned only the revolt which Arminius had told him of. When Arminius assured Varus that the way ahead was most certainly clear, and that he would take the auxiliary cavalry forward to see if there were any other members of the Cherusci tribe that might choose to accompany the Roman column. It was Varus' hope that Arminius would indeed find additional Germanic warriors to add to the auxiliaries, Germans who would be willing to assist in the quelling of the revolt in the north. Arminius was sent forward, then, with Varus' blessings and hope to scout out the passageway ahead as it would travel around the base of Kalkriese Hill. For Varus, more German troops would lend weight and credibility to his crushing of the revolt.

Thus believing that Arminius, to whom Varus had given command of the auxiliary forces serving as the column's vanguard, was moving forward to make sure that the way was clear, Varus marched his column into the deadly trap which Arminius had prepared.

The Battle

"While the Romans were in such difficulties, the barbarians suddenly surrounded them on all sides at once, coming through the densest thickets, as they were acquainted with the paths." – Cassius Dio

Stretched out for over two and a quarter miles, the Roman column was open and vulnerable to attack. More important than this, however, the Roman legions would be completely unable to assist one another should they be attacked upon the road, and along with this inability to supply one another with mutual support, the Romans would be unable to bring their heavy weapons to bear against any Germanic troops who might choose to attack the column. Catapults and carroballista (large, dart throwing weapons operated by anywhere from two to five men depending upon the weapon's size) would be rendered completely ineffective, much like the open field heavy infantry tactics that the Roman legions had mastered.

At the point the Romans were actually ambushed, there remain only fragments of ancient history and speculation as to what actually occurred in the Teutoburg Forest. Some modern historians believe that the initial attack made by the Germanic troops against the Roman column occurred at the rear of the column. These particular ones assert that not only would this have been the best of all tactical decisions, but that it was also the only practical choice to be made by

Arminius and his commanders. Adherents of this theory state that a large number of Germanic troops, probably hidden in the dense woods, lashed out in a lightning attack at the unprotected rear of the last legionaries in the column.

If so, this attack would have forced the Roman legionaries to come to an immediate halt and attempt to form up in a defensive maneuver that would allow them to turn around and repel the attack while preparing to launch a counterattack of their own. These historians also believe that the decision to attack the rear of the column would have forced the entire legion which was attacked to come to a complete halt in order to support the elements attacked. The news of the attack would have been instantly sent along to Varus and the commanders, and from there it would have been forwarded to the head of the column. As a result, the entire column would have been thrown into disarray as the Romans prepared to meet whatever was happening head on.

The three legions would have been forced to come to a stop, and once stopped, each legion would then have tried to fall into formations that would allow them to protect themselves go on the offensive. In addition to this, the standard procedure for each Roman legion required the legionaries to leave a detachment of troops with the baggage train. In this particular case, with all of the camp followers marching along with Varus' column, an even larger detachment of legionaries would have been required to guard the baggage train and civilians. This additional loss of fighting men would eventually prove to be significant in the face of a large group of Germanic warriors attacking a stationary column.

When the legionaries at the end of the column had finally managed to stave off the attackers long enough to launch their own counterattack, the theory is that the Germanic warriors would have broken off the engagement. These Germanic warriors, lightly armed and armored and equipped with a familiarity and fearlessness regarding the Teutoburg Forest, would have slipped away from the battle and into the protective cover of the forest.

There is a second theory that is based heavily upon anthropological and archeological information, as well as what little information was passed on by the ancient historians. This second theory posits that the Germanic attack would not have taken place until a large portion of the Roman column was marching abreast of the wall which Arminius had his men build.

According to this theory, Arminius and his auxiliary troops would have raced forward to the wall to inform their Germanic brethren of the approaching Roman column. Arminius had managed to gather an estimated 18,000, all of whom would have been stationed in four key areas around the ambush site. The first group of Germanic warriors, consisting of an estimated 7,000 troops, were believed to have been placed on the eastern side of Kalkriese Hill, just before the start of the wall. The road used by the Roman column followed the hill, curving up and around to the left, back towards the west. Slightly past the curve of the hill – where the Germans had hidden the access to the second passageway that curved up and around the Great Bog – the wall which Arminius' troops had built began. Here the road narrowed considerably so that the legionaries on the left and right of the road found themselves marching forward through a mixture of mud and water, constantly slipping off of the sides of the road.

At the wall itself, an estimated 5,000 German warriors waited in hiding. According to the archeological evidence that continues to be unearthed, there was a tremendously large group of spear bearing men waiting for the Roman column. Also, at a slight distance from the warriors at the wall, an additional 5,000 Germanic warriors were believed to have been stationed in the woods behind them. This positioning would have allowed the men gathered there to launch spears into the road and then to race down through the woods and over the wall. The shock of the spear attack and the deadly impact of running troops slamming into trapped, stationary troops and engaging in hand to hand combat would have been devastating. That said, other historians believe that while the Germanic warriors in the woods behind the wall could have been there for an attack upon trapped Romans, it was more likely that the positioned Germanic troops were there to lend support in the initial missile attack against the Roman column and to act as a reserve force if necessary.

The final group of Germanic warriors stationed by Arminius and his commanders numbered roughly a thousand men positioned around the Kalkriese Depression. Although lightly armed and spread out, these warriors would be an effective way to keep any panicking members of the Roman column from escaping through the Great Bog.

With the Germanic troops in their basic positions, it has been theorized that the German commanders would have ensured the strength of their lines by dispersing their bravest troops amongst the other warriors. Rather than having veteran and accomplished warriors in one section alone, the commanders would have had them mixed in amongst what were an undoubtedly large number of untried and nervous young men.

That said, the Germanic tribal culture valued valor and ability in combat, and social standing was dictated by a German man's ability to fight. Men who could not perform well upon the field of battle – or who fled – were castigated by their tribes. In order to help ensure the strength of his lines, and also to make sure that the nervous and untried Germanic warriors didn't run at first contact with the greatly feared Roman legionaries, Arminius would have stationed his warriors who had proven their skills and bravery amongst the others.

Arminius had long been a commander of men in battle, so he would have been able to give support to anyone with faltering courage as well. His charismatic nature would have allowed him to calm any that he identified as having difficulty prior to the battle, and the cultural pressure to achieve renown in battle and to be distinguished by strength of arms would have weighed heavily upon the untested members of the ambushing troops. Peer pressure also would have been significant, yet it would also have sustained an individual's courage for a period of time.

The veterans no doubt provided significant help maintaining the courage and calm of the troops. These warriors would be able to tell the younger men what to expect when the fighting started, and prior to the battle, they would remind the young warriors of the basics, including how to hold a shield, how best to throw a spear, and where the armor was weakest on the Roman legionary. They also would have provided an example for the younger men to follow once the battle was engaged.

A German depiction of Arminius attacking Romans

The second group of theorists believe that once Arminius was assured that all of the Germanic forces were in position, he and his auxiliary troops moved farther up around the curve of the road so that they wouldn't be seen by the approaching Roman column. Arminius and his men would then wait until the ambush began before reappearing.

When Varus' troops arrived at the east side of Kalkriese Hill and turned to follow the narrow path around its base, Arminius' commanders held back the initial strike until nearly the entire frontage of the wall was occupied with marching legionaries. Once this was done, the ambush began.

A view of Kalkriese Hill, the suspected site of the ambush

According to the theory proposed by this second group of historians, the ambush started not with an attack upon the rear of the column but with a spear attack from behind the protection of the wall. The hidden Germanic troops would have been able to rise up from behind the wall, which stood only 5 feet high, and throw spears at the Roman legionaries. This initial wave of spears from the Germanic troops nearest to the wall would have been thrown at a nearly horizontal level with full force straight from the shoulder. The Germanic tribes had long since mastered the process of making steel, and the spearheads recovered from the battlefield are excellent examples of their skills. The spears used would have been brutally efficient when thrown by men accustomed to using them.

While the Germanic troops directly against the wall were throwing their spears horizontally, others near them would have served to either pass additional spears to the front rank or would have thrown their own spears at the Roman legionaries. This second set of spears, thrown by the Germanic warriors from farther behind the wall and from behind their own comrades in arms, had to have been thrown in an arc. As the spears reached their apexes and came down, they would have gathered speed and increasingly deadly force as they quickly descended towards the tightly packed Roman troops.

The spear attack would have been brutally efficient when combined with the complete surprise of the attack and the nature of the road that the Roman column was attempting to march upon. With Arminius having narrowed the road down to a slim 15 feet in width, with soft, muddy shoulders on either side due to the Great Bog, the Roman legionaries would have been packed tightly together. The compacted nature of the column would have exponentially increased the effectiveness of the German spear attack. The interior line of Roman troops marching parallel to the wall would have suffered the devastation of the spears being thrown directly at their heads, necks, and faces. The Roman helmet, which was effective at deflecting sword blows launched over the Roman shield, would not have been completely effective against a powerfully thrown spear at point blank range. The spears thrown in an arc would have been effective against exposed arms and legs, and the large, two-foot by four-foot shield that the Roman legionaries carried would have become too heavy or cumbersome to hold should a spear – or multiple spears – become embedded in the wood. On top of all that, the Roman legionaries would have been unable to bring their shields into effective use, such as creating a shield wall or a "tortoise" formation where the shields were interlocked above their heads, due to the fact that they were pressed so tightly together upon the road.

    The Roman legionaries' ability to launch any sort of counterattack, or to conduct any sort of offensive maneuver, would have been negated as well. Due to the confining nature of the road and the way in which the Roman column was marching, the Roman legionaries found themselves completely incapable of responding to the attacking German troops. The Roman legionaries' short sword was useless, as there was no one for the Romans to attack due to the fact that the Germanic troops were using spears. The Roman javelin, the *pilum*, would also have not been brought into play, as there was no way in which the individual legionaries would have had the room to either thrust the pilum at an enemy or to even have enough room to throw them at the Germans. In essence, due to the very nature of their method of warfare, and the military technology with which they were armed and equipped, the Roman legionaries found themselves at the mercy of the Germanic warriors.

    It is at this point in the tale that the two separate theories concerning the ambush converge. What followed next, as the ancient historians readily record, was an absolute massacre. With a large portion of the Roman column trapped along the length of the wall, the rest of the column that was still marching steadily along and unaware of the ambush found themselves pressing their comrades further into the fray. No word was quickly sent back to Varus and his commanders because of the way messages were usually delivered when the Roman legions were in marching order. This method of delivery relied upon members of the cavalry used as dispatch riders, connecting the forward and rear sections of the column to the center, but in the case of the ambush on the road, this method of delivery was all but impossible. The Roman cavalry at the fore of the column could not ride back to the center and warn Varus since there was nowhere for a horse to be ridden, and the road would have been clogged with the dead and the dying. The edge of the road farthest from the wall was a mess of mire and bog, and any cavalryman attempting to leave the fight would have found the going extremely difficult, as well as draw attention to himself. Germanic warriors who had experience serving in the Roman auxiliary forces also would have been looking for a cavalryman attempting to warn the rest of the column and would have been prepared to cut the rider down long before he could get out of the killing zone.

By the time that Varus realized that the column was under attack, it would have been far too late to do anything. Arminius and his auxiliary troops could now come racing down the road to crash headlong into the front of the Roman column, sealing off that potential exit from the Roman legionaries. In turn, the additional 5,000 Germanic troops placed slightly higher up and behind the wall would have flooded the road, seeking to smash whatever resistance might remain among the Roman troops before them. Farther back, along the eastern section of the road before it came to the wall, the other 7,000 Germanic warriors would have attacked, swinging down and to the left. This tactic would have forced the Roman column back onto itself and seal off that section of the road as an escape route. Finally, the Great Bog itself served as a fourth barrier in the killing box which Arminius and his troops had created.

The Roman legionaries fought terrifically against the Germanic troops, but there was little that could be done. Their bravery was no match for the tactical situation in which they found themselves. Some of the Roman legionaries, in spite of the healthy fear they had regarding discipline by their own commanders, attempted to flee from the battle. A few of these men sought refuge within the Great Bog, fighting through the natural obstacles presented within the Kalkriese Depression. Some of them cast away their armor and weapons and reached the other side of the bog and the road to safety only to be stopped by the 1,000 men Arminius had stationed there. These legionaries were butchered where they stood. Back at the road, a few legionaries attempted to race past the Germanic troops and into the doubtful safety of the Teutoburg Forest. Few of these men made it very far, the Germans quickly cutting the legionaries down before the men could make any sort of distance into the forest.

While this small number of legionaries abandoned their comrades and tried to escape, the others continued to fight. Many of these men formed up into small groups in attempt to protect one another from the attacks, but even here the Roman military's heavy infantry training was more of a hindrance than a help. Each legionary had been trained to fight as a unit, but in that unit they were accustomed to having an average of five feet on either side and behind them as they fought. This gave them a tremendous amount of room to employ their shields, swords, daggers and pilum. This generous amount of space, while it could be found on an open battlefield, was absent on the road through the Teutoburg Forest. Naturally, Arminius's in-depth knowledge of the tactics and training of the Roman legionaries took this need of space into account when he was planning both the ambush and the ambush site. It was why he made sure that the road around the Kalkriese Hill and between the Great Bog was cut down to only 15 feet in width.

When the legionaries did manage to maintain enough room to fall back upon their training, they opened themselves up to attack from multiple assailants at once. Germanic warriors could attack an individual Roman legionary in pairs, trios or even quartets. The Roman legionary, exhausted by the sheer effort of attempting to stay alive and more than likely overwhelmed by what he was witnessing on the road around him, would soon find that while he was defending himself from an enemy on his front or on either flank, he could be cut down by a German attacking him from the rear.

As the Germanic warriors swept into the column, Varus and his commanders would have been desperately attempting to form some sort of defense. In addition to this, there would have been the horrific realization that the Roman column's camp followers were being butchered along with the legionaries themselves. The discipline amongst the Roman legionaries would have eroded even further as the men realized that their families were being killed.

Within a short time of the ambush starting, Varus and his commanders likely realized that the situation was beyond salvation, and that defeat would be the inevitable outcome of the attack. With this in mind, Varus and his commanders chose to commit suicide. In addition to the fact that Roman nobility often committed suicide as a result of shame, Varus knew the Germanic warriors had a long history of torturing Roman officers and commanders prior to sacrificing them to the Germanic guards. With such a fate coming ever closer as the Germans pressed in upon the center of the column, Varus and his troops followed acceptable Roman protocol by falling on their swords; Romans who chose to commit suicide in this manner would grasp the sword by its handle and fall upon the point of it.

After Varus had committed suicide, several of his men attempted to hide his body to keep it out of the hands of the Germans, but this proved useless. Varus body was eventually discovered, and Arminius had the man's head removed so that he could send it on to other Germanic tribal leaders in an effort to create an even larger alliance of tribes. Ultimately, Arminius's efforts would fail, as the various tribes fell back into minor skirmishing and warfare with each other shortly after the battle.

Ancient armies and medieval armies often broke and ran upon hearing news of the death of their commander in battle, so news of the suicides of Varus and the commanders likely made it around to the remaining legionaries and destroyed the last shreds of their will to resist. It is believed that at this point, Roman discipline broke completely, and the survivors of the column attempted to fight their way out or flee from the attacking Germans. The Germans, already enjoying superiority on the battlefield due to the surprise and exceptional planning of the ambush, slaughtered almost all of the survivors.

Within an hour, it is estimated that the Germans had killed about 5,000 Roman legionaries, while another 10,000 legionaries were said to have been mortally wounded and left upon the road. At the end of the battle, the Germans made their way through the wounded legionaries and finished them off. Little is known of the fate of the camp followers other than that they suffered the same as the Roman legionaries. A few may have been taken as slaves, but the majority of them would have been put to death on the road. As for the Germanic warriors under Arminius's command, it is believed that only a few hundred of them were killed during the ambush.

A small amount of Roman legionaries were captured by the Germans. Some of the regular legionaries were executed immediately, while others were kept as slaves or sold off as the same. For centurions, tribunes and legates, the officers of the legions, no such kind fate awaited them. In the depths of the Teutoburg Forest, makeshift altars were erected by the Germans and the Roman officers were sacrificed to the Germanic gods for the victory which was given to them over the hated legions of Rome.

Some legionaries did survive the battle by escaping. These men cast away their weapons and their armor and hid during the day. For days, they would hide during daylight and travel slowly at night, carefully making their way to various Roman strongholds. This was primarily how the information regarding the massacre and the fate of the Roman column came to be known back in Rome. By piecing together accounts told by those Roman legionaries who had escaped, and also by accounts told by those legionaries taken as slaves and later rescued from their servitude, the grisly annihilation of Varus' troops became fully known across the Empire.

As a result of information getting back, ancient Roman historians wrote accounts of the battle, and their descriptions give readers a glimpse into just how shocking and horrific the battle was to the Romans. Cassius Dio stressed how total the massacre was in his history:

> "At first they hurled their volleys from a distance; then, as no one defended himself and many were wounded, they approached closer to them. For the Romans were not proceeding in any regular order, but were mixed in helter-skelter with the waggons and the unarmed, and so, being unable to form readily anywhere in a body, and being fewer at every point than their assailants, they suffered greatly and could offer no resistance at all.

> "Accordingly they encamped on the spot, after securing a suitable place, so far as that was possible on a wooded mountain; and afterwards they either burned or abandoned most of their waggons and everything else that was not absolutely necessary to them.

> "The next day they advanced in a little better order, and even reached open country, though they did not get off without loss. Upon setting out from there they plunged into the woods again, where they defended themselves against their assailants, but suffered their heaviest losses while doing so. For since they had to form their lines in a narrow space, in order that the cavalry and infantry together might run down the enemy, they collided frequently with one another and with the trees.

"They were still advancing when the fourth day dawned, and again a heavy downpour and violent wind assailed them, preventing them from going forward and even from standing securely, and moreover depriving them of the use of their weapons. For they could not handle their bows or their javelins with any success, nor, for that matter, their shields, which were thoroughly soaked. Their opponents, on the other hand, being for the most part lightly equipped, and able to approach and retire freely, suffered less from the storm. Furthermore, the enemy's forces had greatly increased, as many of those who had at first wavered joined them, largely in the hope of plunder, and thus they could more easily encircle and strike down the Romans, whose ranks were now thinned, many having perished in the earlier fighting.

"Varus, therefore, and all the more prominent officers, fearing that they should either be captured alive or be killed by their bitterest foes (for they had already been wounded), made bold to do a thing that was terrible yet unavoidable: they took their own lives.

"When news of this had spread, none of the rest, even if he had any strength left, defended himself any longer. Some imitated their leader, and others, casting aside their arms, allowed anybody who pleased to slay them; for to flee was impossible, however much one might desire to do so. Every man, therefore, and every horse was cut down without fear of resistance."

Paterculus focused on the actions of some of the Roman leaders: "The general had more courage to die than to fight, for, following the example of his father and grandfather, he ran himself through with his sword. Of the two prefects of the camp, Lucius Eggius furnished a precedent as noble as that of Ceionius was base, who, after the greater part of the army had perished, proposed its surrender, preferring to die by torture at the hands of the enemy than in battle. Vala Numonius, lieutenant of Varus, who, in the rest of his life, had been an inoffensive and an honorable man, also set a fearful example in that he left the infantry unprotected by the cavalry and in flight tried to reach the Rhine with his squadrons of horse. But fortune avenged his act, for he did not survive those whom he had abandoned, but died in the act of deserting them. The body of Varus, partially burned, was mangled by the enemy in their barbarity; his head was cut off and taken to Maroboduusnote and was sent by him to Caesar; but in spite of the disaster it was honored by burial in the tomb of his family."

The historian Florus described some of the barbaric actions supposedly conducted by the Germans: "Meanwhile Varus was so confident of peace that he was quite unperturbed even when the conspiracy was betrayed to him by Segestes, one of the chiefs. And so when he was unprepared and had no fear of any such thing, at a moment when (such was his confidence) he was actually summoning them to appear before his tribunal, they rose and attacked him from all sides. His camp was seized, and three legions were overwhelmed. Varus met disaster by the same fate and with the same courage as Paulus on the fatal day of Cannae. Never was there slaughter more cruel than took place there in the marshes and woods, never were more intolerable insults inflicted by barbarians, especially those directed against the legal pleaders. They put out the eyes of some of them and cut off the hands of others; they sewed up the mouth of one of them after first cutting out his tongue, exclaiming, 'At last, you viper, you have ceased to hiss.' The body too of the consul himself, which the dutiful affection of the soldiers had buried, was disinterred. As for the standards and eagles, the barbarians possess two to this day; the third eagle was wrenched from its pole, before it could fall into the hands of the enemy, by the standard-bearer, who, carrying it concealed in the folds round his belt, secreted himself in the blood-stained marsh. The result of this disaster was that the empire, which had not stopped on the shores of the Ocean, was checked on the banks of the Rhine."

The Aftermath

The news of the disaster was quickly sent on to Rome, which reeled at the news. There had been military disasters in Rome's past, of course, but there was nothing which could compare to the complete destruction of the legions under Varus' command. Suetonius described Augustus' reaction to the news: "He suffered but two severe and ignominious defeats, those of Lollius and Varus, both of which were in Germany. Of these the former was more humiliating than serious, but the latter was almost fatal, since three legions were cut to pieces with their general, his lieutenants, and all the auxiliaries. When the news of this came, he ordered that watch be kept by night throughout the city, to prevent outbreak, and prolonged the terms of the governors of the provinces, that the allies might be held to their allegiance by experienced men with whom they were acquainted. He also vowed great games to Jupiter Optimus Maximus, in case the condition of the commonwealth should improve, a thing which had been done in the Cimbric and Marsic wars. In fact, they say that he was so greatly affected that for several months in succession he cut neither his beard nor his hair, and sometimes he would dash his head against a door, crying: 'Quintilius Varus, give me back my legions!' And he observed the day of the disaster each year as one of sorrow and mourning. He made many changes and innovations in the army, besides reviving some usages of former times. He exacted the strictest discipline. It was with great reluctance that he allowed even his generals to visit their wives, and then only in the winter season. He sold a Roman knight and his property at public auction, because he had cut off the thumbs of two young sons, to make them unfit for military service; but when he saw that some tax-gatherers were intent upon buying him, he knocked him down to a freedman° of his own, with the understanding that he should be banished to the country districts, but allowed to live in freedom. He dismissed the entire tenth legion in disgrace, because they were insubordinate, and others, too, that demanded their discharge in an insolent fashion, he disbanded without the rewards which would have been due for faithful service. If any cohorts gave way in battle, he decimated them, and fed the rest on barley. When centurions left their posts, he punished them with death, just as he did the rank and file; for faults of other kinds he imposed various ignominious penalties, such as ordering to stand all day long before the general's tent, sometimes in their tunics without their sword-belts, or again holding ten-foot poles or even a clod of earth."

Ancient statue of Augustus

Eventually, the Roman government would recover from their shock at the loss and the betrayal of Arminius, and legions would be sent into Germania to exact revenge. These legions also included some of the legionaries who had managed to escape the ambush and survive the treacherous paths which had led them to the safety of their own kind. With these legionaries as guides, the legions sent into Germania to punish the Germans followed the fateful trail of Varus' column through the Teutoburg Forest and to the site of the ambush. There, upon the road, the legions found the remains of Varus' columns. The skeletons of horses, mules and men lay scattered upon the road, and for years afterward it was said by the legionaries who passed along the road around Kalkriese Hill that the skulls of Roman legionaries could still be found nailed to the great trees of the Teutoburg Forest. Explorations into the woods found the remains of the altars erected to the Germanic gods, as well as the remains of those Roman officers who had had the misfortune of being sacrificed in the name of those same gods.

Tacitus provided some details of what subsequent Roman expeditions found:

> "Varus' first camp with its wide circumference and the measurements of its central space clearly indicated the handiwork of three legions. Further on, the partially fallen rampart and the shallow fosse suggested the inference that it was a shattered remnant of the army which had there taken up a position. In the center of the field were the whitening bones of men, as they had fled, or stood their ground, strewn everywhere or piled in heaps. Near lay fragments of weapons and limbs of horses, and also human heads, prominently nailed to trunks of trees. In the adjacent groves were the barbarous altars, on which they had immolated tribunes and first-rank centurions.
>
> "Some survivors of the disaster who had escaped from the battle or from captivity, described how this was the spot where the officers fell, how yonder the eagles were captured, where Varus was pierced by his first wound, where too by the stroke of his own ill-starred hand he found for himself death. They pointed out to the raised ground from which Arminius had harangued his army, the number of gibbets for the captives, the pits for the living, and how in his exultation he insulted the standards and eagles.
>
> "And so the Roman army now on the spot, six years after the disaster, in grief and anger, began to bury the bones of the three legions, not a soldier knowing whether he was interring the relics of a relative or a stranger, but looking on all as kinsfolk and of their own blood, while their wrath rose higher than ever against the foe. In raising the barrow Caesar laid the first sod, rendering thus a most welcome honor to the dead, and sharing also in the sorrow of those present."

A Roman ceremonial mask excavated from the battle site

Slingshot projectiles found at the battle site

While the Romans continued to launch their campaigns of revenge into Germany, they never again sought to control Germania. The destruction of Varus' column and the complete obliteration of three legions of Roman troops along with their camp followers had marked a turning point in Roman expansion into Germania. Rome, after the battle of the Teutoburg Forest, was content with leaving Germania to the Germans.

A German depiction of Arminius liberating Germania from the Romans (with a reference to the 1813 Battle of Leipzig that led to Napoleon's exile and the deliverance of Prussia)

Arminius, in spite of his stunning victory over Varus' troops in the Teutoburg Forest, was unable to unite the Germanic tribes, and he was also unable to fill the power vacuum which was created following Varus' suicide and the Roman government's subsequent withdrawal from Germania. From 14-16 CE, the Roman general Germanicus twice battled Arminius and defeated him both times. Arminius did not live much longer following his last military defeat; in 21 CE, Arminius was assassinated by several members of his own Cherusci tribe. These men had grown tired of Arminius' increasing attempts to secure a position of ultimate power amongst the other tribes and had grown fearful of him as he finally secured his place of power within their own tribe.

Thus, even though Arminius was wildly successful in driving Rome out of Germania, Rome quickly recovered from the loss and Arminius eventually suffered for the victory. Rome would continue to conquer and move forward, albeit not in Germania, and the Roman military learned the harsh lessons taught to them in the Teutoburg Forest. The legions adapted themselves accordingly, ensuring that Rome would never again suffer such a humiliating defeat at the hands of their enemies.

Online Resources

Other books about ancient history by Charles River Editors

Bibliography

Greco-Persian Wars

Aeschylus. 1942. Lyrical Dramas. Translated by John Stuart Blackie. London: J.M. Dent and Sons.

Briant, Pierre, 2002. From Cyrus to Alexander: A History of the Persian Empire. Translated by Peter T. Daniels. Winona Lake, Indiana: Eisenbraums.

Green, Peter. 1970. Xerxes at Salamis. New York: Praeger Publishers.

Hale, John R. 2009. Lords of the Sea: The Epic Story of the Athenian Navy and the Birth of Democracy. London: Penguin Books.

Hammond, N.G.L. 1956. "The Battle of Salamis." Journal of Hellenic Studies. 76: 32-54.

Herodotus. 2003. The Histories. Translated by Aubrey de Sélincourt. London: Penguin Books.

Jordan, Borimir. 1988. "The Honors for Themistocles after Salamis." American Journal of Philology 109: 547-571.

Kent, Roland. 1953. Old Persian: Grammar, Texts, Lexicon. 2nd ed. New Haven, Connecticut: American Oriental Society.

Morkot, Robert. 1996. The Penguin Historical Atlas of Ancient Greece. London: Penguin Books.

Parker, Robert. 2001. "Greek Religion." In The Oxford History of Greece and the Hellenistic World, edited by John Boardman, Jasper Griffin, and Oswyn Murray, 306-329. Oxford: Oxford University Press.

Pausanias. 1964. Description of Greece. Translated by W.H.S. Jones. Cambridge, Massachusetts: Harvard University Press.

Plutarch. 1968. Lives. Edited and translated by Bernadotte Perrin. Cambridge, Massachusetts: Harvard University Press.

Roaf, Michael. 1974. "The Subject Peoples on the Base of the Statue of Darius." Cahiers de la

Délégation Archéologique Française en Iran 4: 73-160.

Sage, Michael M. 1996. Warfare in Ancient Greece: A Sourcebook. London: Routledge.

Thucydides. 1998. The Peloponnesian War. Translated by Steven Lattimore. Indianapolis: Hackett Publishing

Wallinga, H. T. 1990. "The Trireme and History." Mnemosyne 43: 132-149.

Walser, Gerold. 1966. Die Völkerschaften auf den Reliefs von Persepolis: Historiche Studien über den sogenannte Tributzug an der Apadanatreppe. Berlin: Akadamie Verlag.

Xenophon. 2006. Hellenica. Translated by Carleton L. Brownson. Cambridge, Massachusetts: Harvard University Press.

Zalli, Vasiliki. 2013. "Themistocles' Exhortation before Salamis: On Herodotus 8.83." Greek, Roman, and Byzantine Studies 53: 461-485.

Cannae

Bagnall, Nigel (1990). The Punic Wars. ISBN 0-312-34214-4.

Daly, Gregory. Cannae: The Experience of Battle in the Second Punic War. London/New York: Routledge, ISBN 0-415-32743-1.

Delbrück, Hans. Warfare in Antiquity, 1920, ISBN 0-8032-9199-X.

Goldsworthy, Adrian (2006). The Fall of Carthage. ISBN 978-03043-6642-2.

Lazenby, John Francis (1978). Hannibal's War. ISBN 978-0-8061-3004-0.

Lancel, Serge (1995). Hannibal (in French).

Polybius, Histories, Evelyn S. Shuckburgh (translator); London, New York. Macmillan (1889); Reprint Bloomington (1962).

Palmer, Robert E. A. (1997). Rome and Carthage at Peace. Stuttgart.

Mahaney, W.C, 2008. "Hannibal's Odyssey, Environmental Background to the Alpine Invasion of Italia," Gorgias Press, Piscataway, N.J, 221 pp.

Dodge, Theodore Ayrault (1891). Hannibal. Reprinted by Da Capo Press, Cambridge, Mass. ISBN 0-306-81362-9

Teutoburg Forest

Appian. The Civil Wars. Waxkeep Publishing, 2013.

Appian. The Foreign Wars. Waxkeep Publishing, 2013.

Caesar, Gaius Julius. The Complete Works. 2014.

Clunn, Tony. The Quest for the Lost Legions of Rome. Savas Beatie, 2009.

Murdoch, Adrian. Rome's Greatest Defeat. The History Press, 2012.

Polybius. The Histories of Polybius, Volume One. 2013.

Polybius. The Histories of Polybius, Volume Two. 2013.

Renatus, Flavius Vegetius. The Military Institutions of the Romans. CreateSpace Independent Publishing

Platform, 2014.

Tacitus, Caius Cornelius. Germania. The Acheron Press, 2012.

Tacitus, Caius Cornelius. The Annals. The Acheron Press, 2012.

Tacitus, Caius Cornelius. The Germany and the Agricola of Tacitus. 2012.

Venchus, James L. Rome in the Teutoburg Forest. United States Army Command and Staff College, 2009.

Wells, Peter S. The Battle that Stopped Rome. W.W. Norton, 2004.

Printed in Great Britain
by Amazon